Robert E. Lee

Robert E. Lee

ICON FOR A NATION

Brian Holden Reid

59 John Glenn Drive
Amherst, New York 14228–2119

Published 2007 by Prometheus Books

Inquiries should be addressed to
Prometheus Books
59 John Glenn Drive
Amherst, New York 14228–2119
VOICE: 716–691–0133, ext. 210
FAX: 716–691–0137
WWW.PROMETHEUSBOOKS.COM

Originally published in hardback by
Weidenfeld & Nicolson
The Orion Publishing Group, Ltd.
Orion House, 5 Upper Saint Martin's Lane, London WC2 9EA

Brian Holden Reid has asserted his right
to be identified as the author of this work.

11 10 09 08 07   5 4 3 2 1

Library of Congress Cataloging-in-Publication Data

Reid, Brian Holden.
    Robert E. Lee : icon for a nation / Brian Holden Reid. — 1st American pbk. ed.
        p. cm.
    Originally published: London : Weidenfeld & Nicolson, 2005.
    Includes bibliographical references and index.
    ISBN 978-1-59102-585-6 (pbk.)
    1. Lee, Robert E. (Robert Edward), 1807–1870. 2. Generals—Confederate States of America—Biography. 3. Confederate States of America. Army—Biography. 4. United States—History—Civil War, 1861–1865—Campaigns. I. Title.

E467.1.L4R45 2007
973.7'3092—dc22
[B]
                                                                            2007027079

Printed in the United States of America on acid-free paper

To the residents of "A" Block, Grant Hall, The Lawns,

October 1971–June 1972,

who were "much exposed" to Robert E. Lee

AND

To the memory of Ivor W. Pfuell (1952–2001)

Contents

Map List

1. Virginia Theater

2. Second Manassas

3. Chancellorsville

4. Gettysburg

5. Wilderness/Spotsylvania/Cold Harbor

6. Appomattox

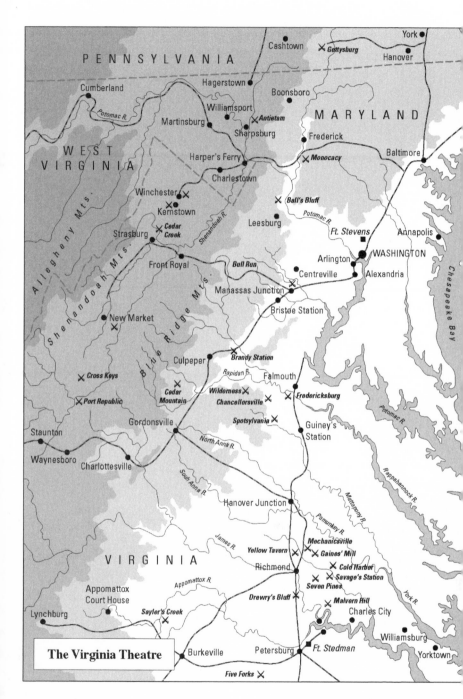

The Virginia Theatre

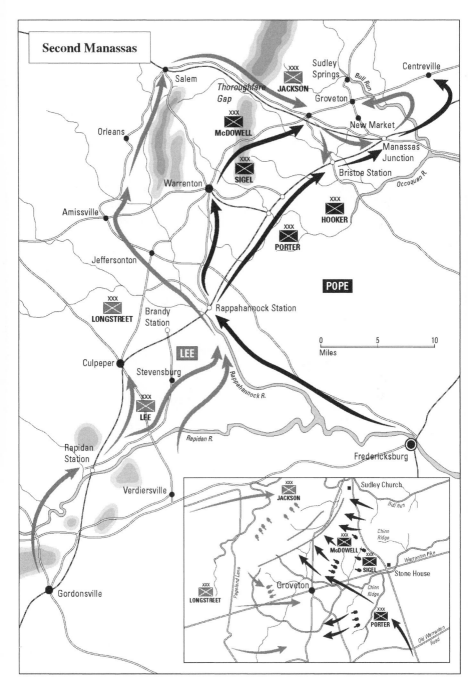

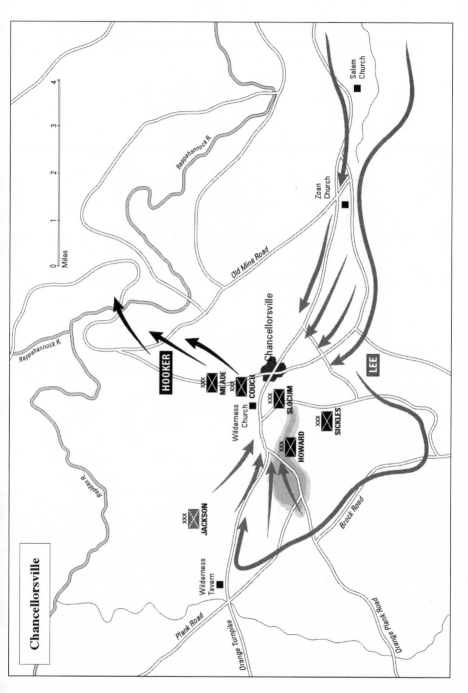

Chancellorsville

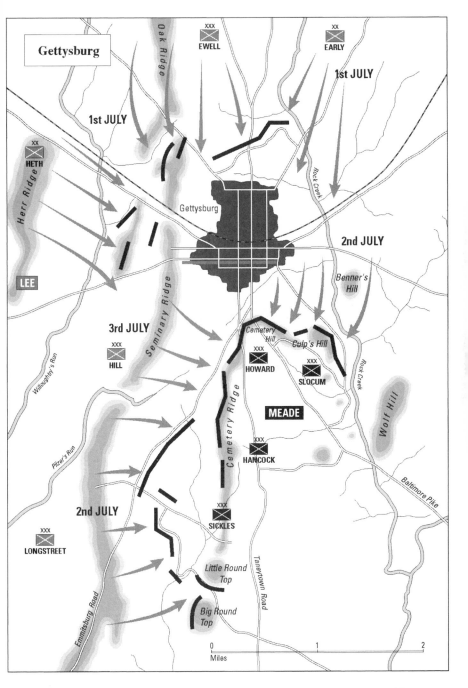

Gettysburg

EWELL

EARLY

1st JULY

1st JULY

HETH

Oak Ridge

Herr Ridge

Gettysburg

Rock Creek

LEE

2nd JULY

Benner's Hill

3rd JULY

HILL

Seminary Ridge

Willoughby's Run

Cemetery Hill

Culp's Hill

HOWARD

SLOCUM

Cemetery Ridge

MEADE

Wolf Hill

Pitzer's Run

HANCOCK

2nd JULY

Rock Creek

Baltimore Pike

LONGSTREET

SICKLES

Little Round Top

Taneytown Road

Emmitsburg Road

Big Round Top

0   1   2
Miles

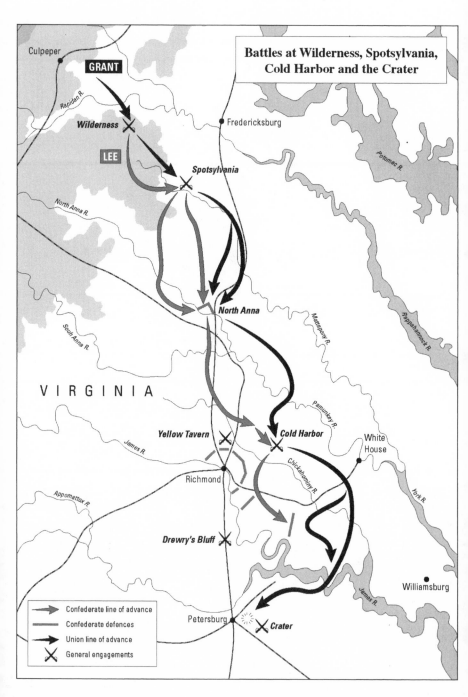

Battles at Wilderness, Spotsylvania, Cold Harbor and the Crater

GRANT

Culpeper

Rapidan R.

Wilderness

LEE

Fredericksburg

Spotsylvania

North Anna R.

North Anna

South Anna R.

VIRGINIA

Mattapony R.

Rappahannock R.

Yellow Tavern

Cold Harbor

Pamunkey R.

White House

Richmond

James R.

Chickahominy R.

Appomattox R.

Drewry's Bluff

York R.

James R.

Williamsburg

Confederate line of advance
Confederate defences
Union line of advance
General engagements

Petersburg

Crater

Potomac R.

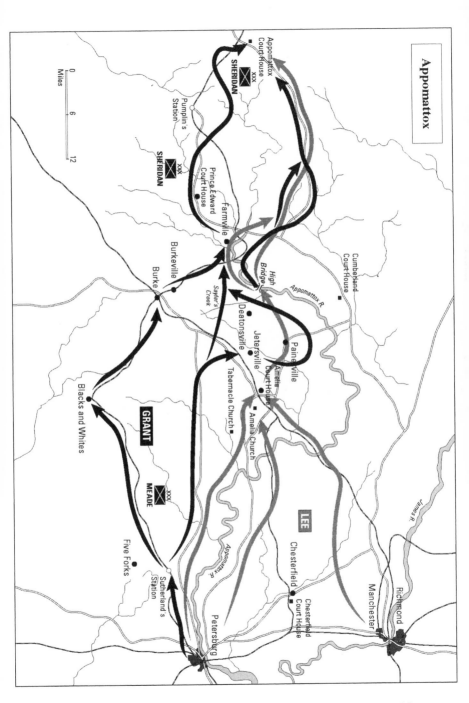

Appomattox

Appomattox Court House

SHERIDAN xxx

Pumplin's Station

SHERIDAN xxx

Prince Edward Court House

Farmville

Burkeville

Burke

Sayler's Creek

Deatonsville

Jetersville

Paineville

Cumberland Court House

Appomattox R.

High Bridge

Amelia Court House

Tabernacle Church

Amelia Church

Blacks and Whites

GRANT

MEADE xxx

Five Forks

Sutherland's Station

Appomattox R.

LEE

Chesterfield

Chesterfield Court House

Manchester

Richmond

James R.

Petersburg

Miles
0   6   12

Foreword

by Julian Thompson

In writing about Robert E. Lee, Professor Brian Holden Reid encountered the problem that all authors face who tackle this subject. Lee is held in such esteem in the United States, not only in the states that formed the old Confederacy but also in the North, that it is difficult for any author to write an objective assessment of his generalship. Lee has become so revered that criticizing him invites an angry response from his many admirers who treat such treatment as tantamount to blasphemy.

It would be hard to find an author better qualified to write a study of Lee than Brian Holden Reid. He has a deep knowledge of the American Civil War, has walked many of the battlefields and written extensively on the subject. His profound scholarship is enhanced by his experience at the Army Staff College at Camberley in Surrey. Here, in addition to his duties as Resident Historian, he was a full-time member of the Directing Staff, teaching tactics and operations alongside some of the brightest and most innovative lieutenant colonels and brigadiers of the 1980s and 1990s. In this capacity he was responsible for instructing a whole generation of the most promising British Army officers in the command and staff work associated with commanding large bodies of troops. He fulfilled a similar function on the Higher Command and Staff Course preparing officers for the most senior appointments in the British Army, as well as the Royal Navy and Royal Air Force. Many of his pupils and associates held high command in all three services, and do so to this day. He is familiar with the demands on commanders and staff officers faced by moving and supplying an army, and fighting battles and campaigns in a practical rather then scholarly sense. Brian Holden Reid's assessment of Lee reflects his own experience as a mentor in the operational art, and what he says about him should be gauged with this in mind.

He reminds us of the enormous self-confidence that Lee had in his own ability. He tells us that Lee believed small armies could beat big ones, and how and why he came to this conclusion. Lee believed in attacking to put his opponents off their stroke, hitting hard and keeping moving. This aggressiveness, as Brian Holden Reid points out, runs counter to much of the defensive-minded military philosophy that emerged in American military circles following the Vietnam War. In modern terminology Lee was the maneuver war general par excellence. But he was not seduced by the mere act of maneuver, as some proponents of the art have been since, to the degree that they would like to believe wars can be won without fighting.

The author shows us how Lee always *commanded*, reminding us that a commander must do more than plan. He must see his plans through to a successful conclusion, altering them as circumstances demand. Lee did not command by committee, or council of war. His gentlemanly manner, which comes across so clearly in this book, was not a cover for weakness and indecision.

In this study of Lee, Brian Holden Reid shows us that a commander does not have to be personally unpleasant and ruthless, in modern terminology a "military shit," to command successfully. His officers and men loved him, and this is one reason why he was able to stave off defeat for so long. Few generals, even successful ones, are loved by their troops. Wellington and Montgomery were respected but not loved. Soldiers may have boasted that they served with Patton, but they did not love him.

Most military organizations reflect the characteristics of their commanders. It was Lee's leadership that gave the Army of Northern Virginia its flair and élan, but also what the author calls its "ferocious power," enabling it to outfight the Army of the Potomac on almost every occasion. The gentlemanly Lee took risks that would leave others gasping in astonishment, in the course of which he inflicted on the armies of the United States some of the most humiliating defeats in their history.

Brian Holden Reid contends that linking Lee with the "Lost Cause" of the Confederacy, depicting him as a flawless knight-like figure, and therefore owing his success to his moral superiority over any of his Northern counterparts, misses the point. He needs no embellishment to qualify him as a great commander. His achievements stand without encrustation with romantic ideals. On the other hand, this account of Lee is balanced, and does not hesitate to point out where and when Lee failed, and why. Like other great generals, he made mistakes.

Lee is often portrayed as one of the last of the old-style generals, about to be replaced by the leaders of mass armies in the age of industrial war—Grant, Moltke, Joffre, Haig, Ludendorff, and so forth—and therefore irrelevant in our early twenty-first-century technological era. Brian Holden Reid rejects this. Not only is such a proposition superficial, overlooking similarities between Grant and Lee, but it is also flawed, in that Lee's operational philosophy is thoroughly modern. It is the commanders of the late nineteenth century and most of the twentieth that are old-fashioned.

This is a marvelous book, written with the style that is Brian Holden Reid's hallmark: informative, with a touch of dry wit here and there, perceptive and thought provoking.

New Preface to the American Edition

I am often asked, especially by Americans, how I became interested in the Civil War. Such questions are usually difficult to answer. In my case, curiosity is sometimes compounded by awareness that earlier in my career I devoted much effort to writing about the history of the British Army in the twentieth century. In particular, I wrote a lot about the two important British military thinkers, Major General J. F. C. Fuller and Captain Sir Basil Liddell Hart. Actually, I came to study both these men via their important books on Union generalship in the Civil War. The Civil War, in short, has always been my central scholarly preoccupation even though I became absorbed by other things.

As a student, I had been especially stimulated by Fuller's *Grant and Lee: A Study in Personality and Generalship* (1933), and its cogent criticisms of Lee's methods and the weaknesses of his personality. Fuller was perhaps the first historian of the Civil War to discern the distorting effects of the legendary qualities that hung over Lee's reputation as a peerless commander. The main source of these distortions could be found in the writings dedicated to the

"Lost Cause." Fuller devoted himself to puncturing these, but his indictment is too severe. It is also on certain points—especially in relation to Lee's supposed submissiveness, lack of authority, and excessive reliance on subordinates—mistaken. These aspects are discussed anew in my book. My interpretation is very different from Fuller's and indeed that of Liddell Hart. The latter disliked Lee as the embodiment of the rigid, fastidious, professional military ethos, and in 1928 turned down the chance to write a book about him.

Nevertheless, their writings helped me to view the nature of the Civil War and its command problems in a different light, free from any partiality toward the Confederacy. I still regard chapter 3 of *Grant and Lee*, "The Personality of Lee," as one of the best things written about Lee. The mythological dimensions assumed by Lee after 1865 is reminiscent of the cult of George Washington, fertilized in Lee's case by the sentimentality that hangs over the defeated, gifted commander. The victors do not by any means dominate the writing of the historical record. The Napoleonic legend after 1815 is another example of a successful literary campaign to cast the defeated general in a romantic, seductive light. Napoleon is depicted as the "real" victor—and those that prevailed, especially the Duke of Wellington, are denigrated. Another more recent example can be found in the stream of publications in the 1950s (with Liddell Hart in their vanguard) that sought to present the defeated German generals in a favorable light that they did not deserve. My book stresses that efforts to belittle the military talents of Ulysses S. Grant actually belittles Lee's achievements too.

The reasons behind the approach taken by this book are sketched in the original preface. Still, if I were to sit down and write it afresh now, I would have made more of the enormous influence exerted over Lee by his hero, George Washington. The task of analyzing the great hold over Lee's imagination by Washington's moral and intellectual example has been discharged most effectively by Richard B. McCaslin in his readable study, *Lee in the Shadow of Washington* (Baton Rouge: Louisiana State University Press, 2001). One must be careful though not to exaggerate the import of just one aspect of Lee's character.

There are other themes of the book that I would probably expand upon. The first is my contention that Lee was an inspired improviser. William L. Miller, in a brilliant essay, "'The Siege of Richmond Was Raised': Lee's Intentions in the Seven Days Battles," demonstrates convincingly that Lee's plans in June 1862 were governed by the need first and foremost to secure the Confederate capital, Richmond, and lift the Union siege. He did not originally intend, as I suggest on p. 86, following all Lee's previous biographers, to "destroy" the Army of the Potomac. But Lee succeeded beyond his expectations and thereafter struggled to gain a greater victory, as the Union commander, George B. McClellan, withdrew across his front toward the James River. This notable contribution to Lee scholarship can be found in *Audacity Personified: The Generalship of Robert E. Lee*, edited by Peter S. Carmichael (Baton Rouge: Louisiana State University Press, 2004).

This illuminating series of essays also contains other material that sustains themes of this book. Robert E. L. Krick's opinions on Lee's use of the staff clarify mine. Lee used his staff to help him administer rather than command his army. A more effective use of its talents might have reduced the burdens that weighed him down. Gordon C. Rhea provides more evidence that Lee was not clairvoyant. His work supports my own view that so much of Lee's greatness as a general arises from an incredible capacity to recover from initial errors. Lee's political skill and tact is also discussed in the book, and so, too, is an aspect that I covered briefly, namely, his short but productive period as general-in-chief of the Confederacy. His main contribution was to succeed where all others had failed: he persuaded Joseph E. Johnston to overcome his pathological suspicion of the political leadership in Richmond and exert himself in the last months of the war.

Two other broader areas deserve comment. The first is Lee's skill in retreat—reminiscent of Wellington. Lee was a gifted logistician, but at the time of the writing of this book we lacked a study that dissected the process whereby he conducted a withdrawal. Kent Masterson Brown has at last provided this kind of treatment in his book, *Retreat from Gettysburg: Lee, Logistics and the Pennsylvania Campaign* (Chapel Hill: University of North Carolina Press, 2005). The second area concerns the problem of desertion. The encomiums lavished on Lee's leadership, and the adulation that the men directed toward him, tended to conceal the cancer of desertion. Mark A Weitz's important book, *More Damning Than Slaughter: Desertion in the Confederate Army* (Lincoln: University of Nebraska Press, 2005), illuminates its effects. Weitz shows that large-scale desertion began in 1861 and not only was the Army of Northern Virginia not immune from it after the summer of 1862, but Lee was no more successful in overcoming it than any other commander. There is much food for thought here about the fragility of loyalty to the Confederate cause. This is a conundrum, for no general, however gifted, could overcome such an insuperable obstacle to military victory.

My book is essentially a military biography of modest dimensions furnished with sufficient information to explain Lee's personality and family life. The temptation to theorize about his career from what we know of his personality has been firmly resisted. Far too much emphasis has been placed in the past on trying to understand Lee's enigmatic personality as an explanation for his defeat. Lee is undoubtedly an arresting individual who cannot fail to fascinate. I can only echo Geoffrey Best's hope, when he attempted (successfully) to write a short biography of another much written about individual, set down in the preface to his *Churchill: A Study in Greatness* (2002), that "I hope that my book will convey a fair impression of this extraordinary human being."

Brian Holden Reid

Preface

The origins of this book lie in a conversation that I had some years ago with Professor Sir Michael Howard, OMCH, one night after dinner at the Staff College, Camberley. Clutching glasses suitably replenished with *digestifs*, we talked of generals and generalship. Sir Michael asked me whether I had any military heroes. I replied that I had several, the first being the Duke of Wellington. "Ah," he responded, "a gent." Then, I continued, General Robert E. Lee had always had a very high place in my affections. "*Another* gent," Sir Michael observed quickly. If I had then admitted that the final figure in this military trinity would also include Field Marshal Earl Alexander of Tunis, perhaps this might have proved too revealing. At any rate, this conversation has subsequently prompted many thoughts and queries in my mind over the reaction of the gentleman to the demands of the conduct of war and how they expose his strengths and weaknesses. This book tries to answer some of these questions, frequently through discussion of the broader issues posed by Lee's tumultuous career.

Lee's series of victories against the odds, however, raise an important problem at the outset. Professor Brian Bond spotted this as soon as I told him that I had agreed to write this book. Lee had been the subject of so much praise, he said, that it would be difficult to reach an objective verdict; any criticisms that I might make would not be well received by Lee's admirers. It would be much easier, he counseled, to write about Ulysses S. Grant. I think Professor Bond is right, but I have persevered all the same. The present work attempts to present an intelligible account of Lee's campaigns to the general reader. I have striven to etch an interpretative portrait based on my own appraisal of Lee's published papers and relevant modern scholarship.

I realized as soon as I had begun to organize my thoughts that the legacy of Confederate defeat in 1865 and its most powerful intellectual response, namely, the writers of the "Lost Cause" that hailed Lee as an icon, should be assessed at the outset. So much of the great praise that had been lavished on both Lee's character and military achievements served as a method of retrospectively validating the Confederate cause. Objectively, the latter had little direct connection with Lee's military methods. It has not been my intention to detach Lee's campaigns from their political and social context—quite the contrary. My prime concern has been to relate them to Southern public opinion at the time, rather than what Confederates thought it had been, or what some modern historians think it should have been.

To clear my path, I decided to include an initial chapter on the way that views of Lee's career and historical significance had been shaped by the cult of hero worship that developed after 1865. Of course, my own views on Lee had changed over the course of nearly forty years of reading about him. The most important point to establish is that to express favorable opinion of Lee's generalship does not carry with it pro-Confederate views. In the pursuit of a certain objectivity, in this regard, two further points need emphasis: first, that Lee's qualities as a commander do not need exaggeration, and second, like all men and women, he made mistakes.

I am only too aware how much my first chapter, indeed general approach to the subject, owes to the late Marcus Cunliffe. I have also followed Cunliffe's example in his short biography of George Washington in eschewing footnotes. It is a source of regret, too, that this is the first book of mine for many years not to receive critical scrutiny from the late Peter J. Parish. I am sure it is the worse for it. I am delighted to acknowledge once again how much I have learned from these two great British scholars of the United States. I am also grateful to Gary W. Gallagher for encouraging my endeavors; the pages that follow reveal how my path has been illuminated by his seminal contributions to Confederate military history.

I owe thanks to Simon Blundell, Librarian of the Reform Club, for answering so many diverse queries with cheerfulness and efficiency, to Liz Triplett of the Richmond, Virginia, Public Library, who produced important details at the last minute, and to Penny Gardiner of Weidenfeld & Nicolson, for all her hard work on the final product. I am also most grateful to my mother for creating such a congenial environment in which to work, especially over the last three distracting years. There is nobody but me to blame for any errors.

Brian Holden Reid

KING'S COLLEGE LONDON

CHAPTER ONE

"A Monument to His Glorious Memory"

The statues a society erects to commemorate its heroes usually reveal much about its values. The three statues put up in Whitehall before the Ministry of Defense in London, for instance, are redolent of the British military tradition. They celebrate in black marble the military achievements in the Second World War of Field Marshals Alan Brooke, Montgomery, and Slim (with Brooke set slightly forward to denote seniority as the wartime Chief of the Imperial General Staff). They represent rugged, determined men, capable of lofty purpose, but are studiously unpretentious; above all, these figures are cool and professional. Although victorious, these commanders reveal no swagger or vainglory.

The United States is not short of military statuary, but one of the most impressive pieces can be found in Richmond, Virginia, and commemorates a defeated, and not a victorious general, Robert E. Lee—a general who waged war against the United States. This great equestrian statue weighs 12 tons and measures from the base to the crown of the rider's head just a fraction under 62 feet. It is carved of

Maine marble (much to the disgust of some unreconstructed rebels, but the Richmond stonemasons had put up their prices in anticipation of a large order). The parts of the statue were dragged to its site in Monument Avenue, Richmond, formerly the Confederate capital, by more than 9,000 enthusiastic citizens. Designed by the French sculptor Marius-Jean Antonin Mercié (1845–1916), the statue contains no rank or title, simply the legend: LEE.

The statue projects an element of defiance as well as celebration which implies that, despite all, this general was not defeated. At its unveiling in 1890, before a crowd of well over 100,000 people, Archer Anderson, treasurer of the Tredegar Iron Works, declared that Lee's character combined "the perfect union of Christian virtues and old Roman manhood." The monument expressed "thanksgiving and praise, for that it pleased Almighty God to bestow upon these Southern states a man so formed to reflect His attributes of power, majesty and goodness!"

Such identification of divine attributes with his own character would have appalled Robert E. Lee at any time in his life. Yet it was an indication of how much his life and career had been mythologized since his death twenty years before. Most of those years had been spent in a rancorous dispute over the right place for such a memorial. In 1873 an earlier recumbent statue had been placed at Lee's tomb in the Memorial Chapel at Washington and Lee University. Many of Lee's lieutenants and staff objected to the neglect of Richmond, the result of Mrs. Lee's decision to bury her husband at his last post at Washington College in Lexington. The year before, Lieutenant General Jubal A. Early, one of Lee's corps commanders, in an influential address at Washington and Lee, called for "a monument to his glorious memory" to be raised in Richmond.

Two societies were created to advance this cause, the Lee Monument Association and the Association of the Army of Northern Virginia. From these gatherings of Lee's veterans would emerge the writers dedicated to the "Lost Cause," the romantic view of a gallant Confederacy doomed to eventual extinction at the hands of an irresistibly powerful North which developed after the Civil War. Before his death, Lee himself had planned to write an "unbiased" history of the Confederate Army of Northern Virginia, the troops he commanded. He had begun to collect material for it, assisted by Early and members of his old staff. After Lee's death in 1870, Early decided to put his commander's case for him in a series of lectures, articles, and books.

Early's interpretation, although it would change in detail, remained consistent and influential for almost a century. His case gained strength from its origins in Lee's own views and writings. The Lost Cause could be shaped into a romantic mythology revolving around the stately figure of Lee precisely because it was *lost*. The death of its greatest figures, Stonewall Jackson in 1863 and Lee himself seven years later, reinforced the Cause's appeal. (Those who lived longer like the former Confederate president, Jefferson Davis, had a much more checkered experience.) These early deaths underlined the sense of tragedy and unfulfilled achievement that is central to the sentimental legends surrounding the Old South.

This chapter is not a study of historical writings about Lee. Rather, it is about how he has been perceived and continues to be perceived, and explains why these forms take their particular shape. Such widespread attitudes informed historical writing about Lee until the 1960s. Thereafter the popular and the academic view tended to diverge. Not all of the former is serious. (Tony Horwitz, a journalist looking at the neo-Confederate revival of the 1990s, found a Civil War web site on the Internet, "Top Ten Civil War Studs." Lee apparently represents "a gerontophile's dream with sugar daddy possibilities.") This is a far cry from the profound forces that shaped Southern responses to the trauma and shame of defeat. Most Southerners accepted their defeat, but opposed the Reconstruction of the South that continued until 1877. Local authority enforced by white supremacy became the means by which Federal policy could be thwarted. The humiliation of military defeat could be washed away and soothed by the application of a balm that upheld the justice of the Confederate cause. This required, above all, the denial that slavery was a cause of the war and its retention a Confederate war aim. Lee served as the perfect vehicle for advancing this case because he had never shown any enthusiasm for slavery. During the war itself he had lost home and property—indeed, everything except his honor. Lee also reflected another response to defeat—envy of the dead. He had expressed this several times in 1864–65. The Southern dead were memorialized as heroic—and none more so after 1870, as it turned out, than Robert E. Lee.

Reducing these diverse responses to Lee, war and defeat, is a complex task. The pervasive Lee image can best be reduced to four closely related aspects or stereotypes: the great Confederate captain; the *chevalier sans peur et sans reproche*; the Confederate Washington; and the American Hannibal. Let us examine each in turn.

The Great Confederate Captain

On January 19, 1872, General Early delivered his address at Washington and Lee University, "The Campaigns of Robert E. Lee." It delineated the essential features of Lee as the ultimate Confederate symbol of greatness. Early's address was later distributed as a pamphlet throughout the South. He strove to outline those of Lee's achievements that warranted his fame as "among the foremost of the renowned historic names of the world."

Early thus became Lee's great champion in the jousting lists of history. He delighted in the name "rebel" (the preferred Southern designation for the Civil War, "the War between the States," only gained favor from the late 1880s). The followers of another Second Corps commander, John B. Gordon, would adopt a more conciliatory tone and show enthusiasm for a New South, but their basic view of the Civil War did not differ greatly from Early's.

Over time Southerners also became more proprietorial over Lee's reputation. His earliest biographers, such as the Virginia novelist John Esten Cooke, in his *A Life of Robert E. Lee* (1871), paid full homage to Lee's virtues but did not hesitate to criticize him. For instance, Cooke thought Lee at Gettysburg in July 1863 had got "carried away" by overconfidence. He went so far as to claim that he had behaved like a "man drunk on champagne." Early took this as a personal slur on Lee's reputation. Early also thought that too much praise had been lavished on Stonewall Jackson, who certainly eclipsed Lee until his death in 1863.

As Lee's reputation soared, its splendor and moral appeal as the ultimate justification of the rectitude of the Confederate cause overshadowed Jackson. By the 1880s Jackson was recast as Lee's loyal lieutenant. Early explained Jackson's contribution bluntly but probably fairly, stressing his "unhesitating confidence and faith in the chances of success." This faith "made him such an invaluable executor of General Lee's plans."

Lee thus became a symbol of admirable behavior after defeat. He conferred dignity on the defeated by virtue of his matchless military talent and quiet acceptance of the inevitable. The American South remains the only part of the United States to have experienced military defeat and occupation; and until 1975 and the final abandonment of South Vietnam, American forces were unaccustomed to failure in battle. The elevation of Lee's qualities became a means of assuaging that shame. By the end of the nineteenth century he assumed a religious importance. Senator Benjamin Hill of Georgia hailed Lee as "a private citizen without wrong . . . a man without guile." A Christlike imagery began to permeate opinions about him. John Daniel's *Robert Edward Lee: An Oration* (Savannah, 1883) compared the offer he had received in 1861 of command of Union forces to Satan's temptation of Christ: "No follower of the meek and lowly saviour," he averred, "can have undergone [a] more trying ordeal." Writers were at pains to stress Lee's modesty and gentleness, his spirit of forgiveness and love of children. And like Christ, as we shall see, Lee endured the betrayal of his Judas Iscariot—James Longstreet.

Despite the efforts of Virginians on Lee's behalf, he became (as in life) a *Confederate* symbol. This had an important impact on his overall "place" in Civil War history. Early and others had no doubt that Virginia was the most important theater of the Civil War. Hence they made a logical leap. Lee had been identified as the perfect product of Southern culture—the cavalier. Virginians most closely conformed to this stereotype. The state contributed more than any other to the supposed Southern military tradition. This had been stressed during the Civil War, even by Northerners, as one of the factors contributing to Lee's success. The preoccupation with Lee and his lieutenants offered a quite misleading view of the overall capability of Southern arms. It led to the erroneous claim that Southern generals were superior to their Northern counterparts. Actually, the Confederacy lacked command talent in depth. The efforts of Lee (and Jackson, J. E. B. Stuart, or Longstreet) were unusual, not typical.

The Chevalier sans Peur et sans Reproche

The iconography of Lee is dominated by his depiction as the spotless cavalier. To one Southern writer, Lee would always be the "untouchable Galahad of the Confederacy." Phrases like "our great cavalier" were frequent at the end of the nineteenth century, as this model was often employed to mark out the Old South as culturally distinctive from the materialistic North. "It is our patent of nobility," Robert Stiles suggested in *Four Years Under Marse Robert* (1903), "that he [Lee] is today regarded—the world over—as the representative of the soldiery of the South." Lee's character was marinated in the gentlemanly code. He was honest, hard working, and dedicated to duty and principle. He showed aptitude (without excessive cleverness) and good judgment. More particularly, his career had revealed a judicious and restrained use of authority.

The image of the perfect gentleman had deep roots in Anglo-American culture. Its appeal in the South was especially potent. Miss M. A. H. Gray, a very appropriately named Confederate loyalist, refused to acknowledge any American president after Davis and transferred her allegiance to Queen Victoria. "We Southerners," she proudly claimed, "are of pure English blood." William Thackeray's novel, *The History of Henry Esmond* (1852) outlined the characteristics of the perfect gentleman that Lee consciously nurtured in himself. Thackeray adopts the fictional device of the inclusion of a preface written by the hero's son. He is thus able to convey how the ideals of the gentlemanly code were transplanted from Britain to America. In 1718 Henry Esmond settled in Virginia. He had, the son recalled, "a perfect grace and majesty of deportment, such as I have never seen in this country, except perhaps in our friend Mr. Washington." He "commanded respect whenever he appeared." The applicability of the image to Lee is evident when he observes that Esmond's courtesy "was not put on like a Sunday suit" but perpetual. Esmond had never been "heard . . . [to] use a rough word, [and] 'twas extraordinary with how much awe his people regarded him . . . and [he] brought down the most arrogant by a grave satiric way, which made persons exceedingly afraid of him." The last aspect tends to be ignored by Southern writers concerned to salute Lee's Christlike mien.

The image of the perfect gentleman was useful to Confederate apologists because it allowed them to stress the superiority of Lee's character by comparison with his shabby and second-rate opponents, notably Ulysses S. Grant (a Reconstruction president, 1869–77). It also permitted the elevation of the Confederate *spirit* that Lee exemplified. In his 1872 address Early highlighted the "contest between mechanical power and physical strength on the one hand, and the gradually diminishing nerve and sinew of Confederate soldiers on the other, until the unlimited resources of our enemies must finally prevail over all the genius and chivalric daring, which had so long baffled their mighty efforts in the field." Veterans fell over themselves to pay tribute to the bond between the Confederate commander and his soldiers—men who had been inspired by his very superior character. In 1875 one former soldier wrote that Lee was "the grandest thing in all the world to us, when he loved us like a father and led us like a king, when we trusted him like a providence and obeyed him like a god. . . ."

As a Christian gentleman disinclined to bully or hector, Lee frequently displayed a resignation or acquiescence in the caprice of fate. Undoubtedly, his profound religious faith accentuated a fatalistic tendency. In 1861, at the beginning of the Civil War, Lee wrote, "I fear it is now out of the powers of men, and in God alone must be our trust that a merciful Providence will not dash us from the height to which his smiles had raised us." He made frequent allusions, once battle commenced, to entrusting the fortune of his troops to a merciful providence.

Here was the rub. Well into the 1960s historians of the Confederacy found it frustrating that Lee failed to impose himself on his subordinates and compel them to do his bidding. Douglas Southall Freeman, the greatest of all Southern biographers, in his monumental *R. E. Lee* (4 volumes, 1934–35), came to the conclusion that Lee had proved too fastidious, too nice, to dominate his subordinate commanders. Freeman and Clifford Dowdey, his successor as the premier chronicler of the Army of Northern Virginia, were both highly critical of Longstreet's failure to obey Lee, especially in July 1863 at the Battle of Gettysburg.

They drew on a long tradition of blaming Longstreet (a non-Virginian) for crucial errors. They both also hailed Jackson as Lee's indomitable lieutenant; Lee would have won had Jackson been present. Much of the animus toward Longstreet, not felt at the time, could be explained by his postwar conduct. As the only senior Confederate to defect to the Republican Party and support his old friend, Grant, Longstreet had become a "scalawag," and was denounced by Early on numerous occasions as a "renegade" who carried with him "the brand of Cain."

By the 1880s Longstreet became an easy scapegoat. He had lost the war for the Confederacy, because on two occasions he had failed to carry out Lee's orders (in August 1862 at Second Manassas and, more seriously, at Gettysburg). Assuming he knew better, he allowed the best chances to win the war slip through his hands like dust. Though Lee did not deign to overcome his gentlemanly instincts and chastise Longstreet firmly, he could not be acquitted from error either (although many tried to do so). Nevertheless, the great bulk of the obloquy could be unloaded on Longstreet. Freeman certainly took Lee to task in his great biography for setting an unfortunate precedent at Second Manassas of giving Longstreet, consumed by frustrated ambition, the unfortunate impression that he had established a psychological sway over his commander.

The transfer of blame to Longstreet also allowed the indulgence of the notion that the Lost Cause might have prevailed after all. The obsession with establishing the point when Confederate independence might have been won—"the high water mark"—reached a peak during the years 1890–1910, but it lasted for decades thereafter. It also fitted an interpretation that saw patrician, heroic leaders, like Lee, who inspired armies of adoring, deferential, above all loyal soldiers to accomplish great deeds.

The Confederate Washington

In 1864 a Confederate general, Clement A. Evans, observed that Lee "is regarded by his army as nearest approaching the character of the great and good Washington than any man living." Lee's standing as a great Confederate symbol and the acknowledgment of his gentlemanly bearing naturally led to comparisons with the other great Virginian, George Washington. The doubled image of Washington and Lee (embodied in his old college's rebranding as a university in 1871) is even more important than the doubled image of Lee and Jackson.

Lee's appeal resembled that of Washington by emphasizing probity of character rather than creativity. In his 1872 address, Early attempted "a just appreciation of the domestic virtues, the moral worth, the unselfish patriotism and Christian purity of General Lee's character" and drew a "parallel between General Lee and *our* great Washington"; he commented on "their great self-command . . . patriotism, and . . . their purity and unselfishness"—although

Early argued simultaneously that they were very different species as soldiers. He also referred to the Cincinattus theme that had so enhanced Washington's appeal. Washington had been happy to retire to his home, Mount Vernon, when his duty was done. Early paid tribute to Lee's "dignified and useful retirement . . . In your midst [at Washington College], the true grandeur of his soul shone out as conspicuously as had his transcendent genius in his campaigns." Early thus strove to forge the links in the chain of Confederate self-justification: the purity of Lee's character and his military genius as the validation of the cause he fought for. This symbiotic relationship has had an enduring appeal.

Lee had his own Parson Weems (he of the cherry tree and the young Washington's inability to lie) in J. William Jones, a Lexington Baptist preacher. He persuaded Lee's family to lend him family papers. In 1875 he published *Personal Reminiscences, Anecdotes and Letters of General Robert E. Lee*, and this book went through several editions, though Jones lacked Weems's inspired talent for invention that brought the latter's *Life of Washington* (1800) immortality. During the Civil War Lee himself, always alert for propaganda opportunities, sometimes assumed a Washingtonian pose to evoke historical or cultural memories. Weems's best-selling biography of Washington included a wholly fictitious engraving of Washington kneeling at prayer at Valley Forge. On July 10, 1864, the infinitely more devout Lee evoked this image. He invited Reverend William H. Platt of St. Paul's Episcopal Church to hold an open-air service at his headquarters near Petersburg. Sergeant James Albright witnessed Lee "humbly kneeling on the ground among the sunburnt soldiers of his army, and joining in the impressive ceremony of the day . . . I shall never forget this sermon. . . ."

What is so remarkable about the doubling of Lee's image with

Washington's is that—despite the numerous defeats that Lee inflicted on United States' armies—it was appropriated by the North and doubled with Lincoln. President Theodore Roosevelt exuberantly claimed that Lee's achievements were a "matter of pride to all Americans." Northerners came to salute the Southern military tradition and to accept the Southern estimate of their achievements in the Civil War at face value. The significance of Lee's Confederate loyalties slowly eroded. Gamaliel Bradford could write a biography of Lee, really a study in character, and without embarrassment entitle it simply, *Lee the American* (1912). The model of Washington as moral exemplar was self-evident.

Such a halo of sanctity left Lee vulnerable to a sharp reaction. Phrases like the "whole man" were used to explain his character. A Northern writer, Earl Schenck Miers, contended in his "great life in brief," *Robert E. Lee* (1956), that: "The wholeness of Lee derived in no small measure from the fact that he was consistently the objective man, attending to duty and trusting in God for his motivation." The acquiescence of Northern writers in this kind of discussion is testimony to the success of Lost Cause polemicists in pushing Lee above the tumult (especially the irritating issue of slavery), stirred up by the political strife that caused the Civil War.

Lee's sainthood ultimately had a detrimental effect on his military reputation. The only way was down. The novelist (and latterly Civil War television pundit) Shelby Foote observed that: "Nothing pleases me more than to find some shortcoming in Lee because it humanizes him." But the effort to remove Lee from the political and social environment in which he lived had one further, enduring legacy. Lee's elevated character made it possible to suggest that the Army of Northern Virginia under his command, and inspired by his example, abstained from plundering and acts of vandalism. More significantly, it reveals Lee's contribution to emerging Confederate nationalism. The moral faith enshrined in the supposed restrained and disciplined conduct of Lee's troops became one of the sole props after 1863 of an unappealing and faltering cause. Confederates could only define themselves *vis-à-vis* Northern barbarity.

The American Hannibal

Lee's resemblance to the great Carthaginian general and opponent of Rome, Hannibal, finds its origins in Plutarch's life of Flavinius Maximus Fabius. Plutarch quotes a remark, supposedly made by one of Hannibal's subordinates, Barca, after his great victory over the Romans at Cannae (216 BCE) during the Second Punic War: "You know how to win a victory, Hannibal, but you have no idea how to exploit it." Hannibal was Rome's most formidable enemy as Lee was Lincoln's. But in both cases, highly skilled exponents of the operational art, who combined imagination, ruse, brilliant timing, and clever maneuver, lost, overborne by their enemy's greater resources. In 1872 Jubal Early referred to the comparison, claiming that "in the march of Hannibal . . . over the Alps, and his campaigns in Italy, we might find a similarity to General Lee's bold strategy." The comparison could not be exact, as Early conceded, because of the great differences in the conduct of war since ancient times. Also when compared with the chivalric Lee, Hannibal committed numerous atrocities.

In one important respect though the comparison is revealing, because both Lee and Hannibal were outnumbered. Lee's apologists thus strengthened their case from a different standpoint: that Lee exemplified a superior military tradition. A member of Lee's staff, Lieutenant Colonel Walter H. Taylor, attributed his final defeat to "the great numerical odds" arrayed against him. As an "all-wise

Providence" had prevented Lee from publishing "a true statement of the odds against which they [his troops] had to contend," Lost Cause writers hurried to make Lee's case for him.

Lee stressed the odds against him during the Civil War in his correspondence and official papers. Lost Cause advocates thus took their text from the great Confederate captain himself. "His [Grant's] talent and strategy," Lee wrote on July 24, 1864, "consists in accumulating overwhelming numbers." Early applied the perspective that Lee was always outnumbered to his entire career. At the end of June 1862, he pointed out, Lee left only 25,000 men to defend Richmond while he went on to the attack. "Timid minds might regard this as rashness but it was the very perfection of a profound and daring strategy." He went on to claim that Northern generals were infected with a self-defeating timidity. Lee could defeat them because his dynamic maneuvers created the *appearance* of numbers. "Truly our boys in grey had a wonderful faculty," Early crowed, "of magnifying themselves in battle."

Early began that practice that is common down to our day of referring to "immense" or "vast" Northern armies—"Northern hordes." They were large, but not vast by the standards of the mid-nineteenth century. At Sadowa in 1866, the Prussians and Austrians concentrated over a quarter of a million men each for this single battle, far more than the North ever managed. Early and his followers also sought to minimize Lee's strength. He claimed that in 1864 Lee put 50,000 men into the field against 141,000. He could thus claim that Lee's operational skill had been negated by the constant bludgeoning of a stronger but unimaginative foe. Early anticipated another theme that would dominate Southern writing for the next century, namely, the desire to deny Grant any skill or credit for the campaigns of 1864–65. Taking up Lee's claims, Early complained that Grant won only due to numbers, and "by 'constant hammering' to destroy our army 'by mere attrition if in no other way.'"

The curious results of such a claim was to detract from Lee's achievement in resisting Grant for almost a year by skill and artifice. If Grant had only mediocre abilities, then Lee needed to muster little effort to repel him, outnumbered or not.

A later generation of Southern writers were not deterred. They agreed that Lee embodied an exceptional genius. Douglas Southall Freeman suggested that Lee had a clairvoyant capacity to see into the very heart and mind of his opponents. Here the neglect of the war outside Virginia served a useful polemical purpose. Southern writers could not make such high-flown claims for the "genius" of Confederate commanders in the west, as these were quietly put to one side in the effort to glorify Lee.

Consequently, the claim could be made that the South was never defeated in a fair fight by the North. It remained *unvanquished*, to employ the title of William Faulkner's Civil War novel of 1938. By extension Lee was not really defeated by Grant—he only succumbed to forces beyond his control. Hence the obsession with verifying the details of the Gettysburg Campaign that preceded Grant's onslaught of 1864. Longstreet's accusers were determined to prove his guilt because the best chance to gain Confederate independence had been frittered away, and Lee's grand design to secure it utterly frustrated. Early and Freeman and many other Southerners were left gnashing their teeth "that our victories could never be pressed to more decisive results"—just like those of Hannibal. "It was genius, and nerve and valor, on the one side," pleaded Early, "against numbers and mechanical power on the other; even the lightning of the heavens being made subservient to the latter." Generations of Lee's admirers found solace in this claim, and continued to repeat it.

Where does this leave us?

The metamorphosis of Lee into first a sectional and later a national symbol has left an enduring stamp on the way his reputation has been perceived. The appeal of his elevated character cannot furnish him with an impenetrable shield of sanctity. In the end, Lee cannot be considered apart from the sectional disputes underlying the Civil War itself. Hence the sensitivity of Lee's partisans to any form of criticism. Lee *does* remain a Confederate symbol. The political legacy of the aftermath of the Civil War may have long since receded, but Lee's name can still stir up controversy. Like all Confederate leaders, Lee had been stripped of his US citizenship on the outbreak of war. Upon his surrender at Appomattox, Lee was deemed officially "stateless" and had to sign an amnesty oath before a notary public in order to regain his US citizenship. He submitted an oath on October 2, 1865, but received no response before his death five years later. After the passage of a century, a clerk looking through papers in the National Archives found his application. On July 22, 1975, Congress passed a special act, endorsed by President Gerald Ford, restoring Lee's citizenship, which provoked denunciation at the time by black politicians and groups such as the National Association for the Advancement of Colored People (NAACP). It is possible that the original application was deliberately "lost" by a clerk determined that Lee should not regain the right to call himself an American.

These controversies remain significant in American political and social history. This study of Lee attempts to estimate his achievements without recourse to the special pleading of the Lost Cause advocates and a later generation of historians who had imbibed their fundamental arguments. It is timely to appreciate Lee's gifts and weigh them sympathetically in the same way that historians would consider any other important nineteenth-century commander. There is a need to acknowledge that (like them, too) Lee exhibited weaknesses and made mistakes.

A study of the mythological Lee should not delude us that Lee has never been criticized. This is far from true. As the appeal of the Lost Cause has waned and the South has changed and become more self-confident, so Lee's reputation has been subject to a sustained onslaught. Such criticism has stemmed from academic historians mainly, and frequently from those works that consider Lee indirectly or in passing. After 1945 Lee was judged by T. Harry Williams an "old-fashioned general." As interests in Confederate history broadened and became less preoccupied with Virginia, another source of criticism emerged. Thomas L. Connelly was only the most strident member of a group of historians who claimed that Lee's neglect of the western theater was strategically disastrous; he also lambasted Lee's offensive methods. "When these things are considered," Connelly went so far as to claim in 1969, "one ponders whether the South may not have fared better had it possessed no Robert E. Lee." Such claims excited furious rejoinders, doubtless irritated by Connelly's use of innuendo; although these scored debating points they tended to hark back to the approach of Freeman and other Virginian historians. Fortifying Connelly's line of argument has been the "Vietnam Syndrome," which deprecates "risk" in war and elevates caution and defensive-mindedness of a kind that Early had denounced.

In the chapters that follow the suggestion is made that Connelly and his imitators have been too severe, and too cocksure in their strictures. Connelly (who is often as polemical as the earlier writers he criticizes) did not argue that the Lost Cause writers *created* Lee's great fame, but he did suggest that his transformation into the pre-eminent Southern hero was a post-1865 development. This was frequently achieved by silencing Lee's critics. Connelly tends to assume that these critics must be right *because* they were critical, and, therefore, that Lee's great military talents were largely "mythical."

Mythology does not always imply an untruth. Some elements of the Lost Cause interpretation of the Civil War were not false, only greatly exaggerated. Lee emerges from a study of his correspondence as a very typical Southerner, who shared many of the opinions and ambivalences of other loyal Confederates. Indeed, it is the commonplace nature of his views, rather than their specialness, that made Lee such a convenient vehicle for mythologizing.

If less emphasis is placed on Lee's elevated character—and it can be assumed that he is not always right—a more informed understanding of his generalship emerges. Nonetheless, Lee did display wisdom on the key issues facing the Confederacy, and thus his critics (both at the time and more recently) were and are not always justified. Again, if it is agreed that Longstreet was unfairly maligned by Early and his acolytes, it does not follow that Jackson (whom they so admired) made little significant contribution to Lee's success. Above all, the jarring, excessive zealotry of Lee's partisans should not lead us to jump to the opposite conclusion, namely, that Lee was not a great general.

This book argues that Lee does belong to that select company. It stresses his vision and technical excellence, but suggests that this was exceptional in the Confederacy rather than typical. In his preference for the offensive, Lee reflected deep currents in the tides of Southern opinion that demanded that the war be taken to the enemy. His great fame, in short, rested on Southern opinion during the Civil War itself, and was not, in any sense, retrospective. Like all successful commanders he enjoyed good luck, although he often made his own luck. He also emerges in his relationships with his subordinates as a good deal more astringent and much less sweet-tempered than the meek

Christ-like stereotype allows. Sandie Pendleton, Jackson's chief of staff, wrote ruefully after displeasing Lee that "I never felt so small in my life. I lost no time bowing myself out . . . firmly resolved never to hazard any inquiry or conjecture to General Lee again."

Finally, it is hoped that a view from across the Atlantic confers not just some distance in considering these vexed matters, but some objectivity. T. Harry Williams once observed that British writers tended to sympathize with Lee because he was such a gentleman. There is some evidence to support his case. Colonel G. F. R. Henderson was certainly of the view that Lee was "one of the greatest, if not the greatest, soldier who spoke the English language." Major General Sir Frederick Maurice's *Robert E. Lee: The Soldier* (1925) claimed that Lee was a greater general than the Duke of Wellington. These books were written when Lee's reputation in the United States reached its height. But Britain has also provided some of Lee's most acute and penetrating critics. In 1872 the pro-Confederate *Times* reporter, Francis Lawley, wrote in *Blackwoods Magazine* that he believed Lee to be a great general, but that he was over-confident and stumbled at the crucial moment. Lawley thought on reflection that Lee was inclined to be "admirably bold when weak, but that he became more cautious when he was, comparatively speaking, strong." This verdict did not please Early, and to placate him Lawley paid tribute to Lee's fine character.

This approach provided Major General J. F. C. Fuller with his prime target. Fuller's *Grant and Lee* (1933) located Lee's weaknesses as a commander in his personality, especially in his tact and humility. All Civil War historians owe Fuller a debt in his detaching Lee the commander from Lee the Confederate symbol. The approach here suggests that Lee's tact was a strength and his humility exaggerated. Also, one device that Fuller favors has been rejected. Although

43

"league tables" have come to permeate many aspects of British life (from speed cameras to university departments), they are of little value when considering great commanders. So the temptation to provide a "league table" of great Civil War commanders and Lee's place in it has been resisted.

Clearly, the methods of great commanders can be compared but not their overall standing. Distinction in war depends on opportunity, environment and culture, and it is difficult to see how these can be compared meaningfully. Lee has perhaps already endured an excess of comparison. It seems a more useful exercise to get Lee's methods and achievements in close focus before proceeding to make comparisons with others. The first point of reference must be Lee's formative experiences.

CHAPTER TWO

Military Apprenticeship, 1807–61

"Great soldiers, like poets, are born not made," claims Major General Fitzhugh Lee, CSA (1835–1905) in his respectful biography of his uncle, Robert E. Lee, *General Lee* (1894). "Military training, discipline, the study of strategy, and grand tactics are powerful reinforcements to natural genius." If the younger Lee is correct, then the source of Robert E. Lee's remarkable talent and outstanding military achievements lies in his family background and the peculiar circumstances of his upbringing.

By the middle of the eighteenth century, the Lees of Virginia had risen to become one of the richest and most distinguished families in the Old Dominion. In 1771 George Washington declared that "I know of no country that can produce a family all distinguished as clever men, as our Lees." Two of their number had signed the Declaration of Independence. Their talents lay in politics, oratory and scholarship—the arts of peace rather than war. At least such was the case until the outbreak of the American Revolution in 1775.

Robert E. Lee's father, Henry Lee III, showed enterprise and dash in 1780–81 as a commander of light cavalry—dragoons or mounted infantry—operating in semi-guerrilla style against Lord Cornwallis's columns in the Carolinas. He acquired the nickname "Light Horse Harry." He had previously served in the Virginia House of Delegates, and then as a delegate to the Continental Congress in Philadelphia. In 1792, on the strength of his military record, he became Governor of Virginia, and in 1799 a member of the House of Representatives. Light Horse Harry was a talented man, widely read in the classics, philosophy and literature. He, too, had returned to the natural Lee sphere of politics and oratory. He hailed George Washington in 1798 as "first in peace, first in war, first in the hearts of his countrymen."

For the remainder of his career, however, Light Horse Harry revealed a sad lack of those qualities so important in the regular officer: commitment, constancy, reliability and sure judgment. In 1793 Lee, a widower with three children from his previous marriage, wed Ann Hill Carter, daughter of another Virginia dynast, Charles Carter. Robert Edward Lee was their fifth child, born on January 19, 1807. The son had virtually no contact with his father, who mentions him only once in his correspondence. "Robert was always good," he observed truthfully. Light Horse Harry's second marriage coincided with the rapid decline in his fortunes. Lee personified the romantic adventurer and rash gambler, and became addicted to land speculation. His ventures were usually wrong-headed and he developed a rather casual attitude to paying his growing debts. He hoped that President Washington would give him command of the US Army, but when disappointed he offered his services as military supremo to Revolutionary France. Like his son, Light Horse Harry did not lack self-confidence.

The Lee marriage was marked by deceit and poverty and, partly as a result, Ann Carter Lee's health declined. "I am much of an invalid," she admitted three years before Robert's birth. By 1809 Light Horse Harry's fortunes had so deteriorated that he was imprisoned for debt. He began to write his memoirs. In 1810 Lee admitted bankruptcy and gained release, whereupon he completed his book. The work appeared in 1812 as *Memoirs of the War in the Southern Department of the United States*, although disappointing sales did little to recoup the fortunes of its author. (In 1837 his son edited his father's memoirs, as—remarkably—he did again in 1868, when it might have been more advantageous for him to have reflected on the course of his own campaigns of infinitely greater complexity and magnitude.)

In 1813 Light Horse Harry fled to Barbados, then returned to Cumberland Island, Georgia, where he died five years later. Despite his father's shameful record of debt, foolishness and dissipation, Robert Lee remained loyal to Light Horse Harry's memory and true to his conservative political values. Yet in truth the course of his father's life gave the young Robert an object lesson in what not to do. Ann Carter Lee brought up her children in Alexandria, Virginia, across the Potomac from Washington, DC, and close to powerful members of her family. She and her children were frequent guests at the great plantations around Richmond, Shirley and Stratford. Her three surviving sons and two daughters were reared in genteel poverty. Although they hardly starved, the style to which accident of birth brought them depended on the largesse of others; they enjoyed the forms and symbols of privilege (Ann Lee had her own modest carriage) without the substance—wealth and security. Young Robert Lee, who was a serious-minded and hard-working boy, attended the Alexandria Academy. He excelled at mathematics and absorbed the Latin and Greek learning so vital to his standing as a gentleman.

Robert developed a close relationship with his mother, nursing her during frequent illnesses. She also depended on his mature judgment and calm, steadying presence. When she contemplated his future, the attractions of attendance at the United States Military Academy at West Point recommended themselves, offering an engineering and scientific course of study that eminently suited Robert's talents. The Academy also enjoyed the signal advantage of being free. Nominations for West Point at this date lay in the gift of the Secretary of War, John C. Calhoun. Influential members of the Lee and Carter families rallied to support Robert's application. He was appointed on March 11, 1824, but could not enter the Academy until 1825. There is perhaps some poetic justice in the act of the high priest of secession, Calhoun, in admitting the premier general of the Southern Confederacy to his initial military training.

At West Point Robert E. Lee enjoyed a distinguished record as an impeccable cadet. He took his place in that long line of Southerners led by Albert Sidney Johnston, another future Confederate general, who set the Academy's tone. Young Lee's upbringing ideally fitted him for Academy life. Accustomed to frugality, self-reliance and organizing himself, Lee proved a model cadet. In his four years at West Point Lee (along with five others) did not receive a single demerit (a punishment that lowered a cadet's class standing). One of his closest friends was another Virginian, Joseph E. Johnston (his father, Peter Johnston, served under Light Horse Harry's command in 1780–81). Johnston, too, would rise to high command in the Civil War, although his record is more controversial than Lee's. In the pantheon of Southern heroes, Johnston is usually ranked second to Lee in overall military ability.

In 1829 Lee graduated second in his class. The course structure ensured that engineering, mathematics and other sciences counted for 55 percent of the marks. It suited Lee's own bent perfectly. The art of war received only cursory attention: no more than one week's study. Consequently, the West Point experience had a negligible effect on Lee's generalship. The real influence of West Point lay in the development of his character. On graduation Lee stood sharply etched as the "marble model"—the perfectly attired and stately *beau sabreur*.

Even as an adolescent, when Lee had prematurely combined the roles of husband as well as dutiful son, he had demonstrated rare moral qualities and was perceptive, conscientious and shrewd. He also appeared reserved and proud, although, unlike Jane Austen's Mr. Darcy, he rarely showed haughtiness or overt snobbery. On joining the Regular Army these qualities were transmitted into a dedication to achieving self-mastery. He always sought to be in control of himself, and to exert a grip over any task that he might be set. As this control never lapsed, never broke, he demonstrated a capacity to lead others because he inspired trust. Lee habitually presented a façade of dignified and polite distance that concealed a profound shyness. Like Julius Caesar, Lee's sense of *dignitas* lay at the core of his being. At just under six feet tall, blessed with good looks, poise and a natural military bearing, Lee looked every inch the soldier, and the role would grow on him.

Lee nevertheless remained sociable, especially among young women, and was reserved rather than stand-offish. The pursuit of the gentlemanly code became his lodestone. It would see him endure many frustrations and disappointments.

Lee's high class standing permitted his entry into the US Army's elite, the Corps of Engineers. His first appointment as a brevet second lieutenant was at Savannah, Georgia, where he helped construct Fort Pulaski on Cockspur Island. During his furloughs he courted Mary Custis, the daughter of George Washington Parke Custis, the grandson of Martha Washington and the first President's adopted son. Parke

Custis was a generous, easy-going dilettante, who never made a success of anything. Lee proposed to Mary, and asked her father's permission to marry. Custis refused to grant it on the grounds of Lee's poverty. However, rarely steadfast, Custis changed his mind after constant badgering from Mary, who was wont to have her own way in all things. Lee transferred to Fort Monroe, Virginia, in May 1831, and the couple were married the following month.

Marriage into the Washington family represented an enormously important step for Lee. George Washington had served as his father's patron. Lee himself evinced a tendency toward hero worship. He read as much as he could about Washington and modeled his own conduct on that of the first President. Despite his own lack of wherewithal, by marrying Mary Custis he assumed the position of heir not just to the Custis plantation and house at Arlington, which lay on the bluffs on the south bank of the Potomac overlooking Washington, DC, but identified himself as the heir to the Washington tradition. Douglas Southall Freeman, in his great biography, *R. E. Lee* (1934–5), stresses Lee's dedication to the ideals of honor, loyalty and political service. "He set himself to be worthy of them, precisely as he had made Washington his model, almost without being conscious of it." If that required the defense of plantation slavery so be it.

Nonetheless, tensions lurked behind the stately surface of the Lees' married life. Mary Lee was opinionated, poorly organized and ill-equipped for tackling the duties of an army wife. She spent at least four months of every year with her parents or with relatives. Long periods spent apart would characterize the Lee marriage. In 1832 Lee's eldest son, George Washington Custis Lee, was born. Gradually, like Ann Hill Carter, Mary became an invalid, crippled by arthritis among other ailments. Lee remained a dedicated and loyal husband, but indulged numerous flirtatious friendships with young women.

Lee always preferred female company, but he made a point of seeking his wife's permission before approaching a new, vivacious female correspondent.

In November 1834 Lee was appointed assistant to the Chief Engineer, Brigadier General Charles Gratiot. His main duty consisted of lobbying Congress on behalf of the corps. His diplomatic skills were appreciated, and in the spring of 1835 he adjudicated in the controversy between Ohio and Michigan over the location of the state boundary. Close acquaintance with politicians and their devious ways did not increase his admiration for the species, although he acquired a skill at dealing with them that would serve him well.

Lee's promotion to first lieutenant was gazetted in September 1836. Bored by the dreary peacetime routine of Washington, DC, Lee volunteered to undertake an urgent engineering task on the Mississippi River at St. Louis, Missouri. Two more children had arrived, Mary in 1835 and William Henry Fitzhugh, known as "Rooney," in May 1837. Lee felt that his career needed a boost. Congress had voted money for "internal improvements" and the army accepted the role of helping put them into effect.

Lee was set the task of altering the flow of the Mississippi to prevent sand bars from blocking St. Louis's harbor, rendering it navigable as far as above the Des Moines Rapids. He believed this enormous job could be completed by a patient, calm and reasoned examination of all the problems. The ambitious solution he reached was expensive, and when the Congressional appropriation ran out Lee successfully persuaded St. Louis's mayor to sustain the work with a further $15,000. Congress adjourned in 1840 without voting further appropriations and Lee's work came to an end, but he had demonstrated his ingenuity and pertinacity and an ability to manage a complex problem. It was on the strength of his performance at

St. Louis, that Lee gained admission to the select band of Winfield Scott's staff in the Mexican War (1846–48). The diligence and resource he revealed would be carried over in a later war in the form of consummate skill in adapting nature to the demands of field fortification.

On July 7, 1838, Lee gained promotion to captain, and arrived shortly afterward in New York harbor to work on the improvement of the Narrows between the Upper and Lower Bays. He became depressed with his prospects. "The manner in which the Army is considered and treated by the country," he complained to a friend in July 1838, ". . . is enough to disgust every one in the service and has the effect of driving every good soldier from it, and rendering those who remain discontented, careless and negligent." Should he leave, too? The question was given point by the arrival in June 1839 of another daughter, Ann Carter. (Three further births followed: Agnes in 1841, Robert Edward Jr. in 1843, and Mildred in 1846.)

Despite his disillusion, Lee never seriously considered leaving the army. His time over the next few years was spent on a series of dreary jobs: verifying the government's title to the land used for national defense; serving on the West Point Board of Visitors; assisting the Chief Engineer once more; and serving on the Board of Engineers for Atlantic Coast Defense (1845–8).

The major turning point in his career came in 1846 with the declaration of war on Mexico. This conflict stemmed from the determination of the United States to annex the republic of Texas and the resolve of Mexico to prevent it. Lee immediately sought "active service in the field," and in August was ordered to San Antonio, Texas. There he joined the main American force in northern Mexico, commanded by Major General Zachary Taylor. He came away impressed by Taylor's skeptical reaction to exaggerated reports of enemy strength.

In mid-1847 Lee received orders to join Winfield Scott's head-quarters at Brazos, Texas. Scott had persuaded President James K. Polk to allow him to carry out an amphibious landing on the Mexican coast at Veracruz followed by an audacious overland march toward Mexico City, some 195 miles away. To help him Scott created the first proper general's field staff in American history, his "little cabinet." Initially, it comprised the Chief Engineer, Colonel Joseph G. Totten (before he returned to Washington, DC, in March 1847), Lieutenant Colonel E. A. Hitchcock, and the chief of staff, Captain Henry Lee Smith, Scott's son-in-law. The crudity of this early effort in staff work is revealed by the chief of staff's junior rank. Lee would be joined by Lieutenants P. G. T. Beauregard, George B. McClellan and Zebulon Tower, and later by three topographical engineers, Joseph E. Johnston, George G. Meade and Gustavus W. Smith. Lee quickly made his mark. Once operations began in earnest he effectively displaced Smith as chief of staff, who suffered from bad health.

On February 15, 1847, Scott sailed to Tampico and then rendezvoused with the US fleet off Lahoc Island. Lee was just 40 years old and had yet to experience anything more dangerous than the inside of an office. On March 9, the first American wave landed at Collado Beach, south of Veracruz; within hours the whole force of 8,600 men were safely ashore.

Scott needed to seize Veracruz quickly. The siege was methodically organized, but Scott's troops lacked heavy artillery. The US Navy lent him six heavy naval guns that were put in place by Lee. After a bombardment lasting a week, Veracruz surrendered unexpectedly on March 29. Scott was forced to wait for a further two weeks while sufficient wagons arrived to transport his supplies. The advance on Mexico City began on April 10, with Scott and his staff following two days later.

The columns toiled into the mountains and a few days later confronted a Mexican army commanded by the President, Santa Anna. It occupied a strong position covered by fortified lines. The Mexican right, Lee explained, "rested on the river [Rio del Plan] at a perpendicular rock, unscalable by man or beast, and their left on impassable ravines"; field works plus thirty-five cannon covered the main road that crossed the Sierra Madre. Dominating the outlook was the mountain of Cerro Gordo itself, encircled by entrenchments and capped by an observation tower.

Scott ordered a detailed reconnaissance of the Mexican position. He immediately sought a way round. He attempted to envelop his enemy; that is, he sought the means to turn the enemy's side—his flank—and advance on his most vulnerable point, the unprotected rear echelons. Scott simply lacked the numerical strength to launch a frontal assault against Cerro Gordo. Furthermore, the longer the campaign continued, the more fragile his lines of communication became. These could be cut easily by Mexican guerrillas, and Scott went to great pains to placate the civilian population. He could not afford to wait; he had to act. Lee would face similar pressures fifteen years later.

Lee was dispatched on an urgent mission to find a way through the ravines that covered the Mexican left. His reconnaissance was interrupted by a company of Mexican soldiers and he was forced to hide for many hours under a large fallen tree. Undiscovered, Lee eventually made his way back to inform Scott that a precarious path did exist. Lee could not be absolutely sure that this trail would bring American troops out on to the road behind the Mexican position, but the risk was worth the effort. On April 17 he guided General David Twiggs's division forward, while that of Gideon J. Pillow distracted the enemy's attention. That night Lee employed three volunteer regiments to move forward the heavy guns needed to support Twiggs's attack; then he hurried to place a brigade on the Mexican rear to cut off Santa Anna's retreat. The assault on the morning of April 18 was successful, although the American failure to cut their escape routes allowed the Mexicans to escape. Nonetheless, Lee's cool and perceptive conduct made his military reputation. Scott described him as "indefatigable," and Twiggs commended him: "I consulted him with confidence, and adopted his suggestions with entire assurance."

Given such praise, Lee felt disappointment at the results. His brevet promotion to major did not arrive until August 24. Meanwhile the American column ascended the Sierra Madre, crossed the Anahuac Plateau, and entered Puebla four days later. Scott was forced to wait here three months for reinforcements after the termination of volunteer enlistments before beginning the final ascent to the defenses of Mexico City itself. Lee spent these months profitably examining the maps captured in Santa Anna's baggage after the battle of Cerro Gordo. Assisted by Beauregard he began to prepare for Scott's use the best possible maps, and he carried out detailed reconnaissances to collect intelligence. These techniques were to provide the basis of his own later method of acting as his own chief intelligence officer.

The following year, on March 7, Scott set off once more, his four divisions now totalling 10,738 men. The Americans clambered painstakingly up the Rio Frio mountains along the National Road and on August 11 Scott made his headquarters at Ayutla, 25 miles from Mexico City. Scott sought the advice of his staff as to the direction of the last phase of the advance. Lee counseled that the shortest and most direct route, south of Lake Texcoco, would also be the most hazardous. He persuaded Scott to take the longer, more indirect route via Lake Chalco and Xochimilco. The advance resumed on August 15 with orders to "live off the country." On reaching

San Augustín three days later, the US Army's path was blocked by another strong Mexican defensive position at San Antonio toward Churubusco. Scott's decision to abandon his supply lines multiplied the strategic and logistic risk. He had to attack at the earliest possible date.

Once more Scott ordered a detailed reconnaissance of the ground, with Lee entrusted with the job of finding a road running westward toward Contreras from San Augustín. Such a route would aid the flexibility of the advance and enable Scott to mount a dual-pronged thrust toward Churubusco, outflanking the Mexican right. Lee's main problem was finding a way through the Pedregal, a 25-square-mile lava field of broken, jagged igneous rocks reputed to be impassable. Lee's initial foray encountered a party of Mexican skirmishers, who withdrew into the heart of the Pedregal. Lee deduced that American troops could use this route, too, and he hastened back on the evening of August 18 to tell Scott.

Scott decided to send half his army (two divisions) westward to clear a road suitable for artillery and then supply trains. The following morning Lee led these troops across the Pedregal to the hamlet of Padierna. They were subjected to fierce Mexican artillery fire and Lee helped to find a way across the precipitous ravines on the Mexican left, before the Americans seized the village of San Geronimo. They were poised on the left flank of the Mexican force guarding the road north from Contreras to Churubusco via San Angelo. Its seizure would enable the general envelopment of Santa Anna's force to the east. But Persifor Smith, in command of the exposed forward units, wanted to acquaint Scott with his intention to attack. Lee volunteered to cross back over the Pedregal at night and report to Scott.

Aided by a violent thunderstorm, Lee fumbled through the hostile country and arrived soaking wet at about 11 p.m. It was now too late to withdraw the troops facing Santa Anna, but Generals Worth and Pillow arrived at Scott's HQ shortly after Lee's return. Lee volunteered to guide them back again, and Scott signed orders that he should sweep up all the troops he could find from their two divisions and distract attention away from Smith's front. Lee found the brigade of the future President, Franklin Pierce, and spent several hours getting his men into position, whereupon they drew a withering fire. Thus Smith's three brigades were able to mount a vigorous attack on the morning of August 20 on the distracted Mexicans whom, Lee reported tersely, "soon gave way in all directions."

Scott arrived on the field and entrusted Lee with yet another mission. He received orders to guide the brigades of James Shields and Pierce north of the Churubusco River in an attempt to cut off the Mexicans at San Antonio from Mexico City. The effort failed but Shields acknowledged Lee's "skill and judgment."

Indeed Lee had played a critical role in the military successes of August 18–20. He proved himself an exemplary staff officer, although on this occasion his success owed as much to physical stamina and endurance as to cerebral dexterity. Scott judged these efforts, unbroken over thirty-six hours, crossing the Pedregal three times (twice in the dark), "the greatest feat of physical and moral courage performed by any individual in my knowledge." Later Lee would receive a second, retrospective promotion to brevet lieutenant colonel, dated from August 20, 1847.

In the first week of September Scott's army warily approached the gates of Mexico City itself. Santa Anna requested an armistice on September 7. However, once agreed, Scott was convinced that the Mexicans were breaking its terms by melting down church bells at a makeshift cannon foundry at Molino del Rey, a short distance south-west of the fortress of Chapultepec. Molino del Rey was seized on September 8, but no evidence of malpractice could be found. Its seizure though had the advantage of providing the Americans with a base to launch an attack on Chapultepec itself. Scott favored an assault on the fortress as its capture would permit the use of two roads into Mexico City. An alternative beckoned, however: a longer southerly route. But on this occasion Scott favored the more direct approach.

Lee received the responsibility of siting the three batteries of artillery that would weaken Chapultepec's walls before the infantry assault went forward. On the evening of September 12 Scott decided impulsively to throw in his attack without the advantage of a long preparatory bombardment. Lee persuaded him to wait until the following morning: the extra time would allow the artillery bombardment to be more effective, destroy any repairs the Mexicans might have made during the night and leave the rest of the day for exploitation. Scott then instructed Lee to help prepare the assault and brief the commanders on his intentions.

Lee returned to the three batteries. When the bombardment finished, Lee guided Pillow's division to its line of departure. The infantry surged toward Chapultepec, but their commander was led to safety by Lee complaining of a "wound." The assault was nonetheless successful without Pillow's presence and Chapultepec fell within an hour and a half. Lee spent the remainder of the day conveying Scott's orders and ensuring that they were carried out. Toward the evening Lee was slightly wounded. The blood loss coming on top of fifty-six hours of continuous exertion led to a collapse. But by the following day Lee had recovered and accompanied Scott as he rode in triumph into the Grand Plaza of Mexico City.

The influence of this Mexican War was a far more important

influence on Lee's military outlook than any other, such as the deductions he might have made from a cursory study of Napoleonic warfare. Lee in fact had only the slightest acquaintance with European methods. The source of his techniques is American and can be located in this antebellum military experience, albeit later adapted to the demands of a great civil war. Further, during Scott's campaigns against Mexico City, Lee was able to witness at first hand how an accomplished general conducted himself. The Mexican campaign had a vastly greater impact on Lee than the reading of any book.

Yet perhaps the most important legacy of the Mexican War for Lee was that despite his key role he had never once commanded troops in battle. He had only ushered forward men commanded by others. For all the remarkable ability and prodigious energy he displayed, he had never planned and carried out an operation under fire. If he had, he would have only been too well aware of how many things could go wrong. His experience as a staff officer marked him out. All his training left him with a life-long habit of offering suggestions to subordinates. For all that, he had demonstrated extraordinary potential. No staff officer could have contributed more to Scott's victories than Lee. He had revealed more than just keenness. He showed zeal in seeing his superior's orders carried out, and did not rest until they were. He also indicated real tactical insight and understood what each critical situation required. Above all, he communicated the true mettle of a future commander of distinction. However great the crisis, he remained calm and in control of his emotions. His seniors looked instinctively to him for guidance, and he was always ready to offer it.

Scott's influence came at a crucial moment in Lee's career. Scott was a born leader, a man of pronounced character who imposed his personality on the troops under his command. A fellow Virginian,

Scott took an almost obsessive interest in his dress; he always looked like a general and he cherished the gentlemanly code. Scott's political views were those of an American Whig and therefore conservative; he trembled at the consequences of guerrilla action. He believed passionately that warfare should remain a clash of organized armies whose conduct should remain strictly regulated. In his drive to Mexico City, Scott had mixed caution with audacity. He disliked the defensive because he needed to *act*, to keep the initiative and to gain every advantage over the enemy. Scott's basic formula would flow into Lee's imagination to form the core of his own military philosophy. Its value and importance can be too easily underrated today given the tendency among some American historians since the end of the Vietnam War to prefer defensive-minded military solutions.

The prime lesson that Scott taught Lee was that small armies could defeat larger ones. Scott moved aggressively and close to the Mexicans, unsettling them. "In battles and military operations in general," Scott once observed, "one ought always seek to take the *lead*, that is to reduce the enemy to the *defensive*." Once this was achieved Scott urged that the attacker should try the unexpected. As soon as freedom of movement was attained, he preferred to divide his army even in the face of superior numbers and envelop a confused and uncertain foe. In 1847 Scott had enjoyed good luck. To a degree, careful planning, reliable intelligence and carefully weighed calculation had combined to create his own luck. Lee would try and do the same.

In the exercise of command, Scott worked within the "Old" army's tradition of delegation. Considerable tactical responsibility fell on subordinates who were responsible for their own plans. "Lee's later methods in this respect," avers Douglas Southall Freeman, "are simply those of Scott. Whether he was right in this conclusion is one of the moot questions of his career." In certain areas, especially in his relations with his civilian superiors, Scott also provided a tutorial in how not to behave. Lee successfully eschewed Scott's unfortunate tactlessness and arrogance and always sought to distance himself from political alliances that would antagonize his civilian superiors.

Lee's twenty-one months in Mexico were brought to an end with an almost embarrassing episode. Scott's querulousness had annoyed President Polk. A court of inquiry was convened in March 1848 to consider charges of corruption that had been levied against the commanding general by his political enemies. He had, in turn, arrested Generals Worth and Pillow and Colonel James Duncan for insubordination. Lee testified on Scott's behalf before leaving Mexico in June 1848. The charges were dismissed but tarnished Scott's laurels after the signature the previous March of the Treaty of Guadaloupe Hidalgo that formally brought hostilities to an end.

Lee's immediate career after Mexico appears anti-climactic. He supervised the building of Fort Carroll, near Baltimore, Maryland. In August 1852 he was appointed Superintendent of the United States Military Academy at West Point. Lee did not enjoy his duties. "The climate is as harsh to me as my duties & neither brings any pleasure." He acquainted himself with some French military books, although these sustained his practical military education rather than opened up new vistas. The same was true of the writing of one of his faculty, Dennis Hart Mahan, who emphasized the importance of field fortifications in war. Lee could hardly have avoided grasping this in Mexico.

In the spring of 1855 Lee took up the position of second-in-command of the Second Cavalry at Camp Cooper, Texas, one of the four new cavalry regiments authorized by Congress to deal with the Comanche menace. Lee's pursuit of small war parties of Comanches up the Brazos, Colorado and Wichita rivers was the nearest he came to commanding troops in battle before 1862. His tour in Texas was interrupted in 1857 when he was forced to return to Arlington because of his wife's declining health. The Lees inherited Arlington that October after the death of Parke Custis. His will stipulated the emancipation of his slaves within five years, but Lee put back the process because of the expense, a decision that generated tension on the estate.

In 1859 his period of compassionate leave was interrupted by John Brown's raid on Harper's Ferry—"the attempt of a fanatic or madman," as Lee described it in a typical Southern reaction—to provoke a slave rebellion in Virginia. Lee commanded the militia and a company of marines that stormed the armory into which Brown had fled with hostages to make his last stand.

During the sectional crisis of the 1850s, Lee had not been especially vocal in championing the Southern cause. He tended to keep his opinions to himself. Lee privately blamed the "aggression" of Northern "abolitionists" for the strife. The hysterical Southern reaction to the election of the first Republican President, Abraham Lincoln, in November 1860 on a platform of *restricting* slavery to its current limits, rendered his sober discretion untenable. In December 1860 South Carolina passed an ordinance of secession. Over the next three months six states of the Deep South followed her example. Lee had always preferred a world of hierarchy and deference. He disapproved of slavery in the abstract but kept slaves nonetheless. At any rate, at this date he did not wish to see any modification of social or race relations in the South. He was prepared to fight to protect these from outside interference. He could not "raise my hand against my relations, my children, my home."

Lee had never been a fervent believer in secession and states' rights, but his views were typical of the majority of Southerners during the secession crisis. His ambivalence over slavery would help later Confederate apologists to argue the extraordinary fiction that the Civil War was not really about slavery. Lee certainly did not favor the slave system's expansion, unlike some, but he was prepared to go to war to defend it. There is no reason to doubt that he was a loyal, dedicated Confederate.

The moment when he would need to choose the cause he preferred was close at hand. On April 12, 1861, the Confederates bombarded Fort Sumter in Charleston harbor. Two days later President Lincoln issued a proclamation calling for 75,000 volunteers to suppress an insurrection in the slave states. On April 18 Lee received an offer of command of this force from General Scott (who remained steadfastly loyal) and Francis P. Blair, an influential Missouri Republican. He met them the following day when Scott detected Lee's "equivocal" response and urged Lee to make his intentions clear. On April 20 Lee wrote Scott a private letter informing him of his intention to resign from the US Army. He submitted it formally to the Secretary of War the same day. Then two days later, leaving Arlington for the last time as its owner, he traveled to Richmond, Virginia, by train. There he accepted the invitation of the Governor, John Letcher, to command "the military and naval forces in Virginia" as a major general. His career as a Confederate was about to begin.

CHAPTER THREE

Quiet Emergence,
April 1861–June 1862

Lee had embraced the new, but for the next twelve months it brought him nothing but frustration, ridicule and disappointment. On April 23 he accepted his new command at an imposing investiture at the Virginia capitol in Richmond. Admirers praised "his erect and muscular frame, firm step and the animated expression of his eye." Crowds had garlanded him during the train journey to Richmond and later gathered outside his hotel at Spotswood House. Within weeks, Lee would feel the fickleness of public opinion. From the first, he denied that the war would be brief. His policy assumed a defensive character as he sought to mobilize Virginia's military resources and strengthen her defenses. Such a policy went against received wisdom and the smug Southern conceit which assumed independence would be gained, at most, within a couple of months. Virginia's soldiers, in Lee's opinion, were raw civilians and the creation of an army would take time. He did not make himself popular by suggesting that an army consisted of more than gathering a crowd of men together.

On May 23 the voters ratified the Virginian Ordinance of Secession, and the Old Dominion thus took her place as a Confederate state. During the previous month Lee had developed an alliance with the Confederacy to integrate Virginian troops into its infant military structure. Confederate troops entered the state, and on May 10 Lee received command of all the troops within her frontiers—but only for their organization, garrisoning and equipment. The Confederate President, Jefferson Davis, probably entertained certain doubts about Lee's ability to command in the field, although he grew to respect Lee's judgment. When Confederate troops were deployed for battle, Lee could only direct Virginian troops into Confederate service. By contrast, his old friend, Joseph E. Johnston (as a brigadier general and Quartermaster General, the most senior US Army officer to go with his state), quickly became dissatisfied with his prospects in the Virginian service. He traveled to the first Confederate capital at Montgomery, Alabama, and enlisted directly in the Confederate regular army as a brigadier general—the only senior Southern general to do so.

Such rapid developments left Lee in a peculiar position in the Confederate chain of command as his appointment to command Virginian forces was rapidly overtaken by events. His personal affairs were also complicated by the occupation of Arlington by Federal troops, in the course of which his invalid wife, Mary, fell into Union hands.

On May 31, President Davis and the entire apparatus of government abandoned Montgomery and moved the capital of the new republic to Richmond, Richmond being, in size and facilities, in every way more suitable to house the expanding Confederate government. This decision placed Virginia squarely in the Civil War's frontline. Richmond was barely 100 miles from Washington, DC, and provided the natural avenue for a Union invasion of the South. Five weeks before, Lee had issued orders to Colonel Thomas J. Jackson to hold the crucial town of Harper's Ferry (at the northern tip of Virginia and the junction of the Potomac and Shenandoah rivers, which housed a US armory and arsenal that manufactured rifled muskets), thus ensuring the maximum possible production of rifled muskets for the Confederacy. Shortly afterward Johnston took command in northern Virginia and ordered Jackson to withdraw. These orders illustrate the contrasting attitudes of the Confederacy's premier generals, Lee aggressive even when on the defensive and never fearful of drawing close to the enemy to secure an advantage; Johnston excessively cautious and defensive. The comparison was given point by Lee's suggestion that should Union forces advance toward Manassas Junction that Johnston combine to attack them—Manassas Junction being a rail junction of the Orange and Alexandria Railroad and the Manassas Gap Railroad that linked the Shenandoah Valley to the rest of northern Virginia where it abutted the Potomac River and thus of critical importance.

On June 8 Governor Letcher issued a proclamation mustering all Virginia forces into Confederate service. Lee thus became a Confederate brigadier general (for several months the most senior rank), but rather oddly, given his acknowledged military reputation, did not receive a field command. Johnston commanded at Winchester in the Shenandoah Valley, and the Louisiana creole, P. G. T. Beauregard, before Centreville, south of Washington, DC. Davis reserved the command of Department No. 2 (all the military forces in the West) for Albert Sidney Johnston. Lee suggested to Joseph Johnston that should Beauregard be attacked, he, Johnston, could move to support him via the Manassas Gap Railroad.

The defense of Virginia was vital to the prosperity and survival of the Confederacy. Virginia and the Carolinas together contained

36.2 percent of the Confederacy's total population. Virginia had been the fifth most populous state in the Union. It had more white inhabitants (1,105,453), more slaves (490,865) and more military-age white men (196,587) than any other Confederate state. In addition, Virginia contained 33.2 percent of the South's total rail track and, being more integral than in other Confederate states, therefore had a disproportionate value. It produced 32.5 percent of the South's manufactured goods, three times that of Tennessee, the next most productive manufacturing state, and accounted for no less than 44 percent of manufacturing capital.

Not the least among her strengths was the vitality of the Virginian military tradition and its robust militia structure. After the passage of the Ordinance of Secession, the Virginia legislature authorized the expenditure of $2 million on the state's defenses. Virginia had more regiments with officers, non-commissioned officers and privates who had some kind of military experience before 1861 than any other Confederate state. She could claim 104 West Point graduates. Of the 304 officers of the "Old" army that had resigned during the secession crisis (not all of them necessarily West Point graduates), 137 were Virginians; South Carolina, by contrast, which had the second largest number of West Point graduates, had forty. In short, Virginia was the best prepared of the seceded states to fight a war. Lee threw himself into the task of organizing these resources. When in July 1861 the Union Army, commanded by Irvin McDowell, advanced toward Manassas Junction, 25 percent of the Confederate troops sent to oppose him were Virginian. Lee managed to raise and equip about 40,000 men with 115 guns, and send forward 114,400 rounds of ammunition and one million percussion caps. His defensive strategy had nourished Virginia's military strength and not frittered it away (only seven men had died during these two months). This was a major contribution, and Lee himself would benefit from his own exertions when he eventually took up field command.

While Johnston and Beauregard together won the Confederate victory at the First Battle of Manassas on July 21, 1861, Lee worked in his office. He had become a kind of freelance military adviser to the President, an informal chief of staff though without clear-cut authority or responsibility. Lee found the position vexing. He was not consoled when a list of full generals issued on August 31 ranked him third below Samuel Cooper, the Adjutant General, and Albert Sidney Johnston but above Joseph Johnston (this added to the latter's dissatisfaction, as he believed that his success at First Manassas should have entitled him to first place).

On July 28 Lee received orders to travel to the insurgent counties of West Virginia. They had refused to accept the authority of the rebel government in Richmond and had welcomed the arrival of Union troops. This action indicated the persistence of Unionist sentiment, especially in the mountainous regions of the Upper South. Lee's orders specified that he "coordinate" a Confederate counterattack. But though he might sign his correspondence "General Commanding," in reality he enjoyed no formal military command over his three captious, opinionated and incompetent subordinates, Brigadier General W. W. Loring, and two "political generals" (not professional soldiers but appointed generals on the strength of their political offices), both former Governors of Virginia, Henry A. Wise and John B. Floyd (the latter had also been Secretary of War in James Buchanan's cabinet). The Confederate effort to occupy West Virginia failed: command authority was too diffuse, while the individual columns were both too small and failed to cooperate because each column leader showed himself too greedy to gain individual glory.

Loring, Floyd and Wise jealously guarded their own interests and ignored Lee's suggestions. Prior to this operation, Lee had held no proper field command, having commanded nothing more than four squadrons of cavalry against the Comanches in Texas in the mid-1850s. At Cheat Mountain, in what is now West Virginia (September 11–13, 1861), he planned an ambitious turning movement along the lines of Cerro Gordo or Contreras. His efforts fell apart at the first hurdle, as Lee's subordinates went their separate ways. "I had taken every precaution to ensure success," Lee complained, "and had counted on it." Lee had yet to learn that no plan could guarantee success. On August 23, 1861, the recalcitrant counties of West Virginia declared themselves a separate state, formally admitted to the Union in 1863.

Lee's career as a general officer had got off to the worst possible start. Further, Wise's family had interests in several newspapers, and highly unflattering reports of Lee's activities were featured prominently. Reporters began to refer to "Granny Lee." When a member of his staff queried why Lee suffered in silence, he replied that it was "better not to attempt a justification or defense, but to go on steadily in the discharge of duty to the best of our ability, leaving all else to the calmer judgement of the future and to a kind Providence." Lee's sense of resignation, or fatalism, tended to contradict his dynamism and keen desire to seize the moment.

Lee found himself recalled to Richmond on October 31. His gloomy and frustrated mood was not shaken when he received orders from Davis to strengthen the Confederacy's southern coastal defenses; "another forlorn hope expedition," he sighed to his daughter, Mildred. The Carolinas had been subjected to coastal raids on Roanoke and the sea islands. Lee established his headquarters at Coosawatchie, South Carolina. He had not been impressed by the half-measures, complacency and selfishness he had witnessed since the Confederate victory at First Manassas. "This is not the way to accomplish our independence," he observed tartly. The South needed dynamic and forceful measures—a concentration on the most urgent issues at the expense of the marginal.

Lee based his actions in South Carolina on his Virginia experience. He put 25,000 troops into the field, reasonably well equipped and armed. He devised a policy of concentration at key points that he would later attempt to introduce into Confederate strategic thinking. He built inland strong points beyond the range of Union naval guns and had obstructions laid in the major rivers. Fortifications were begun at Charleston and Savannah (neither of which were taken from the sea). For all his disappointments to date, in South Carolina Lee began to develop a deep respect for the fine qualities of Southern volunteer soldiers, despite their numerous complaints about the amount of digging they were forced to undertake.

On March 27 Lee returned to Richmond again. His depressed mood matched that of the capital. Defeats on the North Carolina coast were soon followed by the loss in Tennessee of Forts Henry and Donelson and shortly afterward of Nashville; worse would follow with news of the defeat at Shiloh in Tennessee and the loss of the South's greatest city, New Orleans. The widespread view that the war would be short appeared to be the correct one. The Confederacy stared defeat fully in the face. Some Congressional critics, stricken with panic, searched for a military supremo to replace the Secretary of War, Judah P. Benjamin. Lee, despite his checkered record, still seemed the best candidate, and Congress passed a resolution calling on the executive to appoint a general-in-chief. Davis opposed this measure on the grounds that a commanding general would trespass on *his* presidential prerogative as commander-in-chief. Davis offered a compromise whereby Lee would be appointed "under the direction of the President" and "charged with the conduct of military operations in the armies of the Confederacy." The President's solution only formalized Lee's earlier role as Davis's chief military adviser. "I do not see either advantage or pleasure in my duties," Lee wrote. "But I will not complain, but do my best." For all Lee's efforts to avoid politics, at this date his talents were viewed primarily as political and administrative, rather than military.

The controversy over the higher direction of the war highlights significant weaknesses in the Confederate command system. Lee's position resembled that of a chief of staff, but he lacked executive authority. Davis, in any case, was suspicious of any person who sought broad latitude in strategic decision-making. In short, Lee could suggest and cajole (and he was skilled at this, admittedly), but could not initiate. The levels of command became confused. Real authority and prestige were vested at the level of army command, but army commanders were too busy with their own affairs to consider broader questions of strategy, with the result that a vacuum of authority developed above the army level. As in the North, ultimately the commanding general was expected to take the field and thus abandon his most important role as strategic director. The Confederacy failed to fill the gap between the President and his field commanders. And Lee himself longed for army command.

Lee's most striking aspect during this most disappointing time was resilience. For all his frustration, he attended conscientiously to the duties he was entrusted with, however distasteful he might find them.

His job was primarily administrative. Lee could not develop military policy, but he could comment on it; Davis might (or might not) accept his suggestions, but either way it was Lee who had to work out the details of the President's decisions. Lee had not been given time to sort out a suitable staff and the range of problems that came to him at first was diverse. "Our enemies are pressing us everywhere," he complained to his wife. He had to manage departmental needs across the Confederacy, encourage Josiah Gorgas's infant ordnance department, and make himself available for Davis's interminable and often fruitless conferences.

Lee's major contribution to Confederate military policy came in the form of legislation, the Conscription Act of April 16, 1862, the first such law in American history. The Act exemplified two emerging themes in Lee's strategic outlook: to organize Confederate manpower rationally; and to concentrate the maximum possible strength for the approaching climactic phase of the war. There was an additional problem that Lee had to cope with: a large percentage of the twelve-month enlistments were about to expire. The initial concentration achieved in the summer of 1861 in Virginia, Tennessee and Missouri, had slipped from 80 percent to 63 percent of the available soldiers, and Confederate armies were threatened with dissolution. The final draft of the Act was written by a member of Lee's staff, Charles Marshall, who had been a lawyer in civilian life. It permitted the conscription of all white men aged between 18 and 35 for three years or the duration of the war. Those already in the ranks would not be permitted to leave them.

When submitted to Congress, its clauses were diluted as a sop to the champions of states' rights. Substitutes were allowed and a range of exemptions introduced favoring the wealthy and professional classes. The Act was criticized for pushing the burdens of fighting on the backs of the poor. Nevertheless, the Conscription Act sponsored by Lee represented a major step forward in the mobilization of the South's manpower resources. It was superior to anything put in place by the Federal government until 1863 and made possible the waging of the summer and autumn campaigns of 1862.

On March 17 the Confederacy was forced to meet its greatest challenge yet, when the Union commander, George B. McClellan, launched his "grand campaign" to end the war and seize Richmond. His landings on the peninsula between the York and James rivers near the Union enclave at Fort Monroe were not completed until April 2, by which point 389 vessels had landed 121,500 men, 14,592 animals, 1,224 wagons and ambulances and 44 batteries of artillery. McClellan's siege train consisted of 70 heavy siege guns and 41 great mortars. He could thus throw devastating firepower, 7,000 pounds of metal in a single barrage, at Richmond's puny defenses. By March 24 it became clear to the Confederate high command that the Union had landed in strength. Joseph E. Johnston, commander of central and Tidewater Virginia, received orders to hold a line along the Chickahominy River and shield Richmond's lifeline to the Shenandoah Valley, the Virginia Central Railroad. On April 4–5 McClellan opened the siege of Yorktown and closed up to the line of the Warwick River.

Johnston sought to acquiesce in what he regarded as the inevitable by abandoning the line of the Warwick River and pulling back to Richmond itself. On April 14, Johnston and his principal subordinates, James Longstreet and Gustavus W. Smith, attended an important council of war with the President, the new Secretary of War, George W. Randolph, and Lee. Smith put Johnston's case for him: the Confederates should withdraw from the peninsula, continue to garrison Richmond, and shift the war to the North "beyond the Potomac." An advance aimed at Washington, DC, and beyond to threaten Baltimore and Philadelphia, Smith argued, would force

McClellan to withdraw. The ensuing discussion, at times heated, lasted for fourteen hours.

Lee did not favor the abandonment of the lower peninsula because he felt that McClellan might yet be halted in its narrow, crowded fields surrounded by woods and with poor and congested roads. Lee also stressed the importance of not abandoning the naval base at Norfolk. The CSS *Virginia* (formerly the *Merrimack*) covered Johnston's right flank and prevented Federal gunboats from sailing upstream along the James to menace the heart of Richmond itself. Her earlier foray, a month earlier, had caused great alarm in Washington; although the *Virginia* had retired to Norfolk after her fateful encounter with the USS *Monitor*, another sortie was dreaded by Union commanders. Finally, Lee feared for the safety of the Weldon Railroad and the security of the South's Atlantic coast should Union troops from the Carolinas be sent north. Lee was anxious that Ambrose E. Burnside's IX Corps might shift from Roanoke to land south of the James.

Lee argued that the hesitant and cautious McClellan would grant the additional time needed by the Confederates to mount an effective defense of Richmond. His doubts about Johnston's proposed strategy seem soundly based. The transfer of Confederate forces north of the Potomac could not be organized quickly. If Johnston's proposal was accepted, the Confederacy might lose its capital but remain powerless to strike back until the autumn—the political consequences would be incalculable.

The Confederacy had already embraced a strategy to drive Union forces back from its industrial heartland which lay close to its northern frontier. Such a strategy entailed risks, and one element of it had already failed at Shiloh. The only issue to be resolved was whether the campaign to relieve Richmond should be fought close to the capital or far from it. About midnight Davis finally made his decision. He rejected Johnston's proposal and ruled that the Warwick River line should be held.

In the following days Lee began to withdraw troops from the South's Atlantic states, but these were sent to guard the Rappahannock line in case Irvin McDowell's I Corps, held back at Fredericksburg to guard Washington, DC, should advance on Richmond and take its defenders in the rear. If the lower peninsula had been abandoned without a fight, it would not have been possible to mount a diversion in the Shenandoah Valley because Stonewall Jackson would have been called to Richmond sooner. Likewise, McDowell could not have been called away to deal with Jackson and would have been able to play his full part in McClellan's plan to take the city. Faced by such an array, the odds are that Johnston would have abandoned Richmond and McClellan could not have failed to take it.

Lee looked anxiously to find a way of "disrupting the enemy's prearrangements," but the crisis that enveloped the Confederate high command continued to worsen. Johnston evacuated Yorktown on May 4 and the following day fought a rearguard action at Williamsburg that failed to halt McClellan's advance. In a letter to Lee of April 30, having successfully subverted Davis's strategy, Johnston reiterated his desire to cross the Potomac, and suggested an attack in the west to cross the Ohio River. These were mere pipedreams. Johnston resented the rejection of his suggestions and became uncommunicative to an irresponsible degree. Lee became the reluctant intermediary between an angry President and his sulky commander. Lee wrote to Johnston on May 14 that "the President wishes you to confer with him upon your future plans, and for that purpose desires you to see him at his office." Three days later Lee tactfully noted Johnston's failure to comply, and as Davis still needed basic information on "the program of operation which you pro-pose," Johnston should contact Davis directly, "which perhaps would be more convenient to you and satisfactory to him."

The series of evacuations and retreats continued without either rationale or explanation. On May 14 Norfolk was abandoned, with immense destruction of stores and other *matériel*, including the scut-tling of the CSS *Virginia*. Three days later Johnston withdrew into the suburbs of the city. Control of the James River had been given up. Federal gunboats sailed up the James toward Richmond and were not driven back until May 15. The prospects were simply stated: if McClellan could extend his siege lines and bring up his train of heavy guns, the city was doomed. Reflecting the air of depressed expectation, the Confederate government prepared to evacuate its capital. The archives were packed into railroad cars—but where were they to be sent?

Lee had attempted countermeasures on his own initiative. He had no command authority over Jackson in the Shenandoah, and their correspondence was conducted via the Adjutant General's office. On May 12 Lee suggested that Jackson should strike toward Washington, DC, and drive the Union forces back, as "it will prove a great relief to the pressure on Fredericksburg." Jackson used this letter as authority to start his attack. He accepted Lee's advice to feint toward the west, join with Richard S. Ewell's division, and then advance down the valley (that is, advance north-eastward). As a result, Jackson won victories at Front Royal and Winchester. On May 30 Jackson approached the Potomac, a move that engaged the attention of the Lincoln administration, and McDowell's I Corps was summoned northward in an attempt to entrap Jackson's men. Lee learned from this experience the acute sensitivity of Lincoln and his advisers to any threat to Washington, DC.

On May 18 Davis convened an emergency cabinet meeting to consider the unpalatable choices facing the Confederacy. Lee was invited to give his professional opinion on where Confederate forces should rally if the capital was abandoned. The only defensible line south lay about 100 miles to the south-west on the Staunton River, and any such move would expose the Carolinas to invasion. In an emotional outburst, Lee exclaimed: "But, but Richmond must not be given up; it shall not be given up!" These hot words from a cool and reserved man had a marked effect on the President and his civil officers.

On May 26 McClellan shifted two corps, III and IV (some 34,000 men) to the left bank of the Chickahominy, while the remainder stayed on the right bank to shield the axis of the Richmond and York Railroad along which the siege guns would have to be transported. Under cover of III and IV Corps, the Chickahominy would be bridged as a prelude to the concentration of all Union troops on the right bank prior to the final advance. This lumbering and deliberate shift characterized all of McClellan's movements since the landing at Fort Monroe. On May 27 McClellan extended his right flank when V Corps was ordered to drive off Confederate troops around Hanover Court House. Johnston sensed an opportunity for a counterstroke. McClellan had strung out his front over poor lines of lateral communication and had separated a third of his army from the main body. When Johnston received word that III and IV Corps had reached Seven Pines east of Richmond, he decided to attack them. Johnston labored under the misapprehension that McDowell had begun an advance toward Richmond when he had actually withdrawn north-east, and Johnston felt that this might be his only chance to drive McClellan back. Heavy rains had swollen the rivers and transformed the roads into quagmires. The decision to attack had resulted, too, from Lee's success at concentrating troops. He had added more than 40,000 men to Johnston's ranks during May. Johnston would thus be able to attack with a strength of 70,000 and many more men were en route.

At the Battle of Seven Pines (Fair Oaks) on May 31 Johnston attempted to crush the two isolated Union corps. He tried to attack and move around, that is envelop, the flanks of III and IV Corps and guard against a flank attack on his own men across the Chickahominy. In every respect the plan failed in a badly mismanaged battle. All attacks were repulsed despite the advantage of surprise. Lee himself rode to the battlefield to see what was going on, as did the President: both were unaware of the details of Johnston's plan. At the end of the day, Johnston was severely wounded. As they rode to Richmond, Davis told Lee that he intended to give him the command. Lee was, in any case, the only full general available. He would receive his orders as soon as Davis got back to the Confederate "White House." Lee's instructions were to take "command of the army in eastern Virginia and North Carolina" and this would "interfere temporarily" with his duties as the President's military adviser. It may have been an accidental promotion forced on Davis—and considered temporary—but it was the best decision that the Confederate President ever made.

CHAPTER FOUR

Fortunes Transformed,
June–July 1862

Lee's assumption of field command resulted from an unfortunate accident that befell an old friend. Nobody more "deeply deplored" this event Lee told the army on June 1 than "its present commander." Nevertheless, Lee's whole demeanor over the next month reveals a determination to make the most of his opportunity. He succeeded beyond all expectation. He became eventually so identified with the Army of Northern Virginia, as Johnston had previously styled his command, that when Johnston returned to duty in late November 1862 nobody even dreamed that he should be restored to its command. Lee was 55 years old and the remaining chapters in this book deal only with the last eight years of his life—and only three of these would be at the head of an army. Apart from the time spent in Mexico, most of Lee's life had seen his ambitions thwarted. Like Lambert Strether in Henry James's novel, *The Ambassadors* (1903), Lee could say that all he had to show for his 55 years was an acceptance of fate. The boldness and the elegance of the design of his campaigns sustains the view of historian Emory Thomas that they were a response to his earlier tribulations: the struggle between his desire for release—the freedom to take risks, which his father had exploited to the uttermost—and the crushing obligation to maintain control, especially his iron dedication to duty.

So far Lee had served the Confederacy for thirteen months, working at the very center of its counsels. There he developed a very particular strategic outlook. It is appropriate to review the attributes and beliefs that Lee brought to field command and assess the challenges he faced in the overall context of the war, as well as to look at the later controversy over the nature of his achievement.

Though his trials would be eased by the sheer strength of his character, Lee hardly took up command at an auspicious moment. His subordinates were Johnston's men and some resented the imposition of a staff officer on them. Johnston himself had proved a whiner, always the first to complain about something, and his subordinates had picked up the habit. He had proved especially poor at reassuring his political masters. The first thing Lee did was to change the atmosphere in which decisions were taken. Within days "a new impulse" could be felt "from headquarters." Nonetheless, for many Lee remained the butt of ridicule and sarcasm throughout these weeks. The newspapers remained hostile and dismissed him as elderly and cautious. But being underrated is often an advantage, and McClellan was conscious of critical Southern press comment of Lee. In terms more suited to his own autobiography, he believed Lee "wanting in moral firmness when pressed with heavy responsibility, and likely to be timid and irresolute in action." McClellan would be in for a shock.

Actually, Lee's strength of character, aloofness and gentlemanly conduct convinced his new subordinates that he was not an intriguer but could be trusted and that he would concentrate on the affairs of the army rather than keep more than half an eye on Richmond politics. Within two months many of the grumblers would become his most loyal acolytes. Those who failed to prove themselves would be removed, for Lee's gentlemanly bearing disguised a ruthlessness in sizing up subordinates and replacing those unable to live up to his high expectations.

Lee's fatalism was matched by an optimistic spirit. He shouldered responsibility readily, whereas Johnston tended to shuffle it off or blame others. He immediately displayed energy and a capacity to inspire others. "Lee was ceaselessly astir," as Douglas Southall Freeman puts it with characteristic pith. Unlike Johnston's, his military career would be characterized by an overwhelming determination to damage the enemy rather than worry about what damage the enemy would do to him. Within a week he had evolved a concept to encompass McClellan's defeat and had secured a level of presidential approval and trust that had always eluded Johnston. Within three weeks he was ready to launch the most audacious offensive yet seen in the short history of the Confederacy.

Lee's rapid success in transforming the gloomy atmosphere can be measured by his first meeting on June 3 with his generals at a house called The Chimneys on the Nine Mile Road outside Richmond. Lee wanted to gauge their mood rather than get the benefit of their views. They were pessimistic and short of ideas. Chase Whiting picked up a piece of paper and drew a diagram purporting to demonstrate the inevitable triumph of McClellan and the fall of Richmond. "Stop, stop," exclaimed Lee. "If you go to ciphering we are whipped beforehand." President Davis called in at the meeting and complained afterward that he did not like its tone. Lee ended the meeting without acquainting this "council of war" with his plans.

In setting about his task Lee did enjoy certain advantages denied Johnston. First, he had been given a broader command over all Virginia and North Carolina. Second, coming from the inside, he had a working knowledge of the Davis administration that would ease the acceptance of his plans and facilitate his demands for logistical support. Lee had the extraordinary (and rare) ability, as Major General Sir Frederick Maurice acknowledges, to focus on his own tasks and not interfere in the affairs of others. Davis and Lee thus developed a strong partnership, their differences being of emphasis rather than substance.

Third, Lee also enjoyed the great good fortune in being able to draw upon the men mobilized by the April Conscription Act. As a result, the Confederacy managed to field the largest army before Richmond it ever managed to raise. Fourth, it fought in its own country, and had easier access to intelligence and supplies, and, unlike the Union forces, did not have long, vulnerable supply lines. Finally, Lee engaged the enemy vigorously at a time when the Lincoln administration in Washington demonstrated scant confidence in its commanders.

The future difficulties that Lee would encounter were due more to the structural weaknesses in the command system than to personalities. Lee's post as presidential adviser was not filled until 1864, and to some extent Davis still expected Lee to proffer advice. This worked to Lee's benefit during the summer of 1862, but not thereafter. In the absence of a properly constituted general-in-chief, Lee could hardly serve haphazardly as a distant substitute. Lee might have demanded more authority, but it is difficult to see how this would have overcome the structural awkwardness of combining field command with higher authority. Davis appeared keen to grant him greater influence so long as it did not have to be acknowledged formally. Such difficulties did not prevent Lee from displaying exemplary tact and finely tuned political shrewdness in his dealings with the President. Davis's relationship with his other commanders tended to be fractious; that Lee enjoyed such a harmonious working partnership with Davis is not the least of his achievements.

Before taking up field command, Lee had evolved firm views on the grand strategy that best suited the Confederacy and he now wasted little time in implementing them. It is not true, as Major General J. F. C. Fuller suggests, that Lee lacked grand strategic vision. Another critic, historian Alan T. Nolan, admits that Lee had a grand strategy, but believes it to be the wrong one. These and other critics of Lee, such as Thomas L. Connelly, criticize Lee's "parochialism" because he concentrated on the eastern theater and lacked appreciation of the west's strategic importance. In short, they claim, Lee's penchant for the offensive proved self-defeating because it eroded Southern manpower. Nolan even goes so far as to suggest that "it was not feasible to defeat the North militarily as distinct from prolonging the contest until the North gave it up." This is a very pessimistic assessment of the potential of military power, one that clearly deprecates "risk." Nonetheless, much conventional wisdom now claims that the Confederacy's only chance to gain its independence lay in adopting a defensive strategy and this was ruined by Lee's offensive forays.

The charge of "parochialism" is a serious one, and has been made many times. Lee had shown no bias toward Virginia when he served as Davis's military adviser. On the contrary, when Johnston had argued for concentration before Richmond, Lee had pointed toward its effects on the South's Atlantic states. Army command, of course, encourages a constriction of view because the first loyalty of any field general is to the troops under his immediate command. Lee was really the victim of a faulty command system. Born down by his pressing duties, he could not be expected to take matters for which he was not formally responsible more seriously than those for which he was. He did not ignore the importance of the west. Similarly, though he had a measure of influence with Davis, this was not the same as true power or formal responsibility. Criticisms of Lee's strategy overlook the vital importance of Virginia to the defense of the Confederate eastern seaboard. Both the west and the east were strategically interdependent. The only real difference between them is that although the Civil War could be lost for the South in the west, the only chance it had of *winning* lay around the Northern political heart, Washington, DC. Here were fixed the eyes of other powers, like Great Britain and France. If the Confederacy had been defeated in the east the war would have been lost even sooner.

Lee would not have disagreed with Nolan's suggestion that the Confederacy needed to force the North to relinquish the contest. But he believed a defensive strategy misguided because time was not on the South's side. He believed that the Confederacy *did* have a chance to win—and would risk much to achieve it. Lee contended that he should make war on the Northern *will*. To be successful, the process of making war would have to be speeded up. His political instinct led him to understand the influence of elections on the war. He regularly took the temperature of Northern public opinion by his assiduous reading of Northern newspapers. Conversely, he sensed the fragility of Confederate nationalism, one that might not survive a long war; many white Southerners had not supported the secessionist cause until after the Federal response to the bombardment of Fort Sumter. Lee grasped above all that its uncertain loyalties and fickle opinions would demand offensive victories.

Lee's attempt to wage a war of attrition against the North faced even more severe problems than those overcome by George Washington against the British. The Union Army could bring its superior strength to bear far more easily: Lee's enemy lay just across the Potomac not the Atlantic. He sought to "frustrate, embarrass," "baffle" or "mystify" Northern attacks by maneuver, and then defeat them on ground of his choosing. The Confederacy, he told Davis, needed "to carefully measure and husband our strength, and not to expect more than in the ordinary course of affairs it is capable of accomplishing." Northern strength should be worn down at key points. The Confederacy could not afford "inactivity" or delay. The tempo of operations would need to be multiplied and matters brought to the proof. The South would win when the North failed to replace its armies. Lee's formula urged that the Confederacy's resources be conserved as much as possible. Lee's much-vaunted boldness, in other words, was the product of clear-headed calculation not rash, thoughtless gambles.

Confederate public opinion and politicians demanded that Yankees be punished and made to flee. Defensive measures gave up territory, precious war-making resources, exposed slavery to dissolution and brought great political pressure to bear on Davis. Militarily, it surrendered the initiative to the Union. Defensive operations for the Confederacy always seemed to end in catastrophe. Lee believed this pattern would repeat itself on the peninsula. The Confederates would have to seize the initiative and determine the time, place and indeed the style of fighting. So far they had failed to do any of these things. The South's defensive campaign had only permitted McClellan to muster overwhelming strength at a point of his choosing: he was only 5 miles from his goal and about to bring up massive firepower in order to attain it. Lee thus deduced that he should risk much to gain much, to *win*. Simply avoiding defeat, Johnston's course, was not enough. Lee's course was the right one, but he suffered no delusions as to the enormous task that lay in front of him.

He had no alternative but to attempt the relief of Richmond. The city not only provided sustenance for his troops, it provided more munitions than half of the rest of the Confederate states put together. In addition, he needed Richmond's railroad system to sustain his dynamic form of warfare. But Lee set himself a more ambitious objective. He intended to seek the destruction of the Army of the Potomac in the field. This was the key step, in his view, in securing the northeastern frontier of the Confederacy, one that would keep the enemy away from the South's putative industrial heartland and allow an untrammeled assertion of its territorial integrity. Lee's aims were so ambitious that a danger existed that he might over-reach himself.

Lee's operational methods were consciously developed to match his strategic objectives. He wished to see Confederate resources concentrated in two field armies; these, in turn, would force the Union Army to counter them and thus relieve threatened points along the Atlantic coast.

Lee's style of warfare might be dubbed defensive-offensive. He would develop a technique whereby he threw back Federal invasions and then strove to follow up his success. His plans tended to be dependent on the movements of the enemy; but once the direction of the Union advance had been divined, he sought to impose his will on the campaign. But to make the most of his opportunities, above all, he needed reliable intelligence. His army needed to be lean and supple to respond rapidly to changing circumstances. The very first order issued by Lee's headquarters decreed that "all surplus baggage, broken down wagons, horses and mules, and everything that may embarrass the prompt movement of the army will be turned into depot." Not only was the Army of Northern Virginia lighter and more nimble than its Northern rivals, until the autumn of 1864 it also demonstrated superior march discipline.

Lee repeatedly divided his army at the outset of a campaign, confident that it could be reunited if danger threatened. He calculated that a divided army confused the enemy. Lee sought room for maneuver, revealing decisiveness and self-assurance as to the objective of the campaign. He never doubted the importance of bringing the enemy to battle if the conditions favored his troops. Consequently, he sought favorable ground by shifting away from the navigable estuaries dominated by the US Navy and McClellan's heavy guns to the fields and thick woods to the north and west. Here Lee could exploit his advantage in infantry and cavalry. The latter could screen his movements, discern the intentions of the enemy and protect his own columns from prying eyes. Lee expected his infantry to out-march and out-fight the Union troops. He asked a lot of his men, but he came close to creating the balance of stalemate that he sought while other Confederate fronts crumbled.

Lee's dynamic and audacious style of warfare left only a small margin for error. The possibility of defeat might rest on a knife-edge. He therefore made strenuous demands on his own resources and stamina. He was rather old for field command, as J. F. C. Fuller is not slow to point out, but he proved that he had the physical and mental strength of a much younger man; he carried a colossal weight of responsibility lightly. A war of maneuver required a skilled commander who had confidence in his own judgment to see operations through to a successful conclusion. Lee had that sense of purpose and a resilient, buoyant spirit. Another Confederate commander, Braxton Bragg, a near-great general, proved capable of conceiving subtle and elegant plans but crumbled psychologically as they reached the point of decision, collapsing into hypochondria and irresolution.

In pursuit of victory, Lee made effective use of the turning movement. He could rarely exploit what military theorists term "interior lines," that is, the geographical advantage of movement to an objective via a shorter distance than the enemy can cover (like the inside lane of a running track). He usually had to rely on the exterior line of advancing around the enemy's flank to attack the Union rear and lines of communication. Once turned, the enemy could be forced to abandon his defenses. An alternative version would be to seize an important point that the Union would have to take back by launching an attack under a disadvantage. The main weakness of this device, as Lee's own conduct during the Seven Days' Battles showed, was that it encouraged an aggressive defender to snatch the initiative back.

Once Lee had decided to fight for the initiative he showed a surpassing skill in selecting the decisive point and then gaining local, tactical superiority. Lee's reforms in June 1862 made this practice easier. His Military Secretary, Colonel Armistead Long, and the brilliant ordnance member of his staff, the gunner E. Porter Alexander, sought to reorganize the artillery. Big smooth-bores were replaced with field pieces, slack batteries were consolidated and divisional chiefs of artillery were appointed to ensure the creation of reserves of guns. The whole was designed to ensure greater flexibility and mobility of firepower, and ultimately its concentration in grand batteries.

The turning movement and the tactical flank attack might define Lee's defensive-offensive method, but it opened up a cavity that he never successfully filled. To destroy Union cohesion, Lee needed to mount a successful pursuit of a broken army. But the point when an attack switched from being frontal to driving the enemy from the battlefield is difficult to gauge. On two occasions, at Malvern Hill in

July 1862 and Gettysburg a year later, Lee misjudged the level of Union disarray and tottered on the edge of disaster. Lee should have devoted more effort to considering how pursuits could be managed tactically.

In June 1862 thought of pursuits seemed absurd. Lee was under a lot of pressure and caught a summer cold, but shouldered his burdens effortlessly. He had little to go on, and his own plan could not rely on the spadework of his predecessor. On June 3 he sent the Chief Engineer, Major Walter H. Stevens, on a reconnaissance. "It is not intended to construct a continuous line of defense or to erect extensive works," Lee briefed him before his departure. After his return, Lee sent some further thoughts to the President for his consideration: "McClellan will make this a battle of posts. He will take position from position, under cover of his heavy guns, and we cannot get at him without storming his works, which with our troops is extremely hazardous." Consequently, Lee deduced that he should build a series of lighter field works, "that I can hold with part of my forces in front, while with the rest I will endeavor to make a diversion to bring McClellan out." But the main question remained unanswered: what form would this diversion take?

The following day Lee undertook a personal reconnaissance. He trotted out of Richmond on his grey stallion, Traveller, taking his staff with him. "Now, Colonel Long," Lee asked rhetorically (as he would do repeatedly during his campaigns), "how can we get at those people?" (He hardly ever referred to "the enemy" in conversation; they were invariably "those people.") Lee decided that Johnston's effort to exploit the division of the Army of the Potomac had been, in principle, the correct one. However, Johnston had attacked the wrong part of the Union line. Lee switched his attention to the Union right on the north bank of the Chickahominy. Lee believed that this represented the greatest point of Union operational vulnerability, but it was not weakly held. Major General Fitz-John Porter's V Corps covered McClellan's right. A protégé of McClellan, he had followed his master's methods by constructing a defensive line at 90 degrees to his front around Beaver Dam Creek, with advanced posts at Mechanicsville.

Within five days Lee took the decision that this flank should be turned and that the attacking units would be reinforced by bringing the 32,000 men of Stonewall Jackson's Army of the Valley to Richmond. Jackson, the most famous soldier in the Confederacy since his audacious victories in the Shenandoah Valley, would be given direction "to sweep down north of the Chickahominy, cut up McClellan's communications and rear, while I attack in front."

It would be easier to bring Jackson into the fray at this point rather than further south, a journey that required his men crossing Richmond. The plan did not lack disadvantages, nonetheless. Lee would have to advance operationally (though not strategically) on an exterior line and would have to move around the Union Army. It would be far easier for McClellan to reinforce Porter, as he possessed the bridges over the Chickahominy, than it would be for Lee to offer succor to Jackson. A measure of tension also existed within Lee's neat calculations. The Shenandoah had to remain quiet. On June 8 Lee warned Jackson to be prepared to "unite at the decisive moment with the army near Richmond." A week later Lee finally received word from Jackson that his dual success at Cross Keys and Port Republic would enable him to leave the valley and join him. Jackson was to unite with the Army of Northern Virginia at Ashland, 16 miles north of Richmond, though the date of his arrival had yet to be agreed. Jackson pushed ahead of his troops to confer with Lee.

Lee desperately needed more detailed information about the

Federal right flank. He feared that McClellan might reinforce it (indeed Porter had already received the support of one division from VI Corps). On June 11 the cavalry commander, Major General J. E. B. Stuart, received instructions to "make a secret movement" in order to gain "intelligence of his [the enemy's] operations. Communications &c." Stuart interpreted his orders broadly, and took 1,200 troopers within 3 miles of McClellan's supply base at the White House. Stuart succeeded in drawing attention away from Confederate preparations to attack the Union right by completing a circuit of McClellan's entire army, a signal victory in the propaganda war. Stuart confirmed that McClellan's right had not been extended northward and that he lacked a rearguard to parry Jackson's blows.

Now that Lee held responsibility for the defense of Richmond, he assumed Johnston's mantle as the earnest spokesman for concentration. He drew about half of all North Carolina's troops to Virginia. He also completely reorganized the army. About thirty regiments found themselves serving in different brigades and divisions. Gustavus Smith's division was broken up, and a new one under A. P. Hill (the "Light Division") created. Such changes are usually unpopular, and Lee made few new friends with a program of trench-digging. Lee faced a clamor of complaint, but insisted to Davis that hard work instilled discipline and that entrenchment would save lives.

By the end of the second week of June, Lee began to fill in the tactical detail of his conception. For all his brisk attention to business, Lee always exuded an unhurried air. He had not met his subordinates for nearly three weeks. On June 23 he called together his four principal commanders, A. P. Hill, Longstreet, D. H. Hill and Stonewall Jackson to brief them on his plans to divide the army. Lee's planned turning movement would involve all of their troops and enjoy the advantage of concentrating 56,000 men for the attack. He had contrived to gain local, tactical superiority at the decisive point of more than 2:1. In total Lee would field 92,400 men. He would have a sizeable force available to shield Richmond itself, including the divisions of John B. Magruder, Benjamin Huger and Theophilus Holmes.

Lee's conduct at the conference was distinguished by his self-assurance. He did not seek the views of his commanders or convene a "council of war." He explained the plan in general and then expected his subordinates to work out their own tactical roles. Once Lee had finished, he stood up and left the room. During the subsequent discussion, Jackson reported that he could be in place at Ashland by June 25—that is, in two days' time. In this casual manner, the decision emerged that June 25 would be the start date for the offensive. Hence not only had Lee relinquished control over the movement of his divisions, the start date was effectively imposed on him. He would not repeat this experiment in delegation again.

The Seven Days' Battles, as they were later called, were Lee's first experience of command in war. His plan was brilliant, but due to inexperience far from brilliantly executed. It was based on a series of complex movements that made excessive demands on his divisional commanders and their staffs who had not worked together before. Lee, moreover, had given little thought as to what McClellan might do once he had abandoned his entrenchments. If he attempted to seize Richmond, "I will be on the enemy's heels before he gets there." McClellan needed 600 tons of supplies per day. Lee guessed correctly that in a crisis, McClellan would place logistical priorities over the operational and move to cover his lines of communications.

The first day, June 25, passed waiting for Jackson's arrival. McClellan raised fears by probing gingerly toward Oak Grove. Lee worried this might indicate a strong Union assault on Richmond, but he did not allow this proposal to deter him from following his own plan. When on June 26 the Confederate attack began in earnest, McClellan was completely taken by surprise. Lee rode out to Mechanicsville, arriving just before 3 p.m. Jackson had failed to arrive as promised. What was to be done? Lee, who seems to have assumed that his role would be that of a spectator, immediately felt the pressures that bore down on a commanding general. He had never intended to fight at Mechanicsville, only seize Meadow Bridge and move on around the Union flank once Jackson had turned it. At about 5 p.m. and without orders, A. P. Hill impetuously attacked the Union position frontally. The assault was scrappy, poorly co-ordinated and easily repulsed. Hill had also needlessly announced Lee's intention to attack north of the Chickahominy.

Lee intervened, not to stop the attack, but to support it. Lee reasoned that with the divisions of D. H. Hill and Longstreet approaching, the junction with Jackson was endangered if McClellan, now forewarned, attempted to prevent it. Hill renewed the assault. At that critical moment, President Davis and a large entourage rode on to the battlefield.

"Mr. President," Lee snapped angrily, "who is all this army and what is it doing here?"

"It is not my army, General," replied Davis, rather taken aback.

"It is certainly not my army, Mr. President, and this is no place for it."

Davis led them away from the field.

Despite this display of asperity, Lee kept his *sang froid*. He issued no further orders at Mechanicsville, even as Longstreet and D. H. Hill crossed the Chickahominy, widening the gap between the two parts of the Army of Northern Virginia. The troops in the Richmond defenses, commanded by John B. Magruder, whose entire career had been an essay in bluff, put on a fearsome show of frantic demonstrations that distracted McClellan's attention. Hill's continued attacks on Beaver Dam Creek were no more successful than before, but Lee kept his nerve, remaining determined to impose his will on the Union commander. By the end of June 26, it was evident that the V Corps could not stay in position, and that night McClellan ordered its withdrawal. Lee had to stay alert and be prepared to strike in order that the tempo of operations might be maintained. He had discovered already that ambitious plans were easier to conceive on the map than put into practice. For one thing, as Freeman says, the "maps issued to officers proved unworthy of the name."

Porter withdrew to a strong position about 4 miles to the southeast, covering Duane's Bridge astride Gaines' Mill on Powhite Creek. The retreat had surrendered New Bridge that, once repaired, would ease Lee's communications with Magruder and Huger's divisions. At last, a day late, the junction with Jackson was made, and the two generals met at Walnut Grove Church. Jackson offered no apology or explanation and Lee wasted no time in recriminations. Lee ordered that his command would be increased to four divisions and that this force should take the road south-east to Cold Harbor and turn Porter's new line. A. P. Hill and Longstreet's divisions would advance directly on Powhite Creek, but they would not assault the Union lines until Jackson had turned them.

As the day wore on, Lee fell victim to a miscalculation. He believed erroneously that McClellan had moved the bulk of his force north of the Chickahominy and thus the climactic moment of the campaign was rapidly approaching. Lee rode to Gainesville, content to see the debris of retreat scattered around him. His headquarters tent was pitched back at Mechanicsville, but he wanted to be close at hand in case further improvisation was required. He had successfully concentrated 50,000 men to face Porter's 35,000, but his supe-riority could not be described as overwhelming. In addition, Porter had occupied a formidable position behind Boatswain's Swamp and anchored on a rise called Turkey Hill. At Gaines' Mill, Lee would direct troops tactically and lead them into battle for the first time.

He arrived on the battlefield not a moment too soon. For a second time, A. P. Hill had impulsively attacked Federal breastworks and been thrown back so violently it looked as if his division might break. In the middle of the afternoon Jackson's men appeared—at the right moment but in the wrong place. Jackson's guide had got lost and eventually chosen a road that brought his command out opposite the Union right-center, not flank or rear. Lee rode up to greet Jackson. "Ah, General," he said airily, "I am very glad to see you. I had hoped to be with you before this"—a remark revealing more than a hint of sarcasm.

Lee had little choice but to risk a frontal assault. The attack would have to be made in the evening with little information about Union dispositions. Lee's top priority was to keep the offensive moving forward: he had to keep the initiative in his own hands. Lee approached one of Longstreet's brigadiers, John B. Hood, whose Texans would attack Turkey Hill. Lee said simply, "This must be done. Can you break his line?"

"I can try," Hood replied.

In an extraordinary act of vigor, courage and determination, Hood's men stormed Turkey Hill and opened the way for Jackson and the rest of Longstreet's division. Porter was driven off but not destroyed. Lee had won his first battle, in the process capturing twelve artillery pieces, but did not have time to count the cost. The action had been vital and had succeeded. Lee appreciated that some-times commanders lack choices when pursuing their aims.

It was thus all the more frustrating to discover that the offensive remained stalled. "We will sleep on the field and shall renew the contest in the morning," Lee reported to Jefferson Davis. He had driven McClellan back about 10 miles in a semi-circle toward the Chickahominy, but the Union supply line had yet to be cut. That night McClellan decided to abandon his current position and shift his base to the James River. Curiously, McClellan's caution, attention to logistics and defensive-mindedness led him to choose the most dangerous course rather than admit defeat and go back the way he had come. Instead, his troops (80 percent of which had not yet been engaged) would have to march across the Confederate front.

Lee could not know this, and June 28 was spent in trying to locate McClellan's line of retreat. If it was to the south-west, Lee needed to advance the three divisions guarding Richmond, those of Magruder, Huger and Holmes, and concentrate the Army of Northern Virginia south of the Chickahominy. If it was back to the White House and the York River, then a Confederate concentration could be more easily achieved. But a Federal movement to the James had one advantage for Lee. The effort against Richmond could not be renewed because the western side of the peninsula lacked a railroad to send forward the Union siege train.

Lee lacked intelligence. He made poor use of his cavalry as it remained idle north of the Chickahominy: June 28 had been wasted, but the following day McClellan's withdrawal to the James had been verified. His 99,000 men, 281 guns, 26 heavy guns, and 3,800 wagons stretched back more than 25 miles. The Union commander offered Lee the opportunity to slice up his corps while strung out on the march, and destroy his army chunk by chunk.

McClellan did not lack a certain skill, but he thought war could be waged like a business. When his schedules and targets were dislocated he lost heart: paradoxically McClellan's generalship lacked enterprise. Lee had succeeded in driving the Army of the Potomac into the open, and it had retired, as Lee predicted. The Confederate right flank now needed to be thrown forward, and Lee wrote to Benjamin Huger, "you must press him cautiously, and hold your line at all hazards." Yet though he wished to avoid any more incautious actions like Mechanicsville, he was to be disappointed. Lee slept well that night. At 11 p.m. Brigadier General Jubal A. Early came to report and found Lee in bed asleep; he left quietly.

Lee had formulated his operational plan to defeat Union offensives in a letter to Major General Theophilus Holmes as long ago as March 16: ". . . retard his movements, eat him up in detail if possible, attack him at a disadvantage, and, if practicable, drive him back." Lee strove to do just this three months later. Magruder was ordered to attack McClellan's line of retreat. But Lee could not overcome the price that a wasted day had cost him. It was simply too far from Gaines' Mill to the James to envelop McClellan in one bound. A sequence of battles had to be improvised. First, Lee had to hit McClellan's rear guard to slow down the pace of the Union retreat (Magruder's task); second, he would follow this up with a turning movement that would cut the Army of the Potomac off before it reached the James. Jackson would support Magruder on the left to commence the envelopment. On the right, Huger's division would advance down the Williamsburg Road to harass the Union columns. Holmes's division would also move forward but remain in reserve.

Lee grasped immediately that White Oak Swamp would be the crucial feature on the morrow. The swamp lay in a slight valley and stretched like an arc across the battlefield, an unavoidable barrier that the Army of the Potomac must cross. Lee ordered that the envelopment must be attempted at the crossroads near Glendale, so that the path of the Union troops could be blocked as they emerged from the swamp. Longstreet and A. P. Hill were moving southward as well as Jackson. All Magruder had to do was launch a well-timed, coordinated attack on the Union columns before they could escape; once support came up the Union Army could be broken up and its cohesion smashed.

Lee decided to emulate Scott and set up a central headquarters on the Cold Harbor Road. He believed that from this point he could communicate with all parts of his scattered army. This was a mistake. He was too far back and unavailable for consultation. Lee needed to be at the front to reassure and prompt his nervous and inexperienced subordinates, as he had been at Gaines' Mill.

This stage of the campaign demonstrated a lack of firm grip. A confused Magruder, unnerved by an unaccountable withdrawal made by Huger's division, could not decide what to do. He needed to be reassured by the authoritative voice of a staff officer acquainted with Lee's designs. None was to be found: Confederate staff work had virtually collapsed because of a shortage of officers who had the barest acquaintance with the nature of their duties. Magruder lost his head and ordered a series of wild, piecemeal attacks on whatever troops lay in front of him. A messy action ensued that made no contribution to Lee's overall operational design.

The blame was not all Magruder's. Lee wrote censoriously to him during the action: "You are under the impression that General Jackson has been ordered not to support you. On the contrary, he has been directed to do so and to push the pursuit vigorously." In fact Jackson had not received such an order, or if he had, he ignored it. The muddle was symptomatic of the excessive strain placed on the crude staff system by operations of this magnitude.

A powerful thunderstorm then intervened, soaking the roads and fields and the men marching across them. June 29, the day that Lee believed would decide the campaign if not the war, broke "cloudless and calm." Lee himself, as one observer noted, looked "absolute perfection" in "every detail of dress and equipment." In the morning he conferred with Jackson, and the contrast with his grubby and dishevelled subordinate could hardly be more marked. Jackson seemed to be more alert and keen as Lee outlined his mission of smashing into the rear of McClellan's army. So far he had done nothing in this campaign to merit the reputation he had earned in the Shenandoah. As he rode off, Lee watched him intently.

The numerous Confederate columns (eight divisions) that circled McClellan's weary host had so far hardly behaved like hungry wolves. McClellan himself was no longer on the battlefield, as he busied himself inspecting suitable enclaves on the James River in which his army might find safety. Two of his corps had plunged through White Oak Swamp, but the remainder had yet to begin the laborious passage. Lee had assumed that Huger had drawn up on the right to harry them and their vulnerable trains. He trotted up a slight knoll in the rear, but became impatient when he could hear no firing. As he had heard nothing from either Huger or Jackson since the movement began, he rode off himself (rather than send a staff officer) to guide them to their points of attack. En route he met Holmes and ordered his division to fire on the Union trains immediately. Holmes failed to do so. Then Lee encountered Longstreet and A. P. Hill's divisions. In a state as near to frantic as Lee ever allowed himself to get, he ordered that they should begin their attacks in the hope that both Huger and Jackson would throw their men forward as soon as they heard gunfire.

It was no wonder that Lee acted with growing frustration. Around Frayser's Farm he had one half of McClellan's army almost surrounded. He had again secured a local superiority of 71,500 men against 61,500 Union troops. One thrust from Jackson and they would be forced to capitulate in the field. Alas, Jackson sat lethargically, overcome with torpor and weariness after his exertions in the Shenandoah Valley. As it was, Longstreet and Hill (yet again) launched piecemeal attacks: 20,000 Confederates swept forward against 40,000 Union troops and made little headway.

Lee's plan had been ruined by poor tactical execution: the Confederate troops attacked in such a way as to negate the local superiority their commander had contrived to achieve. It is no surprise that Freeman calls Fraser's Farm "one of the great lost opportunities of Confederate military history." Casualties were about even, 3,673 Confederate to 3,797 Union, but the scales of fate crashed heavily in favor of the Union. The Army of the Potomac continued its retreat virtually unmolested. Even D. H. Hill, who came to have reason to dislike Lee, recalled that he "bore grandly his terrible disappointment." He became desperate to inflict a heavy blow on the enemy before he made good his escape. On June 30 Lee had no alternative but to redeploy the three commands that had already failed him, namely, Huger, Magruder and Jackson. He had no choice either but to compress all six divisions on to the narrow Willis Church Road. The cavalry were not available to find other routes (Stuart had only just crossed the Chickahominy that morning). The divisions followed one after the other with the artillery pushed to the rear.

While Lee watched through his field glasses as the Union columns deployed in good order along Malvern Hill, overlooking the James, Early observed that McClellan might yet escape.

"Yes," snapped Lee. "He will get away because I cannot have my orders carried out."

Malvern Hill, a plateau with steep bluffs opposite the Confederate right, forms the most prominent high ground south of Richmond. It served as a more than adequate shield for McClellan's withdrawal. Lee rode to the Confederate left toward Western Run, a sector covered by the bulk of the Union artillery, a clue perhaps to a hidden vulnerability. Lee examined the possibilities for a flank attack.

Lee may have been reluctant to let McClellan escape unscathed, but by July 1 he lacked any clear-cut aim. Longstreet reported the discovery of a clearing on top of a rise opposite the Union position that, combined with a similar clearing on Jackson's front at the Poindexter Farm, would bring a devastating crossfire on the Union gun line and clear the way for the infantry. Lee issued orders for the concentration of sixty guns at each clearing. He also dictated a vague order at 1:30 p.m. stating that the artillery "would rake the enemy's lines" and, once shattered, a brigade of Huger's division (Armstead's) "who can witness the effects of the fire, has been ordered to charge with a yell. Do the same." Once this vague order was circulated to divisional commanders Lee abdicated all control over the battle.

The guns could not be found or brought up in time. This left the Federals free to concentrate their artillery in its most devastating role during the Civil War—killing infantry. During the afternoon Magruder's division had wandered about on the battlefield often lost. At 3:30 p.m. he emerged on the Confederate right and received Lee's order, now two hours old. He assumed it had recently been issued and launched his cheering and enthusiastic brigades against the strongest part of the Union position. D. H. Hill's men followed suit on the left. All of the piecemeal assaults were driven back. Lee contemplated shifting the battle around the Union left, but this would have been futile, and instead waited anxiously for a Union counterattack. Fortunately, as the "utmost confusion" prevailed on the Confederate side, none materialized.

Malvern Hill was quite the most botched engagement Lee ever directed. He imposed no design on a series of disjointed attacks that cost over 5,000 casualties for no gain. Lee was just as inexperienced at field command (probably more) than any of his subordinates. He had not yet grasped that his troops were no longer in pursuit and that he had to prepare the intricate tactics needed to win a set-piece battle. Lee's decision to make July 2 a day of rest seems to indicate that he was on the verge of exhaustion. Finally, on July 4 Lee ordered probing attacks on the new Federal position at Harrison's Landing, but these came to nothing. As Lee informed Davis, "he [McClellan] is too secure under cover of his boats to be driven from his position." Thus the Seven Days' Battles, and indeed the Peninsula campaign itself, came to an anti-climactic end.

The Seven Days' Battles were a deeply flawed series of engagements and failed to secure their tactical objectives. As a result, Lee's deeply wrought and sophisticated campaign plan kept falling apart. He simply demanded too much of his uncertain subordinates and raw troops. The Confederates suffered 20,135 casualties (of whom 11,000 were killed or permanently incapacitated) to the Federal loss of 15,855, a greater bill than Lee had allowed for. By his own strategic yardstick, Lee had not done well. Some tactical errors could be rectified, such as the misuse of cavalry and the artillery. (Only once had firepower been massed, at White Oak Swamp, and then the advantage had been frittered away.) In his report, Lee complained of a want of "correct and timely information" accentuated by the atrocious maps and low, thickly wooded country. Lee's rapid improvisations were bound to fail unless sustained by a flow of reliable intelligence. He could not casually assume that it would be available when he needed it. To some degree, his self-assurance hindered his capacity to shape the campaign, because as a staff officer he took it for granted that opportunities sprang from a detailed plan. He did not realize until after his first campaign how many things could, and would, go wrong.

His staff should have been there to help him, but often he ended up doing their work. Staff work at all levels was abysmal. The American staff system had evolved fitfully and by Prussian standards appeared crude. American staffs were not expected to show decision or take responsibility for operations, let alone take decisions in the commander's name. Lee himself did not appear adept at handling the staff, despite, or perhaps because of, his staff background. To make matters worse, he relied excessively on his subordinates and they let him down. Among the trio of generals who failed (including Huger and Magruder) was Stonewall Jackson. If Jackson had shown half the energy of his Valley campaign then McClellan might have been crushed.

Yet, when all the flaws are laid bare, the Seven Days remain a triumph of will and determination. The siege of Richmond had been lifted, Southern morale had soared, indeed the Confederacy itself had been saved. Lee's strategic victory ensured that the Civil War would continue. He demonstrated that a combination of concentration, ingenuity and audacity enabled a turning movement to drive even the most cautious commanders out of entrenchments.

Lee himself became almost obsessed with gaining an initial, overwhelming victory. Such a victory, he believed rightly, would have staggered the North and eroded its will to continue the war. So much had been invested by the Union in McClellan's "grand campaign" that its shattering defeat would have had incalculable effects. Lee had also gained a moral sway over McClellan and his generals. Lee had "lost" most of the tactical actions, but this mattered little because in terms of the operational direction of the campaign, taken as a whole, Lee had maneuverd to keep the initiative in his hands, and then gone on to win.

Lee suspected that the best opportunity for achieving victory had already been lost. He might have taken 52 guns and 31,000 small arms, but the Army of the Potomac remained intact.

"Under ordinary circumstances," he lamented, "the Federal Army should have been destroyed." His report, submitted in 1863, was written after nearly a year of observation of "ordinary" attention to duty, obedience to orders, march discipline, initiative when required and trust in Stonewall Jackson. A modicum of any one of these in June 1862 would have brought immense dividends; the casualties sustained might have saved far more of the lives lost later.

When Lee later learned of McClellan's reluctant evacuation of Harrison's Landing, he wrote to Davis on August 17, "I feel greatly mortified . . . he ought not to have got off so easily." It is rare in history for a commander in his first campaign to save the nation that he has chosen to serve, but that is what Lee managed to achieve in June and July 1862.

CHAPTER FIVE

Apogee,

July–September 1862

"Our success has not," Lee regretted to his wife, reflecting on the Seven Days, "been as great or complete as I would have desired, but God knows what is best for us." McClellan's army remained intact and in a strong position. Lee had proved successful in drawing Federal pressure away from other fronts. Union forces were removed from the South's Atlantic coast, including Ambrose E. Burnside's IX Corps, and brought north. At the end of June 1862, Lincoln called John Pope from the west to take command of the newly created Army of Virginia. Pope had gained some minor successes along the Mississippi, including the seizure of Island No. 10, and had been present at the fall of Corinth. He appeared more aggressive than McClellan, and enjoyed the advantage of being a Republican in politics. Yet Pope was untested in high command.

Pope had a talent for self-promotion that rebounded on his historical reputation. In pursuit of promotion, he antagonized his peers who thought him pompous, abrasive and intolerant. He is usually dismissed as an incompetent blockhead, completely out of his depth when commanding an army. It is tempting, but quite misleading, to label all Lee's opponents before Grant as wholly bereft of skill. Pope's conduct of operations actually appears energetic and thoughtful—save at the crucial moment when it really counted. Pope's first biographer, David Hunter Strother, discerned his fatal weakness when he noted a tendency to be "irascible and impulsive in his judgments of men."

Lee quickly formed a dislike of Pope. This personal edge—a desire to humiliate his Union opponent—requires explanation. After the Seven Days, Lee had been reunited with his wife. She had dallied at Arlington and then passed through Union lines before staying at the White House, a plantation bequeathed by his grandfather to Rooney Lee. Alas, this lay square in the path of McClellan's advance, and by the summer the house had been set ablaze and many items belonging to George Washington looted or destroyed. Mrs. Lee proved herself more strident in her Confederate loyalties than her husband, and no doubt he received a graphic account of this vandalism. Lee's patrimony had been rapidly consumed by the war. "I expect to be a pauper if I get through the war," he confided to his eldest son, Custis.

Enter John Pope, a general happy to approve the kind of destruction that caused Lee so much heartache. On July 14 Pope issued a bombastic and self-congratulatory order, claiming that in the west "we have always seen the backs of our enemies." He followed this with three General Orders announcing that his troops "will subsist upon the country," with payment only being made to Unionists; any houses harboring snipers were to be burned, and disloyal Virginians were to be arrested. Pope's experience in Missouri taught him the necessity for harsh and punitive measures when confronting guerrillas. His policy was not so much the reflection of a malicious character as a response to the tougher attitudes permeating the Lincoln administration as it contemplated numerous failures to bring the Confederacy to heel. Lee felt outrage at Pope's swipe at fellow Virginians. He wrote to McClellan (not Pope) threatening retaliation "as the only means of compelling the observance of the rules of civilized warfare." A proclamation issued by Jefferson Davis placed Pope and his officers outside the bounds of the usual rules governing the taking of prisoners of war. If captured they would be arrested and imprisoned; if any Southerners had been executed, a like number of Pope's officers would be shot.

Such a controversy could not conceal from Lee that Pope's appearance had complicated the solution of the strategic equation. The Army of the Potomac remained the greater threat; but the Army of Virginia could not be ignored. It posed a serious threat to the Virginia Central Railroad, Richmond's lifeline to the Shenandoah Valley. Lee explained the best way to defend such a vulnerable line to Jefferson Davis. He would mass "troops at salient and commanding points to repress the attack of the enemy and strike him as he advances" rather than scatter "the force along the whole line." To improve articulation of movement and the coordination of large-scale operations, Lee in effect reorganized his army into two corps, under Longstreet and Jackson. His innovation would not be confirmed by Congress until November, but it operated *de facto* for the remainder of the campaigning season.

On July 13 Jackson was sent with two divisions and a cavalry brigade to protect Richmond's lines of communication and gather intelligence on Pope's intentions. Lee's stab northward began a delicate juggle, as he shuttled his forces about in line with his evolving appreciation of Union plans. Union commanders might intend a pincer movement against Richmond or a concentration on the line of the Rappahannock that could herald a renewed thrust on the city from the north. Lee needed all his subtlety and resourcefulness to dodge the weighty if cumbersome blows aimed at his army. On July 13 he received a first warning that Burnside's IX Corps had arrived at Fredericksburg via Aquia Creek.

Lee believed that his only alternative lay in neutralizing Union numerical strength by maneuver and that, should he advance to the Rapidan, Pope would retire. Throughout the next month Lee acted with tremendous skill as his own chief of intelligence. He considered all the reports he received, written and oral, questioned deserters and returned Confederate prisoners of war, listened to local rumors and evaluated captured orders. Lee was not clairvoyant, and his capacity to "read" his opponents has been exaggerated. Indeed, he admitted that "he found his ideas running around in a circle" and struggled "to find a tangent." The evaluation of intelligence he found difficult because (as he had learned in Mexico) "our people take up so readily all alarming accounts" that became so exaggerated in the telling "that it is difficult to learn the truth till too late to profit by it."

By July 23 Lee warned Jackson not to advance too far northward in case he had to return to assist in the defense of Richmond. Still, four days later A. P. Hill's division and one brigade were sent to reinforce Jackson with the order to harass Pope. "I will keep General McClellan quiet till it is over, if rapidly executed." D. H. Hill's division plus forty-three guns would attempt to drive the Army of the Potomac further downstream, "so that I can reinforce Jackson without hazard to Richmond, and thus enable him to drive if not destroy that miscreant Pope."

With three divisions at his disposal, Jackson remained vulnerable. After his lethargic performance during the Seven Days, Lee did not trust Jackson as fully as he would in the future. He probably assumed that Jackson prospered in semi-independent operations and, although he urged a turning movement on his subordinate, he added that he would "leave the matter to your reflection and good judgment." Jackson's stock began to rise when on August 11 Lee received news of the Battle of Cedar Mountain two days earlier. This encounter with Pope's vanguard had foiled the Union advance on Charlottesville to cut the Virginia Central Railroad.

The pace of operations thereafter slowed. Pope took up a strong position along the north bank of the Rapidan, presenting Lee with a tricky problem of how to restore maneuver. Lee deduced that Jackson's success at Cedar Mountain (for all that it had been a messy battle), indicated that it would be profitable to concentrate his full strength against the Army of Virginia (the smaller of the two Union forces) so long as McClellan lay quiescent along the James. He could use the Virginia Central Railroad to shift his troops northward before a significant portion of McClellan's army could be transported by sea to reinforce Pope. The pressure on Lee to reach a final decision mounted. On August 13 D. H. Hill sent news that McClellan had begun the evacuation of Harrison's Landing, at the same time further details of Burnside's advance toward Fredericksburg arrived. Stuart's cavalry received orders to verify the reports.

Lee did not yet plan to go to Gordonsville (a railroad junction on the Orange and Alexandria and Virginia Central Railroads east of the Blue Ridge Mountains) and take personal command. McClellan's evacuation might be only partial. Lee proposed that Jackson (under Longstreet's supervision, whose commission as a major general was senior) repeat his Valley campaign by sweeping around Pope's left, join Stuart's cavalry and position himself between Pope and Burnside's forces. Lee's plans were temporarily disrupted by the alarming news that McClellan had advanced to Malvern Hill again; but once the falsity of these reports was clear, Lee resumed his northward concentration content that Richmond remained secure.

By August 14 half of the Army of Northern Virginia had been transferred to the area around Gordonsville, mostly by rail. A day later Lee himself left Richmond. "I go to Gordonsville," he informed Custis, now serving on Davis's personal staff. "My after movements depend on circumstances that I cannot foresee." Lee had not forgotten that the Army of the Potomac represented the greater threat. Should McClellan be allowed to make an uninterrupted junction with Pope, the odds would be too great to resist. In anticipation of the former's arrival, Pope crossed the Rapidan and encamped in the V-shaped area west of the confluence with the Rappahannock. Lee realized that if he could turn Pope's right flank the Union Army could be trapped between the two rivers.

The Confederate maneuver had to be postponed until August 20 because of inadequate logistical support (especially the supply of ammunition). The artillery, coming up by road, had also lagged behind. In the meantime (thanks to the capture of Stuart's adjutant, who carried valuable dispatches) Pope recognized his vulnerability and withdrew to the north bank of the Rappahannock. Lee watched the Federal retreat from the top of Clark Mountain. He turned to Longstreet, cloaking his disappointment with sardonic humor at Pope's expense. "General, we little thought that the enemy would turn his back upon us thus early in the campaign."

Lee quickly produced a new plan. He asked Davis to release the Artillery Reserve and two of the four divisions left behind to defend Richmond. Pope had actually benefited from his hurried withdrawal because he had shifted nearer to Fredericksburg and his reinforcements. But if he continued to withdraw toward Warrenton, then his columns might get strung out along the roads, offering an opportunity for Lee to strike and destroy Union cohesion. A larger conception also took shape in Lee's mind. As the Army of Northern Virginia advanced northward, it pushed back at every bound the start-line from which Federal commanders would have to mount their offensives. The pressure on the agricultural resources of Virginia would be commensurately relieved. As the campaign developed, Lee sought nothing less than to secure the northern frontier of the Confederacy.

Lee had yet to evolve a coherent concept of operations in order to achieve his aim: Pope had so far successfully countered every one of his gambits. Lee predicted that Pope would remain satisfied "to hold us in check" on the Rappahannock until reinforced by the Army of the Potomac. Foul weather did not deter Lee from launching the dynamic and aggressive operations he knew were needed to dislocate Pope's prudent scheme. He again asked Davis for the remaining troops left in Richmond. The President sent them north plus two further brigades of North Carolina troops that Lee had not asked for. "Confidence in you," Davis told Lee, "overcomes the view which would otherwise be taken of the exposed condition of Richmond. . . ." Presidential support was a key factor in Lee's early successes.

By August 24 Lee had finally decided to push Jackson's corps around the Union right flank, with Jackson using the Bull Run Mountains as a screen. Its main objective would be to operate along Pope's line of communications with Washington and cut the Orange–Alexandria Railroad. As Pope's reinforcements came along a line running parallel with the Rappahannock, that is from the east, disrupting lines to the north-east would only be a nuisance. Lee could not operate around the Union flank downstream where the better fords could be found because Pope had them well covered. Stuart had already made an effective contribution to this audacious stroke by mounting raids that spread alarm and confusion in Pope's rear area, culminating in a raid on Pope's headquarters at Catlett Station, in which many valuable papers were captured.

Lee did not issue written orders or detailed instructions. Too many had already been captured in this campaign by both sides. He had faith in his ability to shape the campaign as it developed and exploit opportunities as they presented themselves, even if such opportunism ran the risk of allowing a subordinate to commit him to a course of action that he might prefer to avoid.

Lee had not yet committed himself to fight a battle close to the Washington defenses, an area that afforded little space for exploitation. Instead, he intended to needle Pope, enticing him away from the Union capital toward the Shenandoah Valley. As Pope pivoted on his left flank in response to the Confederate offensive, he might be brought to battle attempting to protect the Union line of communications—but this remained only a possibility. The ultimate aim was to throw Union forces out of Virginia and bring moral and political pressure to bear on the Lincoln administration in Washington.

Most of the cavalry departed with Jackson to screen Lee's advance. His "foot cavalry" set a scorching pace in the summer heat, 23,000 men covering 25 miles in 14 hours on the first day, and covering the same distance on August 25. Jackson's corps arrived at Bristoe Station by the evening of the following day. Jackson only committed one error: he failed to secure Thoroughfare Gap with Stuart's cavalry, a route Longstreet might need to take to link up with him. Instead, he looted Pope's supply base at Manassas Junction. When a furious Pope concentrated to take his revenge, Jackson withdrew northward (and further away from Longstreet) and took up a well-sited defensive position at Groveton.

Lee had ordered no precise point or date of rendezvous. His distribution on August 26 positively invited destruction in detail. His nerve in scattering the Army of Northern Virginia around the Bull Run Mountains is breathtaking. He deployed 58,000 men in an arc from Waterloo to the Rappahannock. Jackson had four divisions (including Stuart) totalling 28,500; Longstreet, with four smaller divisions of 23,000 men, lurked behind the mountains at Salem, while R. H. Anderson's division had not yet left Waterloo. Eighty miles to the south, D. H. Hill and McLaws's divisions and the Artillery Reserve plus a cavalry brigade were hurrying to join the main body. Fifty miles beyond them were the two North Carolina brigades, boarding trains at Petersburg. In all, 89,000 men in 12 divisions were scattered along a line that stretched 120 miles. A division of force on this scale in the face of a more powerful enemy tempted fate. Fortunately, Pope, myopically obsessed with Jackson's destruction, failed to exploit it.

Lee showed little outward signs of anxiety as he and Longstreet marched to link up with Jackson. On the evening of August 26 he dined with the Marshall family at Orleans, and appeared every inch "the genial cavalier." The real crisis of the campaign came the following day when Longstreet's troops found Thoroughfare Gap, only 100 yards wide and strewn with boulders, blocked by Union infantry. Fortunately it was held by only a single division, that of Brigadier General James B. Ricketts. Lee issued orders to find other routes and then accepted an invitation to dine at a Mr. Robinson's nearby house, giving no hint of worry. Ricketts, isolated and fearful, with no support from Pope, withdrew during the night, and Longstreet's Corps marched through the Gap unopposed on the morning of August 29. They surged down the Warrenton Pike, one of the best roads in the region, toward Jackson's lines. "We must hurry and help him," exclaimed Lee when he heard the roll of cannon and rifled-musket volleys.

Jackson had sent Stuart's cavalry to guide (and screen) Longstreet's corps to the battlefield. The first of his men to arrive were the two brigades of Hood's division, who linked with Jackson's right flank at about 10:30 a.m. The remainder of Longstreet's troops deployed at 90 degrees to Jackson's line during the late morning, with Stuart's cavalry shielding his protruding and exposed right flank. The junction with Jackson had been successfully achieved: "One of the boldest moves," boasted Walter H. Taylor of Lee's staff, "of our so-called *timid*? General"—a sarcastic jibe at Lee's earlier critics and those who put the blame on Lee, rather than on Jackson, for the errors of the Seven Days.

Jackson had been in action since August 28, having provoked a battle because he feared that Pope might withdraw into the Washington defenses. Lee probably did not share his enthusiasm for a general action at this moment. He certainly made no effort to conceal his arrival, assuming that surprise had been forfeited. He set up headquarters in a cleared field about one quarter of a mile behind the front. Immediately Lee suggested that an attack be launched to take the pressure off Jackson while the Unionists were comparatively unprepared. He did not intend this to be a decisive stroke. Longstreet counselled detailed reconnaissance and the investigation of reports that Union troops had appeared on the right flank (these turned out to be Fitz-John Porter's V Corps of the Army of the Potomac).

At about noon, Lee suggested to Longstreet a second time in his gentlemanly way, "Hadn't we better move our line forward?" "I think not," replied Longstreet firmly. The advice was wise because Stuart shortly afterward confirmed the arrival of V Corps on Longstreet's right. Lee agreed that it presented a threat, but deferred a final decision until he had taken a look for himself. He returned after an hour and voiced the opinion that Union forces would not resist strongly. He urged an advance along the Gainesville–Centerville turnpike. Longstreet disagreed, and several failed probes carried out by Hood's division confirmed his judgment. Lee then accepted Cadmus Wilcox's advice that it would be fruitless to continue attacks along this line.

Even Lee's most admiring biographers, including Freeman and Dowdey, are critical of his failure to overrule Longstreet and attack on August 29. They both assume, wrongly, that Lee had decided to launch a decisive stroke that morning when it is likely that he had far more limited aims in mind. These two writers also believe that Longstreet's headstrong, obstinate and obstructive attitude, which wrecked the Gettysburg campaign, dated from the false impression he acquired at Second Manassas that Lee could be dominated, that Lee was essentially too nice, too civil, to overrule an over-mighty subordinate. This incident does not deserve the retrospective significance that has been piled on it. In any case, Longstreet offered sensible tactical advice that Lee was right to accept.

It is probable, however, that Lee sensed more quickly than Longstreet that the events that had brought his army to this field offered a tremendous opportunity and that they must hasten to exploit it. How often had victory been thrown away during the Seven Days by the waste of time? If Lee did not attack soon his army could not stay in its present location for long. Lee could not know that Pope had still not guessed that the Army of Northern Virginia had reunited in front of him. The ridge above Manassas was tactically strong but would have to be abandoned should the two Federal armies join up unimpeded. On the morning of August 30 it still seemed likely that

Lee would maneuver west toward the Shenandoah. He wrote to Davis, offering a magisterial opinion on the conduct of the campaign so far. "It has been my desire to avoid a general engagement, being the weaker force, and by manoeuvring to relieve the burden of the country referred to [Virginia]." Two further alternatives offered themselves: tempt Pope into attacking him (a prospect that appeared less likely as the morning passed); or turn Pope's right flank and move between his army and Washington, DC.

Events beyond Lee's control then intervened in his favor. Pope insisted on throwing forward a reinforced V Corps in an attack on Jackson's right flank. Under the changed circumstances of August 29–30 he was unwittingly hitting the Confederate center and thus exposed his own left flank to a Confederate counterstroke. At 1 p.m. the Union onslaught, in three great columns, advanced over the undulating ground in front of an astonished Lee. Initially, A. P. Hill's division buckled and Jackson signaled urgently for reinforcements to shore up his line.

Fortunately, Longstreet had concentrated a reserve battalion of artillery, eighteen guns in all, at the angle of the junction of the two corps; they opened a deadly fire on Porter's troops. Lee wired back, "Do you still need reinforcements?" Jackson replied, "No, the enemy are giving way." Lee galloped across to Longstreet and ordered him to throw in his entire corps. Longstreet had anticipated the order and at about 4 p.m. launched a concentrated counterstroke that moved forward with simultaneous power. Jackson also received instructions to "look out and protect his left flank."

Union cohesion disintegrated. As Pope's troops ran back toward the Stone Bridge over the Bull Run, Lee became swept up by the excitement and rode along with the advanced Confederate echelons over the mile and a half of the battlefield. This was an error on his part. He should have been thinking about the form the pursuit should take: it is not just a matter of chasing the enemy. Tactical cohesion on Longstreet's left began to break down and units got mixed up, with men wandering off to plunder Union camps. Lee ordered Stuart's cavalry to keep Pope's men on the run, but that was insufficient.

Lee reported to Davis three days later that "the darkness of the night, his [Pope's] destruction of the Stone Bridge after crossing and the uncertainty of the fords stopped the pursuit." Lee did not have at hand the third element of the Army of Northern Virginia under D. H. Hill, at least another two divisions, that could have been ordered forward to support Stuart. He had to rely on his most exhausted troops, Jackson's Corps, to undertake the most taxing part of the battle. Pope gained time to reorganize his forces at Chantilly after a day's grace. On September 1 Jackson's troops were repulsed. To make matters worse, Lee tripped on August 31 and injured both his hands—they had to be wrapped in bandages and his right arm put in a sling. Unable to ride, or even to mount a horse, Lee found it impossible to command effectively. Torpor fell over the battlefield. The fleeting chance to annihilate Pope's army passed as quickly as it came. But though Lee's effort at pursuit had failed, success in battle cannot be gauged by recourse to abstract standards of textbook perfection. Lee faced the Hobson's choice of waiting for fresh troops to arrive or letting the opportunity to attack slip away.

In the campaign of Second Manassas, Lee made the most of the chances thrown his way. It represents an astonishing achievement. No other Civil War commander accomplished such a transformation of his fortunes in such a short space of time and against such great odds. The campaign also witnessed an enormous improvement in Lee's operational technique. Confederate formations moved across the theater with confidence, aggression and initiative. Taken as a whole, the campaign forms a superb example of "operational articulation"—the separation, maneuver and junction of large forces on the battlefield itself. Despite such complex moves, at the climax of the campaign Lee's plans were simpler, relied on fewer subordinates and were better coordinated than they had been during the Seven Days. By the autumn of 1862, Lee had transferred the war in the east back to the northern frontier of the Confederacy. He had placed his army in a strong position to strike the Union at its most vulnerable spot rather than attempt merely to dodge its blows.

During the following month Lee himself gave the impression that the climactic moment of the war approached. He would not stand idly by and forfeit victory. Taking advantage of this strategic dividend nonetheless presented Lee with a thorny problem. His army lay only 20 miles from Washington, but he could not besiege the capital. Union forces had escaped behind its defenses and Lee lacked both the room in which to maneuver and the equipment to winkle them out. His string of victories had forced President Lincoln to call for another 300,000 volunteers. Meanwhile, the Confederacy, too, was being reinforced by men from its more southerly coastal states and from the Kanawha Valley which runs from Ohio into West Virginia. How could these men be deployed?

Lee could not stand still and allow the enemy to concentrate overwhelming forces in Virginia. He needed to advance and force them to follow him so that he could catch portions of the Union Army unawares, as he had with Pope. The Army of Northern Virginia, he felt, should cross the broad waters of the Potomac River and invade Maryland. For many months Lee had consistently argued that the Confederacy would have to gain its independence through its own exertions and not expect foreign help. He could nonetheless create the strategic conditions that might prompt foreign intervention. Lee also hoped that a prolonged stay north of the Potomac might promote the cause of the Democratic Party in the North and those who would not oppose Confederate independence, and thus, as Walter Taylor hoped, "bring about a speedy peace."

Many Democrats supported the war wholeheartedly; others supported the war so long as its aims embraced the restoration of the Union and not the destruction of slavery. After the disappointments of 1862, many Democrats became disillusioned with the "Republican" war and its heavy casualties. The "peace" Democrats argued for some kind of accommodation with the South. For the moment, they appeared passive and discouraged, but Lee hoped that if he could continue to erode the morale of the Northern armies in the east, it would help them to find a strident voice before the November elections. It was this that prompted Lee on September 8, once the invasion of Maryland was underway, to suggest to Davis that the Confederate government demand recognition of its independence, "when it is in our power to inflict injury upon our adversary," and "show conclusively to the world that our sole object is the attainment of an honorable peace." Over the longer term, Lee calculated, Lincoln's rejection of this offer would add to Union demoralization and increase the popular appeal of the peace party.

Though a Confederate move north would be hazardous in the extreme, earlier similar risks had been justified by the results. The stakes in Maryland were higher. Lee reported to Davis that around 100,000 Union troops were stationed in the Washington area, the disparate elements of five different armies, demoralized and disorientated. The conditions facing his enemy were far from propitious. Even if the Southern armies had probably passed their peak numerically, the Army of Northern Virginia appeared resurgent. Lee might enjoy an even smaller margin for error than before Richmond, but he might be given the priceless benefit of three or four weeks to develop his offensive before Union forces would feel able to confront him. As Lee told William Allan in 1866, "the disparity of forces . . . rendered the risks unavoidable."

Several of Lee's assumptions would prove excessively sanguine. Yet the crucial point is that his offensive strategy rested on sound military logic and careful assessment of the risk involved. The Maryland campaign was not a rash adventure. A turning movement north-west of Washington would expose the political and psychological vulnerabilities of Union strategy and cut the lines of communications to its strategic heart in the White House. Once the railroads were cut, organizing any riposte to the Confederate thrust would prove very difficult. Ultimately, Lee sought to end the Maryland campaign with a battle fought under conditions that most favored his army and placed the Union commander at a disadvantage. "I went into Maryland to give battle," he told Allan after the war. Like the Seven Days, Lee hoped that a dynamic operation would create opportunities not even hinted at in the plans that launched it.

In December 1861 a Confederate Congressional Committee resolution had demanded the "liberation" of Maryland. Lee could justify such an effort on the grounds of safeguarding Virginia: the best way of defending Richmond lay in securing the northern frontier. Such a scheme, however, assumed a community of interest between the Confederacy and Maryland. Would Marylanders welcome Lee's army and share their foodstuffs and wealth with their enthusiastic "liberators"? Lee did not intend his excursion to be a full-scale invasion, which he in any case lacked the necessary means to sustain. One day he would have to return to Virginia, as Porter Alexander suggested, "as a stone thrown upward is certain to come down."

Lee concentrated his army at Leesburg and called up its third wing under D. H. Hill. This force now consisted of the two divisions of Lafayette McLaws and John G. Walker, as well as Hill's own, plus Hampton's cavalry brigade. As these troops had marched 145 miles, they arrived at Leesburg on September 2 footsore and tired. (It is unclear why Hill had not taken rail transport, saving him much wear and tear.)

The total strength of Lee's army is a controversial point. Lee himself, and his later champions among Lost Cause writers, and some modern historians, make claims that it numbered between 51,000 and 55,000. A persuasive case can be made, however, that at the beginning of the operation the Army of Northern Virginia was considerably larger. An estimate nearer to 70,000 can be suggested based on calculation of returns, the arrival of considerable reinforcements and the close counting of Union spies as the Confederates advanced into Maryland. What is beyond doubt is that levels of desertion and "straggling" (when soldiers leave the ranks with the intention of returning) were high, not least as the railroads could not be used by Lee's army in making their north-westerly advance and the troops accordingly had to march in the heat and humidity typical of late summer on the Eastern Seaboard.

Once the campaign was renewed in earnest, the drain on Confederate strength began again. Lee called it "our great embarrassment" and asked for firm measures to prevent the hemorrhaging of his ranks; he also created a provost guard to round up deserters. Discipline in the Army of Northern Virginia continued to be casual and, contrary to Confederate propaganda, the looting of private property did occur. It is also likely that the men were not as enthusiastic to follow Lee's lead as they were the following year: he remained a comparatively new commander, and morale in some units was questionable. But those that stayed in the ranks were loyal and keen. "They all believe in *themselves* as well as their generals, and are totally in earnest," a Unionist doctor observed with some exaggeration.

Lee personified this tremendous self-confidence. It is easy to overlook that behind the dynamic stimulus of the Confederate advance lay an invalid confined to an ambulance. Lee's energy was remarkable, but he might have done still more had he enjoyed his customary good health. Unable to write himself, the campaign was still planned and launched in three days. Some of the errors that led to its dramatic unravelling can be explained by this haste. Remarkably, although Lee had taken the trouble to consult Longstreet and Jackson, he began the campaign without obtaining presidential sanction.

On September 5 Jackson's corps crossed the Potomac at White's Ford, near Leesburg. The bands played "Maryland, My Maryland." Longstreet and then D. H. Hill followed. Stuart's cavalry threw out an effective screen as the infantry columns headed north to Frederick to refit and rest. Lee then intended to cross west of South Mountain toward Hagerstown. He expected to use this as a base (as he admitted some days later in an earnest effort to give Davis the impression that he had been consulted) for an invasion of Pennsylvania. Chambersburg was the preferred objective in the Cumberland Valley, the northward extension of the Shenandoah Valley. Its seizure would give the Confederates control over their long lines of communication that ran south-west from Washington, DC. Only if Chambersburg fell without difficulty would Lee consider mounting thrusts toward Harrisburg or Philadelphia, hoping that Confederate raids toward them would provoke desperate and poorly managed Union attacks that would play into his hands. Lee did not know for several days that his opponent in the campaign would again be George B. McClellan, not a man to risk all on the throw of the dice.

On September 4, Lee received a careful brief by Colonel Bradley T. Johnson on conditions prevailing in Maryland. He labored under no illusions concerning the state's enthusiasm for the Confederate cause. Bradley had been keen to point out that "a large portion of the people were ardent Unionists"—especially in the western counties that Lee proposed to occupy. Here the population was mainly of German origin, thrifty folk who worked small farms and were hostile to slavery. Nonetheless, on September 6 Lee became aware of the other Confederate thrusts into Kentucky and thus of the enormous importance of his own campaign in the broader scheme of things. The social and demographic disadvantages of the terrain he proposed to traverse did not deter a man of Lee's optimistic nature.

Two days later Lee decided to issue a proclamation to calm the fears of Maryland citizens as to his intentions. Davis had not cleared this either (and was superior to his proposed draft received later). Lee did not expect to be greeted by a pro-secessionist uprising; indeed his troops had been welcomed by the citizens of Frederick with nothing other than sullen silence. Nonetheless, Lee announced that it was his mission to restore to Marylanders "the rights of which you have been despoiled." This commitment constrained Lee's strategic freedom of action in two ways. First, as he advanced west, subsistence became ever more precarious. Lee could not force Marylanders to "sell" when all he could offer was worthless Confederate currency; neither could he make them give up foodstuffs without antagonizing them fatally. In the haste to set the invasion in train Lee had not brought the gold that might otherwise have persuaded Marylanders to part with their produce. Second, he could not withdraw from the Old Line State hurriedly without incurring an enormous penalty in the propaganda war. Given this unpromising situation, Lee asked for (but never gained) the services of Enoch Lowe

(1820–92), a former Governor of Maryland, to help advance the Confederate cause in Maryland.

Lee thus fell back on his tenuous lines of supply. He had assumed rather casually that the Federal garrisons astride these at Martinsburg and Harper's Ferry would be sensible enough to retreat north before his troops arrived. But by September 9 he concluded that he could no longer rely on them to do what he wanted, even should the advance to Hagerstown continue unimpeded (the latter had the additional attraction of a large stock of flour). At Frederick, Lee consulted with both Jackson and Longstreet. The former put the case for staying among pro-secessionist friends in the eastern counties of Maryland to allow Lee to wait with his army concentrated and ready for a Union attack. The latter urged that the entire army move to the Shenandoah to deal with the Federal garrisons there. Both of these suggestions were not without tactical merit, but Lee felt that they would forgo the primary objectives of the campaign in favor of the secondary. Indeed they might convey a misleading impression that could revive Northern morale.

As a result of these discussions, Lee decided to resort to a device that had served him well previously—a division of the army in the face of the enemy. On the night of September 9/10 his staff issued Special Orders No. 191 detailing the plan. The cavalry were ordered to screen and to "cover the route of the army" to ensure the best intelligence. Jackson with 38,000 men and 32 batteries (about 58 percent of Lee's total strength) were ordered to "intercept" the Federal garrisons. Lee did not envisage any need for a protracted siege of Harper's Ferry. The "main body" under Longstreet, some 28,000 men, the Reserve Artillery and the trains, would continue (as planned) to Hagerstown. John Walker's division would cooperate with Jackson by pushing on to Loudon's Heights on the Virginia side above Harper's Ferry, having destroyed an aqueduct on the Chesa-peake—Ohio Canal en route. Finally, D. H. Hill's division would serve as the rear guard at Boonsboro.

At the time this order was being dispatched to Lee's subordi-nates, Federal troops were only 15 miles away and closing on Fred-erick fast. Lee continued planning his design, unaware of the poten-tial disaster he faced. Indeed Special Order No. 191 was fundamen-tally an attempt to tidy up the first phase of the campaign rather than to start a new phase. Alas, by midday on September 13 a copy of this order had been placed in McClellan's hands. It is likely that this copy (despite passionate denials to the contrary) had been acci-dentally lost, wrapped around three cigars, by a member of D. H. Hill's staff. Hill later claimed that this copy had never arrived and that he had worked from a copy provided by Stonewall Jackson. Lee's staff must share the blame for the blunder. They sorely missed the presence of Major Walter H. Taylor who had been sent by Lee on a secret mission, probably to intercept Jefferson Davis who han-kered after joining the Army of Northern Virginia on what he believed would be its climactic campaign. Possession of Lee's order certainly electrified McClellan. It led him to advance west with a greater edge than he might otherwise have done.

Even if it had remained secret, Special Order No. 191 is riddled with errors that would have found Lee out in any case. Lee was wrong to think that Union forces had yet to venture out of the Wash-ington defenses. He divided his army unaware that McClellan's columns were so close. On September 12, units of the Federal IX Corps entered Frederick. They were closer to Lee's flanks than they were to one another. Further, Lee was wrong to assume that the gar-risons at the head of the Shenandoah Valley would offer no resist-ance. And he had also allowed too little time for Jackson to march the 32 miles there and back—and occupy Harper's Ferry. The Union garrison consisted of 10,000 troops, three times the number that Lee had planned on. Moreover, Lee failed to appreciate that the quality of his intelligence had deteriorated. Though he could no longer rely on sympathetic civilians, he took no corrective action. The issue of Special Order No. 191 placed the entire Army of Northern Virginia in jeopardy.

Hence by September 10, contrary to his belief, Lee had already lost the initiative. He moved to Hagerstown with Longstreet and the "main body." Meanwhile Jackson had to seal off the escape routes from Harper's Ferry by sub-dividing his force further. McLaws's division (plus most of R. H. Anderson's, some 18,000 men) peeled off to enter the Pleasant Valley and advance to Maryland Heights. Scattering the army in this way made it easier to subsist off the country but placed the entire campaign in peril. The full extent of the danger did not bear down on Lee until the evening of September 13. About 8 p.m. he obtained word from Stuart (who had talked with a Confederate spy) that his plans had been compromised by the discovery of the "lost order." Even before receipt of the baleful news, his position had deteriorated gravely: McClellan had been "following our rear" with 95,000 men. Lee had heard nothing from McLaws and little from Jackson. D. H. Hill remained at Boonsboro but had not yet covered the passes through South Mountain. This is hardly surprising because Lee had never planned to hold them. Stuart thought McClellan's main aim was the destruction of Jackson, and he ordered the cavalry to cover Crampton's Gap.

Late that night Lee received news from McLaws that he had occupied Maryland Heights, but evidently operations were running far behind schedule. Lee worked into the early hours of the morning, his tent suffused with candlelight, as he pored over maps and dispatches. Urgent improvisation was the order of the day. In addition to confirming Stuart's action, Lee sent D. H. Hill orders to "go in person" to occupy Turner's Gap covering the Confederate center along South Mountain. As a reserve force, he wanted Longstreet to move to cover the passes at Boonsboro and aid any threatened point. McClellan's advance guard was a mere 5 miles from cutting across a straight line running from Hagerstown to Harper's Ferry. Should this be reached and the Confederate army cut in two, the campaign would have to be abandoned, and Lee would suffer a severe defeat in the propaganda war.

Lee decided that the Reserve Artillery and the trains should stay at Hagerstown, indicating his faith that he would eventually resume the offensive. Longstreet had counseled withdrawal, but that might involve leaving McLaws to his fate, a price that Lee would not countenance. But his countermeasures relied on two eventualities that he had no control over: Stuart and Hill holding the gaps "at all hazards until the operations at Harper's Ferry are finished"; and Jackson's hastening back in time.

The Battle of South Mountain followed on September 14. Lee was not present, but a single Confederate division held on for twenty-four hours. Afterward, Major General William B. Franklin's VI Corps lay only 3 miles from McLaws's rear, though fortunately he did not exploit his opportunity to raise Jackson's siege. It is quite possible that after this setback Lee concluded that he would have to abandon the campaign. If so, he kept the decision to himself. The most direct escape route to the fords across the Potomac at Shepherdstown lay along the road from Boonsboro to Sharpsburg, but Lee declined to take it because a concentration at Sharpsburg failed to provide any protection for McLaws. Instead, he issued orders to fall back on Keedysville. Even more significantly, Jackson was ordered to abandon the Harper's

Ferry siege. The ordnance trains were dispatched to safety across the Potomac at Williamsport and told to head for Shepherdstown. So began the first retreat the Army of Northern Virginia had known under Lee's command. Over the course of two vexing days, September 14–15, the commanding general may have snatched two hours' sleep.

The position at Keedysville was poor from a tactical point of view. But at about 7 a.m., while drinking a cup of coffee, Lee espied the Sharpsburg Heights and immediately grasped their strength. He also received a dispatch from Jackson predicting the imminent fall of Harper's Ferry. Buoyed up by good news, Lee calculated that McLaws would be able to extricate himself from Pleasant Valley and there could be no obstacle to a concentration of the army at Sharpsburg.

Later that morning Lee entered the town. He at once realized that the confusing, interlocking series of rolling hills circling Sharpsburg might conceal his numerical weakness and that he could deceive McClellan's pursuers until he was ready. Lee's logistical difficulties had sharpened his readiness to bring McClellan to battle sooner rather than later. At this date, however, Lee had probably not elected to fight a battle on this ground. Rather, he employed it as a convenient rallying point, a shield behind which to complete the Harper's Ferry operation and concentrate his army. Thereafter he could either cross the Potomac back into Virginia and re-enter Maryland when ready, or shift sideways toward Hagerstown and resume the offensive.

In many ways, the ground did not look promising. Fighting a superior enemy with his back to a great river, with the nearest ford, Boteler's, 5 miles away, did not recommend itself. In addition, the proximity of South Mountain prevented the development of sweeping maneuvers. However, his flanks rested on meanders and could not be turned easily. The left was stronger than the right, being transected by the Hagerstown Pike, and Lee pulled back (or "refused") the left flank to cover it. The weakest point lay in the center, a dale across which ran a circuitous, deep-set country lane. The Antietam Creek ran through the battlefield, and to reach the Confederate line the Union Army would have to cross it by way of three bridges: Upper, Middle and Lower (Rohrbach, now Burnside's). The bluffs above the last favored the Confederates, the opposite was true of the Middle, and the refusal of the Confederate left rendered the Upper Bridge a less critical point. The front ran for 2 miles, but Lee had 62 battle flags with him and these were conspicuously spread about with his 15,000 men and 100 guns, giving the impression of a much larger force.

At 12 noon, news arrived that Harper's Ferry had fallen. "This is indeed good news!" exclaimed Lee, dropping his customary reserve. He summoned Jackson to join him as quickly as possible, with A. P. Hill following once the booty had been sent back to Virginia. The longer Lee remained at Sharpsburg the fewer choices he could make as to his future course. He took a tremendous, and avoidable risk, in waiting for Jackson. His choice could be justified, mainly by a desire not to jeopardize the political dividends of the campaign. Cool calculations were given strength by Lee's faith in the Confederate heart. His run of successes not only imparted self-confidence but *faith* that Southern pluck and moral superiority would vanquish mere numbers and material superiority. His troops were superior to the enemy's and would triumph in the end. McClellan might yet be intimidated or repulsed. Lee's fatalism enticed him to believe he could still win.

On the morning of September 16 Lee awoke refreshed after a good night's sleep at last. Jackson had arrived, too, and Lee invited him to join Longstreet in a discussion of the alternatives facing the army. Lee predicted that they would be given a further twenty-four hours either to escape or renew a campaign of maneuver. Lee proved correct, but in a broader sense his comment is revealing of his under-estimation of the Union capacity and determination to attack the army. Late in the afternoon, Stuart informed him that Hooker's I Corps (plus the XII, although Stuart did not know this yet) had crossed the Antietam. Lee entrusted Jackson with command of the left and Longstreet the center-right. Lee himself would be involved in the close tactical direction of the battle. As a result, with his resources stretched to breaking point, precise areas of corps respon-sibility dissolved.

Lee later claimed that the Battle of Antietam (or Sharpsburg), fought on September 17, had been "forced" on him by McClellan. He had blocked any further attempt by Lee to maneuver around him and brought up 60,000 men and 275 guns with another 15,000 men on their way. Most of the advantages were on the Union side, al-though McClellan failed to make the most of them. The campaign so far had confirmed his ability as a careful and wise strategist but a mediocre tactician. McClellan convinced himself that the Confed-erate Army was larger than his own (when Lee had about 36,000 present on the field). McClellan proposed to attack both Confed-erate flanks and then smash Lee's weakened center. This plan needed tight control, for such a frontal assault could easily break down into a series of separate, piecemeal attacks. Despite a marked superiority in artillery, this is what McClellan permitted to happen. Each attack lacked the strength on its own to achieve decisive results. Lee made the most of this opportunity to muster his available troops to repulse each separately.

The Union attack began at about 5 a.m. on the Confederate left. Joseph Hooker's I Corps aimed to seize the high ground around the Dunker Church, a small white timber chapel. Its possession would render the Confederate line untenable. Confederate guns had been placed on Nicodemus Hill, slightly to the north, under the tactical control of Stuart. They brought enfilading fire to bear on the exposed flank of the columns of Union infantry plodding forward. On a front of 500 yards, charge and countercharge followed remorselessly for over two hours: 5,000 Confederates engaged 8,000 Unionists. Combined casualties were 4,368. Wofford's brigade suffered 64 percent casualties.

The biggest mystery surrounding Lee's conduct of Antietam is why the defending side suffered such high levels of casualties. Lee had not entrenched, a surprising error even if he never planned to fight a defensive battle on this ground. At the same time, many Confederate regiments were still equipped with smooth-bore muskets and thus had to be deployed for maximum firepower in the open, close to their enemy, exposing them to the greater weight and range of Federal artillery, concentrated on the Poffenberger Hill behind the North Woods.

The Union onslaught was renewed at about 7:30 a.m. with the attack of XII Corps, launched piecemeal on the left of I Corps. Jackson sent Sandie Pendleton, his acting chief of staff, to plead for reinforcements. Lee had been on the battlefield since about 5:30 a.m. He could now mount his horse but the reins had to be held for him. A brigade had already been sent to Jackson before Pendleton's arrival. But on hearing the gravity of Jackson's message, Lee immediately sent forward McLaws's division. Early's brigade was also sent to support Stuart on Nicodemus Hill, and Walker's division called up from Snavely's Ford on the far right. The greater the concentration on the left, however, the more vulnerable the right flank became. But for the moment, Lee had no time to worry about it.

The second phase of the battle opened at about 9 a.m. with the assault of Edwin V. Sumner's II Corps on the Confederate center-left. D. H. Hill's division covered the vital hinge along the Sunken road. The three divisions of II Corps were thrown forward hastily and piecemeal and became confused by the ground. Even the individual brigades were sent forward separately, allowing their assaults to be repulsed one by one. Nevertheless, Lee suffered two setbacks. First, although McLaws's counterattack was successful, the Federals seized the Dunker Church for about two hours. Second, at 1:30 p.m., even with the support of R. H. Anderson's division, Hill's men were driven out of the Bloody Lane, as it had proved vulnerable to enfilading fire. Lee was so preoccupied by the crisis around the Dunker Church that he failed to recognize his own son, Robert E. Lee Jr., serving with the Washington Artillery. When he asked whether they would have to attack again, Lee replied, "Yes, my son, you all must do what you can to help drive those people back."

By about 2:30 p.m. Lee had managed to stabilize the front but he had committed all his reserves. A mere 2,400 infantry, a cavalry brigade and eleven batteries of artillery covered the entire right flank. He briefly contemplated launching an attack on the left to distract McClellan's attention away from its vulnerability. Stuart probed the Union flank, but the all-powerful Union artillery rendered such efforts a forlorn hope.

Lee had no choice but to wait and hope that A. P. Hill's division would arrive in time from Harper's Ferry. Fortunately for him, IX Corps moved painfully slowly. Hill galloped up to report to Lee personally. His men had marched 17 miles in less than 8 hours, but would take another 30 minutes to deploy. Lee expressed delight at Hill's dramatic appearance. "General Hill, I was never so glad to see you, you are badly needed. Put your force in on the right as soon as they come up." Hill's Light Division had arrived not only in the nick of time as the Federals fanned out to seize Sharpsburg, but at just the right place. If he had reached the battlefield earlier, he might have been committed to the defense of the Sunken road. His force of 2,000 men (three of his five brigades) hit the Union flank at right angles and drove IX Corps back to, but not across, the Lower Bridge that it had taken so long to secure. Once more the goddess Fortuna smiled, through gritted teeth, perhaps, on Lee and the Army of Northern Virginia on the hard-fought and bloody ground of Antietam.

On September 18 Lee stood his ground. He had suffered 10,000 casualties, and now had perhaps 25,000 men at their posts. Nonetheless, he defied McClellan to attack again, determined to demonstrate that the Union Army had not gained the field and thus the victory. He also calculated that an immediate, chaotic retreat could not have been less disastrous than a renewal of the battle. The final withdrawal the next day was well planned and executed.

On returning to Virginia, Lee frantically attempted to revive the Maryland campaign. However, the unedifying loss of the Reserve Artillery at Shepherdstown, and its rapid recapture, indicated the levels of exhaustion that enveloped Lee's army. As Walter Taylor put it, Lee had been persuaded that "the condition of the army did not warrant such a move." As Lee himself admitted to Davis, "I am, therefore, led to pause."

After Gettysburg, Antietam is the most controversial battle Lee ever fought. Even a great admirer, General Maurice, judged it "unnecessary." Lee's army faced destruction at several critical moments, but like Wellington at Waterloo Lee always found the inner strength to take the right decision. In the exercise of tactical command in a defensive battle, Lee's conduct of Antietam was superb. Moreover, tactical excellence (especially in the calculation of timing and risk in the commitment of reserves) compensated for his earlier mistakes.

His choice of and trust in his subordinates, notably Jackson and A. P. Hill, was vindicated. He also enjoyed good luck. Colonel William Allan's verdict in 1868 is the correct one: "Lee handled his forces with a judgment so cool and calm as to leave nothing for criticism."

Criticism does revolve, however, around the degree to which the Maryland campaign itself can be justified. Lee considered that a defensive stance could not secure his strategic goals. Lee succeeded in taking the war out of Virginia, and in allowing the gathering of food and fodder to sustain the next two campaigns. He threatened Washington, DC, and postponed a further Union offensive for another three months. Yet the Battle of Antietam did not so much damage his army as render the re-entry of Maryland more difficult. Lee might have attempted too much with slender resources, but to have let the opportunity slip of taking the war to the enemy would not have been forgiven by Confederate public opinion. The degree of choice he faced in the late summer of 1862 has been exaggerated. He needed to gain political advantage and exploit the initiative. A prudent consolidation would have frittered both away.

CHAPTER SIX

Resurgent Again,

October 1862–May 1863

The disappointing end to the Maryland campaign forced Lee to set aside for the time being his attempts to consolidate the Confederacy's northern frontier. The initiative had fallen out of his hands, and the Federal forces were potentially free again to invade Virginia. Lee hoped to draw McClellan into the Shenandoah Valley, outmaneuver him and catch fragments of the Army of the Potomac by surprise. It took McClellan six weeks to leave the environs of the Antietam battlefield. On October 27 Union forces advanced on a broad front of 40 miles between the Shenandoah Valley and the Orange and Alexandria Railroad. Lee sent Longstreet's First Corps to Culpeper Court House to shield the railroads to Gordonsville and Richmond. McClellan had placed himself skilfully to exploit any weakness in Lee's distribution of forces. His dismissal on November 7, 1862 (after Lincoln lost patience with the glacial pace of his movements), renders it impossible to say whether he had yet learned to garner the tactical opportunities that his clever plans threw up.

Lee and McClellan would have agreed on one thing. They were being forced to wage war in an increasingly harsh climate. The Preliminary Emancipation Proclamation issued in September 1862 served notice that in order to win, the North would seek the destruction of the Southern social system and its bedrock—slavery. Indeed, the Militia Act of two months earlier permitted the enlistment in the Union Army of "persons of African descent." From the autumn of 1862 McClellan's cherished policy of reconciliation was abandoned. The conduct of the Civil War became less forgiving, threatening the end of all that Lee had known and loved.

McClellan's replacement was Major General Ambrose E. Burnside, once a friend of McClellan, but regarded henceforth by McClellan's acolytes as a traitor. Burnside entertained justified doubts about his ability to command an army. He took the job because he feared that otherwise it would be offered to Joseph Hooker, whom he loathed, a case perhaps of ambition outweighing his doubts. Although genial, Burnside lacked the respect of his subordinates, found it difficult to delegate and communicated his plans and views indifferently. Nonetheless, it was he who would set the pace of the new campaign, because he held the initiative. Burnside, not Lee, would determine when and how the culminating battle would be fought.

McClellan's initial thrust had placed Lee in some difficulty. The defensive line of the Rappahannock formed his central line of defense and his next two, closely related campaigns would be fought over this ground, setting the scene for the culminating and ill-fated climax of Lee's military career at Gettysburg. But fighting on the Rappahannock line offered few chances for gaining a decisive victory; the war could be lost there, but not won. So Lee used these operations as a means of snatching back the initiative while simultaneously attempting to erode the will of Northern opinion to continue the war.

In the short term, Lee struggled to find a suitable position to protect northern Virginia from a Union invasion and then launch either an enveloping swoop or an attack on the exposed Union flank. The longer Burnside marched south, the more stretched and vulnerable his lines of communications became; at the most propitious moment, Lee intended to "strike a successful blow." But Burnside acted much more swiftly than McClellan. He concentrated his army at Warrenton and then side-stepped around the Confederate right. By November 15 his advance guard had reached Falmouth, a mile from the pretty town of Fredericksburg. Should he cross the Rappahannock here the road to Richmond would be clear.

"I am operating to baffle the advance of the enemy," Lee confided on November 10 to his eldest son, Custis. Since the end of October, Lee had slowly regained the use of his hands. He could now dress without assistance and hold a pen. The consequent rise in his spirits was dashed, however, by news of the sudden death of his second daughter Ann. "I cannot express the anguish I feel at the death of sweet Annie," he wrote to his wife, Mary. This bereavement may account for some uncharacteristic fumbling in Lee's appreciation of Federal intentions. He admitted frankly to Davis on November 12 that "I cannot tell" the direction of the Union advance.

Nonetheless, he quickly grasped the need to gain more time. Stuart received orders to erect a cavalry screen stretching from Martinsburg to Fredericksburg that would prevent Burnside from discovering the Confederate distribution. He also issued orders for the destruction of the railroad from Aquia Creek to Falmouth. Lee hoped to avoid battle, for to attack "without too great risk and loss" would require considerable reinforcement. Lee had certainly not been idle since Antietam. The losses sustained in that battle can be exaggerated. By November 10 he had under his command 70,909 men, and after a brief visit to Richmond, had been promised a further 6,000. The Confederate corps structure had been confirmed by Congress four days earlier; Longstreet and Jackson were to command the First and Second Corps respectively and received promotion to lieutenant general. This reform accorded an important tactical advantage, because the two corps numbered about 35,000 men each, whereas a Union corps might deploy only 15,000 men. Lee could concentrate tactical superiority more quickly at the decisive point despite an overall numerical inferiority. Lee also endeavored to exploit this trump card by concentrating his artillery into battalions, so that they could be massed more easily once battle commenced. Finally, he streamlined the organization of the cavalry division into four brigades.

Lee also paid careful attention to the morale of his men. New uniforms arrived and rifled muskets issued, though footwear remained a problem: some 6,000 men of First Corps remained barefoot. But Lee could still be pleased with much (despite outbreaks of drunkenness and indiscipline which he deplored). In the first eight days of October alone, 20,000 men returned to the ranks. When he noticed the British observer, Garnet Wolseley, looking askance at the ragged uniforms of Hood's Texans, Lee made plain his faith in the fighting qualities of his men. "Never mind the raggedness, Colonel, the enemy never sees the backs of my Texans."

Burnside had got off to a brisk start in the new campaign, stealing a march on Lee. The Confederate general would have to remain alert for an opportunity to strike back. Fortunately for him, the very speed of Burnside's advance worked against him. Due to an administrative oversight, the pontoons he needed to cross the Rappahannock were left behind. For six days the Union troops were forced to occupy Stafford Heights and wait. Lee rapidly exploited the extra time he had been granted to recover his poise. On the day the pontoons arrived, November 25, and after conferring with Stuart, Lee finally decided that Fredericksburg was Burnside's objective and not a feint. He ordered half of First Corps to advance toward the town, with the other half following the next day. He instructed Jackson to remain in the Shenandoah Valley, but to be prepared to move at a moment's notice. Lee himself had been at Fredericksburg since November 20.

Shots had been fired at Federal troops from houses in the town. On November 21–22 an increasingly frustrated and irritable Burnside demanded the expulsion of its citizens. Lee refused to surrender the town but offered to provide wagons to help transport the civilians from the war-zone. Civilians were forced from their homes and Confederate propaganda made the most of their plight by branding Burnside's action heartless and barbaric. It is worth remarking, however, that, despite Lee's outrage at Burnside's conduct, he was not prepared to give up a military advantage for the sake of the residents of Fredericksburg.

On November 23 Lee sent Jackson orders to leave the Shenandoah Valley and rejoin the army. Lee still did not finally make up his mind to concentrate at Fredericksburg until four days later. He left Jackson discretion to move into Burnside's rear. On November 25, he wrote to Davis, "I think from the tone of the Northern papers, it is intended that General Burnside shall advance from Fredericksburg to Richmond"—an indication of his reliance on newspapers as a source of information. Even after the arrival of the pontoons, Burnside discovered that he could not sustain his advance until he repaired the railroad from Aquia Creek to Falmouth. "The longer we can delay him," Lee concluded, "and throw him into the winter, the more difficult will be his undertaking."

Jackson's corps arrived on November 29. D. H. Hill's division was sent to cover the Confederate right flank at Port Royal, extending

Lee's front to 20 miles. Nevertheless, he had the army well placed to cover the critical points. Lee had also grasped that so much Federal political capital had been invested in Burnside's campaign that if he forced Burnside to change direction it "would be equivalent to defeat." As ever with Lee, the political and propaganda dimensions of war were at the forefront of his thoughts.

Burnside had indeed come under pressure to challenge Lee and score a decisive success. Despite deteriorating and unpredictable weather during the first week of December, he decided to attack the Confederate position, hoping that he might take Lee by surprise. In a certain sense he did. Lee could not believe that Burnside would attack him in position, assuming rather that Burnside would attempt to turn his right. Consequently, he made his headquarters at Hamilton's Crossing. At 2 a.m. on December 11, Lee rode along the entire front, examining the employment of artillery. He thought one battery badly placed and inquired who had put it there. "Colonel Chilton," came back the reply, his ineffective chief of staff. "Colonel Chilton takes a lot upon himself," Lee announced frostily.

The first phase of the Battle of Fredericksburg opened later that morning in thick fog. Lee decided that, given their superiority in artillery, he could not prevent the Federals crossing the Rappahannock. Instead, he sent 1,500 infantry into the town to harass the engineers laying the pontoon bridges. Burnside replied with a ferocious bombardment of the town. "These people," Lee exclaimed, "delight to destroy the weak and those who can make no defense; it just suits them." He gave indignant voice to a powerful sentiment that would underwrite Confederate propaganda. The character of Confederates was defined by reference to what it was *not*. Northerners were brutal, their conduct savage and their successes due entirely to overwhelming numbers and resources. The South had the moral advantage, as well as greater courage and the fortitude to triumph over the odds.

Lee withdrew his troops from the town at about 6 p.m., but they had bought another day's delay. Burnside blundered in not following up the crossing immediately and in force. He gave Lee time to prepare for the next move. The Union commander sat down to wait another day, but he was running out of time himself. Though he dare not withdraw, his best chances to attack had been frittered away. Lee in the meantime from the right called Jubal Early's division from Buckner's Neck and D. H. Hill's division from Port Royal, and thus completed the concentration of his entire army for battle.

At about 10 a.m. on December 13, the fog dispersed to reveal the entire Army of the Potomac arrayed for battle. The bulk of the Confederate Army lay hidden behind the ridges to the south of the town, holding a position about 6 miles long. Longstreet's First Corps occupied the left, Jackson's Second Corps the right. The position, characterized by long ridges of no great height, was strong but by no means impregnable. The narrow flood plain running to the Rappahannock gave a good field of fire, and offered a series of obstacles to attacking formations in the shape of fences, ditches and hedges. Longstreet massed his artillery on Marye's Heights on the left-center.

The weakest points lay in the center, where Deep Run cuts through the higher ground, and on the right. Jackson held the most exposed sector, about a mile and a half along Prospect Hill. The Richmond, Fredericksburg and Potomac Railroad ran parallel to it across marshy ground. Stuart's cavalry guarded the right flank. Lee thought the ground satisfactory for a delaying action, but unsuitable for launching a counterstroke because of the proximity of the Federal artillery on the high ground rising above the north bank of the Rappahannock; he lacked room for maneuver. Lee would have preferred to fight Burnside at another, even stronger, position on the North Anna River to the south, but had not been eager to withdraw in case he exposed this country to Federal ravages.

Burnside's plan was muddled and he had not explained it well to his subordinates. He had also tried to reduce Confederate tactical superiority by combining Union corps into formations of two that he called "grand divisions." This reform ran along the right lines but caused resentment. Burnside believed that the left grand division under Major General William B. Franklin would "stagger" Lee by taking Prospect Hill and then "roll up" the Confederate position from the right; thereupon Sumner's right grand division would smash Longstreet from the front, allowing Hooker's central grand division to exploit the breakthrough. But Burnside's final instructions, not issued until the morning of December 13, lacked detail and precision. In making arrangements to fight a great battle, Burnside seemed both out of touch and out of his depth.

Lee, by contrast, had received word that the attack might fall on his right, and in the early hours he again rode along the front accompanied by a rolling barrage of cheers. On reaching the right flank, he went forward on a personal reconnaissance with Stuart, riding into a field adjacent to the Union left flank. At about 7:30 a.m. he took up position in the center of the Confederate position on Telegraph (later Lee's) Hill. Even at this hour he was still uncertain of Burnside's intentions, and believed it more likely that any attack on his right flank would mask a Union turning movement into his rear.

Jackson had available thirty-five guns, plus Stuart's horse artillery, massed in three groups to traverse the entire position. But though the railroad grade provided a natural breastwork, his men could not entrench properly because of the frozen earth. The weather grew milder as the morning wore on and the ground became soft and damp. An artillery duel flared up and was quickly lost by Jackson's guns. Under cover of the intense fire, Franklin's lead division (quickly supported by another) took the defenders by surprise, reached the summit of Prospect Hill and cut the Military Road that ran laterally along the top. Jackson's corps faced imminent destruction, but Burnside's orders did not specify a massive onslaught and Franklin did nothing to follow up his initial success. Jackson quickly organized a counterattack, spearheaded by Early's division, that drove the Union troops back.

Burnside had been encouraged by this initial success and decided to bring forward the time of Sumner's assault on Longstreet's front to assist Franklin's advance. This move reversed the respective priority that he had allotted each commander, as Sumner's advance should have been contingent on Franklin's success, not a means of securing it. The troops of Sumner's grand division marched out one after the other. Their attacks went forward in the same piecemeal fashion—as at Antietam. Longstreet had five divisions at his disposal and the Federal pattern of attack enabled him to concentrate all his resources to drive them back. His position was strengthened by a stone wall that ran for about 400 yards along Marye's Heights, close to the Federal lines, covering the sunken Telegraph Road. Hood's division covered the vulnerable inner flank at the point of junction between the two Confederate corps.

Sumner's advance began at about noon. Immediately the alignment of his formations became disrupted by a network of fences, hedges and ditches. The tightly packed and confused Union ranks provided Longstreet's artillery with a splendid target as they were enfiladed from right and left (and his cannon were reinforced with two large cast-iron Parrott rifled guns that threw 21-pound shells). Longstreet's chief of artillery, E. Porter Alexander, did not exaggerate when he claimed that "a chicken could not live on that field when we open fire on it." As each Union brigade deployed successively, so it was shattered. No Union assault got closer to Longstreet's line than 100 yards.

Lee enquired uneasily of Longstreet whether the brigade holding the stone wall, commanded by Thomas R. R. Cobb, might be overwhelmed. Longstreet replied exuberantly, "I will kill them all before they reach my line." Anxious not to tempt fate, Lee reinforced Cobb with a further brigade and three North Carolina regiments. Cobb was thus able to deploy his troops in four ranks, so that, as the front rank fired and the second prepared to fire, the other two ranks were in the process of reloading. This deployment resulted in one of the fiercest and most continuous volleys of fire delivered in the Civil War.

It was at about this point that Lee uttered one of his most self-revealing pronouncements. Just as the integrity of the right flank had been restored, Hood threw one of his North Carolina brigades at the exposed flank of the retreating Union troops. Lee watched the men surging across the battlefield through his field glasses. He turned to his subordinates and staff and declared, "It is well that war is so terrible—we should grow too fond of it." Lee clearly evinced his pride in his troops, his buoyant self-confidence and his evident enjoyment in meeting the moral and intellectual challenges posed by the conduct of war.

At 2 p.m. Burnside reinforced failure by ordering forward Hooker's grand division to support Sumner. Hooker made desperate efforts to get ten 12-pounder guns up to within 150 yards of the stone wall, but these were easy targets for the massed Confederate artillery on Marye's Heights. A lull spread over the battlefield for about an hour before Hooker resumed his attack at about 3:30 p.m.

The lead Union division met a hail of Confederate fire, and the men were observed "half crouching, and moving *sideways*, as though breasting a "blizzard" or a wind and hail-storm." After this effortless repulse, another Union division marched forward. Its commander, Andrew A. Humphreys, reported that "the stone wall was a sheet of flame that enveloped the head and flanks of the column, officers and men were falling rapidly." Lee drew more troops from the right to reinforce the units close to Fredericksburg, but at 7 p.m. Hooker, on his own authority, brought the battle to an end. On the Confederate center, between Lee's Hill and A. P. Hill's division, the weakest point, no Union assaults were mounted.

Lee returned to his headquarters that evening assuming that Burnside would renew the assault the following day. As the ground had softened, Lee ordered the army to entrench. Even if Burnside tried to turn his position, he remained confident that he could hold it with a small force and strike Burnside's exposed flank and rear. Yet though Lee likened entrenchment to a reinforcement of 20,000 men, he was short of ammunition, a consideration that persuaded him to be prudent. He and Jackson (accompanied by Hood) examined the Union position on the December 14 to judge the feasibility of a counterstroke. Jackson's artillery had again come off badly in a further duel with the Federal guns on the late afternoon of December 13. Jackson himself believed an attack would be suicidal. Lee needed no persuasion as to the strength of his case. "Few realize how fragile an army is," he said quietly.

A flag of truce was raised on December 14, and was spent quietly, allowing the Unionists to remove their dead and wounded. Then, in the early hours of December 16, the Army of the Potomac slipped quietly away. Lee felt the Union withdrawal could not have been prevented, but would have preferred earlier notification of it.

He could not help feeling depressed. "Had I divined that was to have been his [Burnside's] only effort, he would have had more of it," Lee remarked crossly.

So once more Lee ended a successful campaign, pleased that he had gained a necessary victory but dismayed that more was not achieved. Lee had maintained the integrity of the Rappahannock line and conserved all the logistical resources that lay between it and Richmond. He had inflicted 12,653 casualties on the Army of the Potomac (12 percent of the 106,000 engaged) and sustained only 5,309 (7 percent of 72,500) and had captured 11,000 stands of arms (the complete set of equipment for one Civil War soldier—commonly held to describe just the rifled musket and cartridge belt). The Battle of Fredericksburg was not a foregone conclusion, let alone a model of how Lee's future campaigns might have been designed. An indication of the danger that Lee faced may be measured by the loss on the right flank (of 3,054 men) that for more than an hour faced complete destruction. To permit another Union commander of greater ability and tactical flair than Burnside to concentrate his greater resources at a place and time of his choosing would court complete and eventual defeat.

Burnside had indeed committed many errors, but Lee had made the most of them. He succeeded in turning the campaign upside down. From being caught out at the beginning, Lee had emerged the victor and foiled another attempt to take Richmond. Tactically, Lee's methods, Colonel G. F. R. Henderson suggests, "could scarcely have been improved upon." His reserves were placed with great care in a layered defense, exposing only one-third of his force to view, while simultaneously covering the entire front. Lee would have also been able to strike Burnside easily if he had attempted to turn the Confederate right. The command system worked well. Order and cool efficiency had prevailed, without Lee becoming absorbed (as at Antietam) in minor tactical direction.

Notwithstanding all these positive aspects, Lee confided to his wife on December 16 that Fredericksburg did "not go far enough to satisfy me." Four days later the troops were ordered into winter quarters. Lee had defeated, but not fatally wounded, the Union Army, and had no choice but to await Burnside's next move. In January 1863 Burnside attempted to turn the Confederate right again; but his advance was stymied by thirty-six hours of continual rain, dubbed thereafter "Burnside's Mud March." Burnside asked to be relieved, and Lincoln quickly replaced him with Major General Joseph Hooker—"Fighting Joe." Hooker had ability but his bibulous habits, boastful nature and love of intrigue raised suspicions among his peers.

Hooker threw himself into his new task and commenced a major program of reform that consumed his energies for several months. He broke up the grand divisions and reinstated eight corps that included the cavalry as a single force; he worked hard at improving discipline, training and morale; he emphasized the role of his chief of staff, Daniel Butterfield, to help him command; furthermore, he succeeded in enveloping his plans in a cloak of secrecy. However, he made one significant error: he broke up the centralized organization of the artillery, scattering his batteries throughout the corps. But there could be no mistaking that the Army of the Potomac had revived and could mount a formidable challenge when Hooker chose to begin the spring campaign.

During the early months of 1863 Lee remained outwardly cheerful. Privately, however, he became more pessimistic, emphasizing "the absolute necessity of raising more troops." Although he believed that current Confederate strength was insufficient "to bring this war to a successful and speedy termination," he did not lose his sense of humor. When his military secretary had a baby daughter, Lee put on a severe expression and teased him. "Colonel Long, I wonder that you should try to evade the conscript laws in this way. You must try it again!"

In mid February 1863 Lee had no choice but to send Longstreet and two divisions to Richmond. He needed to guard against the possibility that IX Corps, recently detached from the Army of the Potomac down the coast, might sweep up the James River. This movement indicates the degree to which the Union retained the strategic initiative even when the Confederacy won defensive victories. A resounding success like Fredericksburg could protect the Southern hinterland, but could do little to stop renewed Federal efforts at other, vital threatened points. Longstreet's 16,000 men were assigned to Suffolk, Virginia, on the coast. His departure left Lee with 62,000 men.

Longstreet's temporary transfer eased Lee's logistical burdens. Even so, with the movement of stores remaining dependent on one line, the Richmond, Fredericksburg and Potomac Railroad, Lee found it impossible to build up enough food stocks and fodder to sustain his maneuvers. He only had seven days' provisions set aside; in addition, the condition of his horses and mules had begun to deteriorate and the army also continued to be short of wagons to transport foodstuffs and ammunition. Somehow Lee managed to keep his men fed, but logistical handicaps were a significant constraint on his freedom to plan and make the most of his advantages.

Lee, too, sought to recast his army and rectify certain weaknesses. He had been annoyed by the plundering of Fredericksburg by Confederate troops and continued to inveigh privately against indiscipline and desertion. When he learned that 5,953 men were absent without leave, he sent squads back to their home towns to round them up. His most significant reform again applied to the artillery. Lee considered that the reserve artillery could not be brought forward quickly enough, so he decided to divide battalions of guns (each of four batteries) between his two corps and invest their ultimate command authority in the corps commanders. Lee hoped to concentrate artillery fire *before* the Federals could reply with their more numerous and heavier pieces. He thus improved his capacity to throw firepower at the enemy just at a time when Hooker had dismantled centralized command over his own artillery.

It is from the Fredericksburg campaign that Lee's moral sway over his army really dates. He had been in command for seven months. His faith in himself had been bolstered by the prodigious efforts of his troops. He had fought four campaigns and sustained 50,000 casualties. When aggregated this seems a lot, but it is well to recall that in 1815 Napoleon lost 25,000 casualties at Waterloo alone (excluding Quatre Bras and Ligny). Lee had inflicted 70,725 casualties on the Union Army, and seized 155 guns (for the loss of only eight). The term "casualties" in the Civil War often includes prisoners of war and should not be misconstrued as fatalities permanently lost to the army. Lee had made significant progress in his aim of eroding Northern support for the war; but he clearly sensed that, given his own losses, time was running out. He must act quickly to land a final, victorious blow.

The Army of Northern Virginia did not escape the personal quarrels among generals that plagued Confederate military efficiency. Stonewall Jackson was the source of most of the friction. In recent months, tension had grown between Jackson and A. P. Hill's staff. Curiously, despite great contrasts in outlook and character, Stuart and Jackson worked well together (perhaps because both shared a profound Christian faith). Within his corps, however, Jackson took the opportunity of renewing his feud with A. P. Hill. He demanded Hill's relief, but Lee ignored his requests. Both generals were still at their posts when the spring campaign opened. But Lee himself worked to ease D. H. Hill's transfer to the Army of Tennessee. He had proved an opinionated and caustic fault-finder whom Lee had tolerated rather than respected. Lee never allowed himself to become personally involved in these (often petty) disputes. His managerial skill, tact and diplomacy allowed his army to escape the open warfare among its commanders that engulfed the Army of Tennessee.

In March 1863 Davis summoned Lee to Richmond to discuss strategy. The President expressed anxiety about affairs in Mississippi. He suggested that Longstreet attack Union forces at Suffolk, Virginia, to take pressure off the Vicksburg front. Lee felt this unwise, fearing it might draw strength away from the vital Rappahannock front. A skirmish at Kelly's Ford on the Rappahannock River, about 25 miles north-west of Fredericksburg, warned Lee that the opening of the spring campaign might begin sooner rather than later. In the middle of the month Lee fell ill and suffered chest pains that foreshadowed his later, fatal illness. He did not start to recover until March 27. The following day IX Corps moved to Kentucky and reduced the danger to the south-east. Lee realized that if he could defeat Hooker and strike toward Washington, DC, it would enable him to help Bragg in Tennessee. He made no detailed preparations, except to evolve a general concept, and waited on events. He also had to take personal command of two of Longstreet's divisions left behind, those of McLaws and Anderson.

Apart from illness, the main reason for Lee's slowness in developing plans lay in Hooker's ability to keep him in a "state of expectancy." Lee rather mocked "Mr. F. J. Hooker" in his correspondence and underrated him. Nonetheless, Hooker's new cavalry corps permitted him to counter Stuart's technique of dominating the area between the opposing forces (scouting the roads, occupying the high ground, interrogating the inhabitants) that allowed him to glean information and simultaneously prevent the Federals from doing so. In the early months of 1863 these tactics were directed against the Confederates. "Their lines are so closely guarded," Lee complained, "that it is difficult to penetrate them." Little of value could be gleaned from the newspapers either because Hooker had been uncharacteristically discreet.

Lee also came under pressure to gain a victory to boost Confederate morale as matters deteriorated before Vicksburg, Charleston and in Richmond itself, worsening conditions leading to outbreaks of popular discontent such as the April Bread Riots (that had spilled over into Atlanta and Columbus). Hooker solved a part of Lee's problem for him. During April he had conceived probably the best operational design sketched by a Union commander in the east during the Civil War. One-third of his army would remain at Fredericksburg under John J. Sedgwick; the other two-thirds were to march west to cross Kelly's and US fords over the Rappahannock; thereafter half of the Union infantry (three corps) would push on to the Rapidan River and cross it at Germanna and Ely's Ford. Hooker aimed to envelop the Confederate left flank and strike Lee's rear simultaneously from left to right. Should Lee turn to face the Rapidan front, Sedgwick could attack his rear, and vice versa. The Cavalry Corps would plunge south and attack Lee's lines of communications and provoke the maximum alarm and confusion.

Between April 27–29, Hooker (like Burnside before him) had done very well. He had placed 134,000 men and 400 guns in a strong position and was poised to deliver his *coup de grâce*. But a successful commander must do more than plan. He must see his plans through to a successful conclusion, making adjustments as circumstances demanded, and demonstrating a capacity to shoulder the moral burdens that taking decisions under pressure requires. Hooker thought his plans "perfect" and that Lee would retreat: all he need do was pursue him and take Richmond. Hooker would be in for a shock when his adversary declined to play the role that had been assigned to him.

In the first part of the campaign Lee had undoubtedly been wrong-footed. "General Early, what are you making all this fuss about?" he asked briskly on the morning of April 29, when Early's division tried to prevent Sedgwick bridging the Rappahannock at Fredericksburg. A gap of about 20 miles had opened up between Stuart's cavalry and the Confederate left flank, and intelligence reports took up to twelve hours to reach Lee's headquarters (the telegraph office at Centreville unhelpfully closed down at night). At first, Lee thought the Union cavalry was heading for the Shenandoah Valley, and ordered reinforcements to Gordonsville to support Stuart. But as events became clearer during the rest of the day he took a series of sensible decisions. He ordered up the artillery, and withdrew the army on to the high ground above Fredericksburg. At 6:30 p.m. he ordered Anderson's division to the left to guard the army's rear. But significantly, he decided not to call Longstreet back from Suffolk immediately. The order would follow eventually, but Lee's decision to act without Longstreet (whose troops did not board trains in Richmond until May 6) indicated Lee's low esteem for "Mr. F. J. Hooker." Lee would rely on his own instincts and cunning to shape events to his advantage.

Lee could muster an army only half the size of Hooker's—65,000 men. "Their intention, I presume, is to turn our left, and probably to get into our rear," he informed Davis. Lee still feared that he might be forced to abandon the Rappahannock line if Union infantry "have come in between us" and Stuart's cavalry. By the evening of April 29, three Union corps (XI, II and V) were indeed on the south bank of the Rapidan and only 10 miles from the hamlet of Chancellorsville, an important crossroads. Lee thus recalled Stuart to shield his exposed left and gain the intelligence that he urgently needed. Henceforth, no longer facing significant opposition, the Confederate cavalry began to gain control over all the roads in the area and harass the Union advance.

On the morning of April 30, Lee turned his full attention to shoring up his left flank. Anderson received detailed instructions to "cover the road heading for Chancellorsville down to the river" and to "dig in." "Set all your spades to work as vigorously as possible," Lee emphasized. This order marks Lee's first acknowledgment of the importance of entrenchment in a campaign of maneuver, a tactic he could use to compensate for a significant numerical deficiency in the open field. Even with this precaution, however, the choices facing Lee were far from easy. Jackson's first response to the looming peril had been to urge an attack on Sedgwick as he crossed the Rappahannock. With Union artillery still dominating the heights on the northern bank, Lee failed to see that anything had changed since December 14–15, 1862. Even though Lee thought the proposal unwise, such was his trust in Jackson he offered to give him the order to attack "if you think you can effect anything." But after second thoughts, Jackson changed his mind and hastened to agree with Lee.

Lee took away from this discussion the idea that he might stand on the defensive at Fredericksburg and switch his strength to the left flank. He would entrust the defense of the hills south of the Rappahannock to Early's division with 11,000 infantry but one-third of the Army of Northern Virginia's artillery. The remainder, some 42,000 infantry, would confront Hooker's flanking column at Chancellorsville. Lee had reduced the odds somewhat by concentrating rapidly at what he perceived would be the decisive point. McLaws's division would support Anderson "as soon as possible." Jackson's Second Corps (minus Early) would follow at dawn on May 1. Jackson's orders specified that he should "make arrangements to repulse the enemy."

Lee once more divided his army in face of a superior enemy force. He defied tremendous and imminent danger. He relished the personal challenge that Hooker's clever opening gambit offered. The only alternative to fighting it out on the Rappahannock line lay in retreat—and that would only expose the Confederate rear echelons and trains to the kind of blows that Hooker had prepared to inflict on his army. Retreat (perhaps to the North Anna River) would have played to Hooker's strengths and reinforced his brittle self-confidence. Lee's bold instincts were the right ones. "I determined to hold our lines in rear of Fredericksburg with a part of the force," he reported to the War Department without melodrama, "and endeavor with the rest to drive the enemy back to the Rapidan."

One factor undoubtedly favored Lee—the ground. Hooker had plunged two-thirds of the Union Army into a thickly wooded area of some 70 square miles, almost resembling a jungle, known as the Wilderness. Federal troops were confined to the roads and the clearings. Hooker had only one brigade of cavalry available and could not use his observation balloons. His plan had rendered him blind. By contrast, Lee could make use of the impenetrable woods to mask his movements. Hooker's right wing could muster 48,300 men. Lee had reduced the odds: he could throw perhaps 30,000 men against them.

Jackson's Second Corps came up by 8:30 a.m. on May 1. Lee

Robert E. Lee (1807–70), by William E. West, 1838. Lee is wearing the dress uniform of a lieutenant of Engineers. His self-assurance belies his frustration and impatience with the tedium of peacetime soldiering. (*Washington and Lee University*)

ABOVE William Henry Fitzhugh Lee (1837–91), always known as 'Rooney', with his father in 1845, just before the Mexican War. (*Virginia Historical Society, Richmond Virginia*)

LEFT Robert E. Lee Monument in Richmond Virginia. This equestrian statue conveys the message of 'Lost Cause' mythology that Lee prevailed despite the harsh reality of defeat. (*Buddy Mays/Corbis*)

ABOVE Arlington House, the home of General Robert E. Lee. Although the Lees lived here periodically, it did not become Lee's first permanent home until the death of his father-in-law in 1857. (*Corbis*)

BELOW General Winfield Scott's entry into Mexico City at the head of Worth's division in September 1847. (*Anne S. K. Brown Military Collection, Brown University Library*)

ABOVE RIGHT General Winfield Scott (1786–1866), a hero of the Mexican War. By 1861 he was elderly and obese, but his mind was clear and so were his Unionist loyalties. (*Medford Historical Society Collection/Corbis*)

ABOVE LEFT Major General Rooney Lee, who commanded cavalry in his father's army. (*Corbis*)

ABOVE Major General 'Jeb' Stuart (1833–64), Lee's flamboyant but highly effective cavalry commander. (*Corbis*)

RIGHT Stonewall Jackson, Lee's indomitable lieutenant (1824–63). In the field he never looked as tidy as in this photograph. (*Bettmann/Corbis*)

ABOVE Lee and Jackson discuss the possibility of seizing the initiative at Chancellorsville on the night of May 1, 1863. (*Anne S. K. Brown Military Collection, Brown University Library*)

BELOW The view towards Cemetery Ridge from Seminary Ridge on the Gettysburg battlefield. (*David Muench/Corbis*)

ABOVE The town of Gettysburg and its surrounding fields seen from Seminary Ridge. (*Medford Historical Society Collection*/Corbis)

LEFT Robert E. Lee photographed in the early months of 1864. As ever, Lee's attention to dress and appearance is immaculate. (*Corbis*)

LEFT General Robert E. Lee surrendering to the Union commanding general Ulysses S. Grant at Appomattox on April 9, 1865. (*Bettmann/Corbis*)

BELOW Mathew Brady's portrait of Lee (center) a few days after his surrender at Appomattox. He is accompanied by his eldest son, Major General George Washington Custis Lee (left) and Lieutenant Colonel Walter H. Taylor (right). (*Medford Historical Society/Corbis*)

ABOVE Robert E. Lee poses on his horse, Traveler, after the end of the American Civil War. This is one of the very few equestrian photographs of Lee. (*Corbis*)

LEFT A prematurely aged 63-year-old Lee towards the end of his life, when he served as president of Washington College, Lexington. (*Virginia Historical Society, Richmond Virginia*) had given him authority to attack and he did so two hours later. This spoiling attack knocked Hooker off-balance as the initiative slipped from his fingers. Union columns were withdrawn to entrench in the vicinity of Chancellorsville. For all his bombast, Hooker sought solace in the defensive thinking of McClellan. Lee moved decisively to exploit this fateful hesitancy.

In the early afternoon of May 1, Lee rode to the front. On the final part of his journey to the Zoan church—the small timber church on the road between Chancellorsville and Fredericksburg, where Federal and Confederate troops first clashed on May 1—Jackson accompanied him amid boisterous cheers. The pair then rode along the Orange Plank Road and, at the Catharine Furnace Road, they dismounted and sat on a log just by the roadside to discuss the position. The Federal withdrawal had come to a halt and an attack on the fortified center seemed out of the question. Darkness began to fall as Stuart rode up to report that Fitzhugh Lee had discovered that the Union right flank (held by XI Corps) had been left unguarded—"in the air," as military parlance puts it. Lee then uttered a rhetorical question quietly to himself, one deeply revealing of his military outlook: "How can we get at those people?" Jackson replied that it was for him to decide.

And decide he did, quickly and with self-assurance. He would not worry about what the enemy would do to him—that much was self-evident. He was intent on what he could do to the enemy, and therefore he would seek victory despite the odds. In other words, this discussion (often erroneously described as a "council of war") concerned itself not with whether the enemy's defeat was a possible or realistic goal but with how such a victory could best be secured.

Lee occupied a central position closer to Hooker's flanks than they were to one another. The envelopment of the Union right seemed to recommend itself. Many can often see the solutions to an operational problem in the abstract; it is quite another matter, as Hooker had already discovered, to take responsibility for them and take timely decisions to see them carried out. With a smaller army, more tightly concentrated, Lee had already begun to take decisions more rapidly than Hooker. He also ordered the preparation of maps, and while these were being drawn, both he and Jackson took the opportunity to snatch a few hours sleep. They rose early and could be seen sitting on two hardtack boxes talking quietly. During this private, unrecorded conversation, Lee revealed later, he took the decision "to endeavor to turn his [Hooker's] right flank and gain his rear"—a characteristic Lee approach. He was a modest man and invariably used oblique language like this to describe his own contributions, while singling out others for direct praise. In January 1866, in a unique affirmation of his dominant role in a letter to Jackson's widow, he emphasised that "I decided against" a frontal assault, "and stated to General Jackson, we must attack them on our left as soon as practicable." Lee, after all, had been the senior partner in their relations since the spring of 1862.

The main witness of the remainder of the discussion was Jackson's mapmaker, Major Jedediah Hotchkiss. Hotchkiss heard Lee ask Jackson what he proposed to do (that is, how he would fulfill the concept of operations that Lee had earlier laid down). Jackson replied, "I propose to go right around there"—that is, the Union right—with his entire corps. Once all these decisions had been taken, the execution of the plan would become the most difficult part of the scheme. "What will you leave me here to hold the Federal Army with?" Lee asked. "Longstreet's two divisions," Jackson responded. Lee then answered without hesitation, "Well, go ahead."

Jackson, on departing, saluted and informed Lee that his corps would depart at 4 a.m. on May 2. Characteristically, Jackson did not inform his staff that the troops would have to depart at sunrise. Long delays resulted, with some Second Corps units not setting off until between 10:30 and 11 a.m. This unforeseen hitch may have complicated Lee's problems, but even with the delays the gamble of dividing his army for a second time was not rash. Although close by, Hooker could not bring his overwhelming strength to bear. Furthermore, the terrain disguised Lee's weakness and, most important of all, Hooker lacked the cavalry to discover its true extent. The risks that Lee accepted, though great, were nicely calculated. Lee felt compelled to snatch the initiative while he had the chance before Hooker recovered his equilibrium. In short, he believed passionately that "a very bold game . . . was the only *possible* one."

Finally, Lee had calculated that Hooker would choose to remain between Washington, DC, and the Confederate Army. He would not shift to the west toward Gordonsville and attempt another side-step around the Confederate left. Consequently, Lee attempted to distract Hooker's attention and persuade him that an imminent assault on his center was likely, while Jackson's troops marched across his front. Second Corps's snaking column was so long that its head reached the objective as elements of Major General Daniel E. Sickles's III Corps attacked its rear. Hooker stopped this attack on the curious grounds that the enemy was retreating. This, after all, is what he expected to happen. In his mind, all was going to plan.

Lee played for high stakes but he had covered the odds. He waited calmly, if slightly anxiously, for news of Jackson's progress. "He sat on his horse a great deal of the time," an eyewitness recorded, "and you could see a shade of anxiety . . . on his face." In the middle of the afternoon he received a scribbled note from Jackson: "I hope as soon as practicable to attack." But Jackson took almost two hours to align his corps across the Orange Turnpike that runs toward the Zoan Church. His attack went forward finally at about 5:15 p.m., and the XI Corps dissolved in panic. Of its 11,000 troops, XI Corps suffered 2,400 casualties. Jackson enjoyed a local superiority of more than 2.5:1; his initial advance was so rapid that it became disorganized. Jackson tried to reorientate it toward the fords. At about 9 p.m. Jackson fell wounded while on a personal reconnaissance—shot by his own men. Lee showed immediate distress when informed of this ominous news. When Hotchkiss tried to give him further details, Lee stopped him. "I know all about it and do not wish to hear any more—it is too painful a subject."

The drama and excitement of Jackson's maneuver tends to disguise the importance of events on the Fredericksburg front and the vulnerability of Lee's army on the night of May 2/3. The battle was far from won and could still have been lost disastrously. Earlier on May 2, due to garbled orders delivered by Lee's chief of staff, Chilton, in an excessively peremptory manner, Early gave up Marye's Heights. Chilton had intimated that Lee wanted to concentrate all his forces on the left. His foolish intervention precipitated a crisis on the right; fortunately, by the time Sedgwick received orders from Hooker to advance, Lee had already firmly told Early to get back into position.

Lee's priority remained to reunite the scattered fragments of his army on the left. Hooker still retained many advantages, not least numerical superiority and the strong anchor provided by his center at Chancellorsville around which he could reorganize his army. Lee might still have to abandon the Rappahannock line if Hooker could not be defeated. Lee instructed Stuart to take command of the Second Corps, and he took great pains to provide detailed guidance. "Keep the troops well together and press on . . . work by the right wing, turning the position of the enemy so as to drive him from Chancellorsville, which will unite us . . . proceed vigorously." Lee would attack the Union left in unison.

Lee launched dawn attacks to keep Hooker off balance. His instincts told him that the side that struck first would gain the victory. The crucial moment occurred when Stuart's troops seized a piece of high ground at Hazel Grove, overlooking Chancellorsville. Confederate artillery concentrated here and bombarded Union formations crowded around the Chancellor House, a two-storey brick house used by Hooker for his headquarters. When he abandoned Hazel Grove, Hooker, in effect, ceded the battle. At 9 a.m. on May 3 a cannon ball struck the porch of the Chancellor House as Hooker conferred with his subordinates, and he was hit by a piece of timber; ninety minutes later, a concussed Hooker handed over command to Major General Darius Couch of II Corps. At this very moment, Lee launched one more push to drive the Army of the Potomac back to the Rappahannock. Casualties were heavy (one brigade, commanded by Dodson Ramseur, lost more than half its strength), but persistence was rewarded by the occupation of the clearing at Fairview. At last the separated wings of the Army of Northern Virginia clasped hands.

Stuart's troops swept into the clearing around the burning Chancellor House, a veritable bonfire of Hooker's vanity, casting a red hue over all. Lee rode through masses of his troops as immaculate as ever, at probably the climactic moment of his military career. Former Confederate writers invariably paint his picture in graphic and romantic colors. Charles Marshall of his staff wrote years later that Lee's appearance sparked a spontaneous outburst "of enthusiasm which none can appreciate who have not witnessed them . . . One long unbroken cheer . . . rose above the roar of battle. . . ."

It was an arresting moment undoubtedly, but Lee had so far won only a tactical and far from complete victory. Further exertions would be needed. At 12:30 p.m., Lee received bad news: Early had been driven from Fredericksburg. Lee calmly ordered a cessation of the pursuit of Hooker. Anderson's divisions and two brigades of McLaws's division were turned around and sent east to block Sedgwick's path at Salem Church. If Hooker and Sedgwick were allowed to link up, all that had been gained so far would be set at nought. Sedgwick, too, found it difficult to bring his full strength to bear; he was fought to a standstill, and left 1,523 casualties on the field compared with a Confederate loss of 674.

On the morning of May 4, Lee sensed that he had been given an opportunity to destroy Sedgwick's isolated force. He ordered Early to drive back toward Marye's Heights and cut off Sedgwick from his bridges over the Rappahannock. Reinforced, Anderson and McLaws's divisions were to launch a simultaneous assault on Sedgwick's front and flank at Salem Church. At about 11 a.m. Lee arrived to direct operations personally. When informed that McLaws had not yet carried out a reconnaissance he became very angry and carried it out himself. Due to such delays, the attack did not begin until 6 p.m. The troops got confused in the woods, and, as Sedgwick began to pull back toward Bank's Ford, his force escaped intact.

Lee ordered Anderson and McLaws to return to Chancellorsville, but could not resuscitate operations against Hooker the following day as heavy rain fell. Hooker took his chance to retreat and "a perfect sea of men" stumbled back in great confusion to the fords. Yet even as the Army of the Potomac began to lose its cohesion, the Confederates seemed incapable of taking advantage of their vulnerability for all the desperate efforts of their commander. When, on May 6, Stuart reported that the Union Army had withdrawn to the north bank of the Rappahannock, Lee could not disguise his anger and frustration. After he had received confirmation of the report, Lee turned on one of his brigade commanders, Dorsey Pender, bitterly. "That's the way you young men always do. You allow these people to get away. I tell you what to do, but you don't do it. Go after them! Damage them all you can!" In fact this repetition of a similar failure after Fredericksburg suggests a fundamental Confederate shortcoming for which Lee should share responsibility.

Lee's disappointment at missing another opportunity to shatter the Army of the Potomac should not disguise the magnitude of his achievement. Lee had won even though Hooker enjoyed a greater margin of numerical superiority than any other Union commander in the east. Over five days Lee had exploited Hooker's errors and hesitations with astonishing audacity, creativity and celerity. At all levels, Lee out-generalled the timorous Hooker, despite his initial success. Hard-fought victories like Chancellorsville can never be purchased cheaply. Union casualties were 17,304 (these were sustained by only four corps; the other three were not engaged), while Lee lost 13,460, about 23 percent of his infantry. The intensity of the fighting at Chancellorsville compares with the great battle in the same area in 1864. But the cost could be justified on the grounds that Lee had secured the vital Rappahannock line and had won back the initiative. He could thus take his strategy forward to inflict a crippling blow on the Union forces. In order to gain its independence, the Confederacy had to find the room to maneuver so that it could strike the Union strategically as well as tactically—and this could not be done by remaining passively on the defensive.

It may seem incongruous to compare gruesome fields of battle to works of art, but in its elegance, careful calculation and timing, the Battle of Chancellorsville does form Lee's masterpiece of operational art. What is so impressive is the speed and thoroughness with which Lee made his appreciation and then put his plans into practice. Yet the battle grew out of the campaign and Lee did not begin this strongly. Consequently, taking advantage of his success required harder work as combinations had perforce to be hastily improvised at short notice. Without Longstreet's two divisions, the complete destruction of Hooker's army perhaps always lay just beyond Lee's reach.

The prime significance of the battle probably is to be found in the moral sphere. Whatever the future course of the war, Lee had built on his earlier success at Fredericksburg to forge a bond with his troops, an unrivalled *esprit de corps* that would see the Army of Northern Virginia through many vicissitudes. Lee would supplant Jackson hereafter as the great hero of the Confederacy. "This is the best army in the world," wrote one soldier. "We are all satisfied with General Lee and he is always ready for a fight." Yet one important figure did not share in this common experience—Longstreet. The factor that did most to shape the outcome of this campaign, as it did that of the summer of 1863, must surely be Longstreet's absence from the field of Chancellorsville.

CHAPTER SEVEN

Fateful Climax,
June–July 1863

Lee had only postponed a return to Northern fields. Before Chancellorsville he had mooted a scheme to relieve pressure on "middle Tennessee and on the Carolina coast" by advancing north of the Potomac; he secretly ordered Jedediah Hotchkiss to prepare a map that "extended to Harrisburg and then on to Philadelphia." Fredericksburg and Chancellorsville had played their part in Lee's plans, namely, "to baffle them [the Unionists] in their various designs." Even before Chancellorsville, Lee had confided to his wife that "I do not think our enemies are as confident of success as they used to be." The main aim, he contended, should be the defeat of the Republicans in the 1864 presidential election, and then "the friends of peace will become so strong as that the next administration will go in on that basis."

Lee struck a more confident note than a few months earlier: "I think our success will be certain," he claimed. News of the death of Jackson on May 10 accordingly came as a severe blow to Lee's hopes. Four days later he received another request to attend a conference with President Davis and Secretary of War Seddon on future operations. For some weeks the latter had urged Lee to send reinforcements to the beleaguered Vicksburg front. At the meeting Seddon strongly urged sending two divisions. Lee expressed reluctance to part with such a large force, due "to the uncertainty of its employment": would it arrive in time to achieve anything significant? A "Western Concentration bloc," composed largely of Davis's critics, Senator Louis T. Wigfall, Johnston, P. G. T. Beauregard (and Longstreet when it suited him), advanced the case for a greater effort in the Kentucky–Tennessee theater, but they devoted less attention to affairs in Mississippi.

Lee listened patiently to Seddon before seizing the chance to offer a counter proposal. He declared a wish to renew the invasion of the North. He subtly implied that should his army be reduced to 50,000 men there might come a time when a Union thrust on Richmond *would* succeed. Lee's troops would be forced back and pinned down in the Richmond defenses. The Confederacy would thus be faced with two great sieges (Richmond and Vicksburg) rather than one. The only way to alter the strategic balance of the war would be to reinforce the Army of Northern Virginia and make the most of the initiative so recently won: strike directly at the Northern will and its readiness to continue the war. Lee thus extended to grand strategy his fundamental desire to do damage to the enemy without allowing his plans to be determined by what the enemy was doing to the Confederacy.

Lee's arguments were made forcefully, their persuasiveness buttressed by his enormous prestige. He took care though to place the onus on Davis and Seddon to make the key choices: between shoring up failure in Mississippi, or undertaking a new, ambitious expedition in the east. To put it another way, they had to choose whether to support John C. Pemberton, the hapless Confederate commander in Vicksburg, or Lee. In any case, Confederate commanders did not lack troops in Mississippi, they only needed to use the forces that they already had more effectively.

Lee pressed his case as an army commander responsible for the troops under his command; here lay his primary duty. He had influence, of course, and this offered him advantages denied others; but the lop-sided command system was of the President's, not his making. Lee has been accused of strategic myopia for failing to grasp the importance of the west. Actually, he could hardly fail to be aware of it. Lee's critics themselves overlook the enormous importance of the east in Confederate strategy. It offered the only chance to *win* rather than not lose. "Every victory," Lee had counseled Seddon, "should bring us nearer to the great end which it is the object of this war to reach." Only Lee had won victories and offered the chance to turn the tide. It might *only* be a chance but Lee thought it worth exploiting. An invasion of the North would attack the North's war-making resources and preserve those of the Confederacy. It would inflict a savage blow both on the Army of the Potomac and Northern morale. This object did not exist just in Lee's imagination. Lincoln himself admitted to Hooker that the effect of Chancellorsville on domestic and international opinion "would be more serious and injurious than any previous act of the war."

Davis eventually sided with Lee. His support counted for a great deal. Lee's investment in soothing and reassuring Davis, taking him into his confidence and seeking his advice, earned a strong dividend in May 1863. Nonetheless, Davis tended to postpone decisions. On May 16 he summoned a full cabinet meeting, even though in many ways the key choice had already been made, to confirm that Pickett's division would leave Richmond that morning to join Lee's army. Lee attended the meeting, and carefully hedged his bets by understating the claims he could make for his plan. He stressed the logistical advantages of moving north while carefully avoiding alarming the politicians with the risks he readily accepted.

Davis continued to question Lee closely, especially about Richmond's safety. Lee replied that "by concealing his movements and managing well, he could get so far north as to threaten Washington before they could check him and this once done he knew there was no need of further fears about their moving on Richmond." Lee faced one dissenting voice, the Postmaster General, John H. Reagan of Texas. He argued that Lee should feint toward Washington and then transfer between 20,000 and 30,000 men to Pemberton. He did not explain how such a complicated move could be made without a great waste of time. Reagan's view did not prevail (even though he continued to repeat it afterward). Lee's plan thus received the endorsement of the cabinet.

His success pleased him. On May 18 Lee breakfasted with a friend, who was "very glad to see that the great and good man was so cheerful." Lee's plan had triumphed in spite of rather than because of his opportunistic arguments. He depended on luck but felt that it had deserted him at Chancellorsville. Most important of all, he felt that he should escape the constraints of the Rappahannock line. He frankly admitted that at Chancellorsville "we had not gained an inch of ground and the enemy could not be pursued." He hoped to find more advantageous ground north of the Potomac. Reagan's *Memoirs* (1906) hint that Lee had fallen victim to hubris: "He believed he commanded an invincible army" that had prevailed "against greatly preponderating numbers and resources." These are good reasons for seizing the initiative and making the most of it by turning the odds against the foe. Hooker's army numbered 80,000, a big reduction on two months earlier. Lee's critics have consistently failed to demonstrate that surrendering the initiative in the east would have transformed affairs in the west. Our retrospective knowledge that the Gettysburg campaign failed should not lead us to the conclusion that Lee's reasons for urging it were wrong or that it should not have been launched in the first place.

Lee had a lot on his mind that May. He also intended simultaneously to reorganize his army. "To explain the reorganization," avers Douglas Southall Freeman, "is largely to explain Gettysburg." The loss of a subordinate as able as Jackson would have been a crippling blow to any army; for the Confederacy, handicapped by a dearth of talent at the highest level, it was grievous. Jackson's death, moreover, gnawed at the sinews of Lee's devolved system of command. Jackson had many talents, loyalty, self-discipline, alacrity, an intuitive sense of what Lee wanted done and, above all, daring. There is a danger of under-valuing Jackson's contribution to Lee's success if excessive attention is devoted to boosting Longstreet's reputation because it has suffered unfairly at the hands of Lost Cause polemicists. Lee and Jackson were not close personally, but they did share a profound religious faith. Lee admitted to his son, Custis, "a terrible loss" with Jackson's passing. "I do not know how to replace him." Yet Jackson's presence at Antietam had not transformed a drawn battle into a victory. Even if he had lived, Jackson would not have recovered in time for Gettysburg. It seems unlikely that events would have been drastically altered.

Nonetheless implicit confidence in a lieutenant is a priceless asset. As Lee once wrote of Jackson, "Straight as the [compass] needle to the pole he advances to the execution of my purpose." Lee concluded that the only solution to Jackson's absence lay in reducing the corps commanders' span of responsibility. Lee selected a risky course, not least as the size of the Confederate corps had ensured a large measure of local, tactical superiority. In recommending his changes to Davis on May 20, Lee justified them on the grounds that corps of 30,000 men "were too large for one commander." Lee decided to give the Second Corps to Richard S. Ewell, who had recovered from the loss of a leg at Second Manassas, rather than confirm Stuart in the position. Lee probably felt that Stuart could not be spared from an enlarged cavalry command, even if the latter had good reason to feel slighted. Both the Second Corps and Longstreet's First Corps were reduced to three divisions to provide for a new Third Corps (its third division would be composed of reinforcements) to be commanded by A. P. Hill, whom Lee rated as his best divisional commander. Each corps also received its own artillery of three battalions of four batteries, all responsible to their own chief.

The elevation of two Virginians provoked grumbles, but this major reorganization resulted in little disaffection by comparison with the many ructions that crippled the Army of Tennessee. Confederate commanders in the west quarrelled incessantly. The most ferocious disputes involved the Army of Tennessee's commander, Braxton Bragg and his supporters, opposed by his critics led by the senior corps commander, Leonidas Polk. Tensions lurked under the surface of the organization of the Army of Northern Virginia, but thanks to Lee's skillful management of his subordinates, it always remained repressed. The maintenance of high morale was vital: as Lee told Davis, "it is time I was in motion." On June 3 Longstreet's divisions began Lee's turning movement by marching west. They were followed by Ewell's. Lee's efforts at deception were not wholly successful. On June 5 Hooker ordered Sedgwick's VI Corps to cross to the south bank of the Rappahannock and probe toward Deep

Run. This move could have dislocated Lee's plans, but he quickly satisfied himself that Hooker intended only a local incursion and assigned to A. P. Hill the role of rearguard.

On June 8 Lee had moved his headquarters to Culpeper Court House, and here he ordered the entire army to assemble. On the same day he also reviewed Stuart's cavalry, now augmented by six regiments and a battalion. Stuart's men put on an impressive show of horsemanship, one that in Confederate eyes perhaps created a false sense of superiority, given the advances in command and effectiveness made by Union cavalry in recent months. As if to underline the point, the following day 7,000 Union troopers, commanded by Major General Alfred Pleasanton, supported by 4,000 infantry and artillery, attacked Stuart in a pre-emptive strike to thwart Confederate cavalry raids. At Brandy Station, Stuart, deploying 10,000 troopers, was able to force Pleasanton to withdraw, but he had been fought ragged. Stuart did not relish the unaccustomed criticism thrown at him by the Richmond newspapers. After the disappointment over Second Corps he determined that during the next campaign he would undertake a grand stroke that would burnish his reputation afresh.

On June 10 the Confederate turning movement began in earnest, when Lee issued orders for a northward advance, across the Blue Ridge Mountains. The advance was then to turn north-east into the Shenandoah Valley, before heading for the Potomac River once more. Ewell's corps formed the van, and he set a pace worthy of Stonewall, covering 50 miles in two days. In the meantime Hooker tracked the Confederates, keeping his army between them and Washington, DC.

On June 10, during the march north, Lee wrote a long and thoughtful letter to Davis about the broader strategic context of the war. He reminded Davis of the need for speed as "our resources in men are constantly diminishing, and the disproportion in this respect between us and our enemies, if they continue united in their efforts to subjugate us, is steadily augmenting." In recent years, some historians have argued that Lee was wrong to take the offensive and that the Confederate cause would have been better served by a defensive strategy. Yet Lee's insistence that a rapid offensive against the North was essential to fracture "their [the North's] efforts" was clearly right. Outnumbered and with obviously inferior means, the only hope for the South was to inflict a crushing defeat on the North. Clearly, this could happen only if the South took the fight to their opponents. Yet Lee was also conscious of the wider political dimensions of the conflict, urging Davis that the Confederates do everything they could to encourage "the rising peace party of the North." In doing so, his talents as a soldier-statesman, a blend of George Washington and Alexander Hamilton, are made quite clear. As significant, he also raised the question of what the South was fighting *for*. He wrote of the need to save "the honor of our families from pollution, our social system from destruction." This was a rare acknowledgment, suitably clothed in euphemism, of the centrality of slavery to the South's cause.

Lee then went on, however, to caution Davis against discouraging the North from agreeing to a deal that would admit the South's right to secede, but would also acknowledge that Confederate victories should enable the South to be readmitted to the Union on its terms (with slavery intact). At any rate, Lee advocated the need for continued military success to maintain the pressure on the North. He thought it not "prudent to spurn the proposition in advance"; but the point is so tactfully expressed that the letter is unclear whether Lee himself accepted reunion as a legitimate war aim.

Lee was revealing the ambivalence that surrounded the Confederate cause. Far from being an exceptional figure, he often expressed the thoughts, doubts and ambiguities that perplexed innumerable white Southerners. This process rendered Lee's transformation after death into a symbolic figure that much easier. The death of the "great and good Jackson" hastened the process of apotheosis, but raised an ugly question. Was Jackson's death really a sign that Providence favored the Southern cause? "Any victory would be dear at such a price," Lee thought, "but God's will be done." Perhaps the question could be answered only by seeking a clear-cut decision one way or the other.

A further matter that demanded Lee's urgent attention involved the propaganda war. Thanks to Stuart's skill at screening the Army of Northern Virginia, Ewell's Second Corps surged into the Shenandoah Valley. A striking victory at Winchester resulted in 4,000 prisoners, 23 guns and 300 wagons. It looked as though it might perhaps set the tone for the entire campaign. Ewell pushed on through Maryland and into Pennsylvania, successively entering Greencastle and Chambersburg, then, on June 27, occupying Carlisle. Lee ordered Ewell to fan out on a three-division front in order to collect as much foodstuffs as possible; if he thought it possible, Ewell should also take the state capital, Harrisburg. Lee himself crossed the Potomac on June 25 and within two days issued General Order No. 73. If the advance into Pennsylvania meant that Lee could not pose as a liberator, he could still depict Southern conduct in the best possible light.

Lee enjoined his troops "to abstain with most scrupulous care from unnecessary or wanton injury to private property" or to seek revenge for Northern ravaging. Officers were ordered to punish offenders severely. Lee claimed that he sought to "make war only upon armed men," and there is no reason to doubt his sincerity. However, the effort to portray the Confederate invasion as morally

171

superior to Federal behavior was belied by the Southern troops. The conduct of Lee's soldiers differed little from that of Federal forces the following year. Workshops, warehouses, mills and depots were destroyed and personal property "pressed" when required. Northern civilians frequently report that Southern soldiers were busy "ransacking the barns, stores and chicken coops." They also mentioned a good deal of thieving and random vandalism. Lee's claim to moral superiority added a powerful propaganda dimension to his campaign, but it is contradicted by his effort to supply his army from the country. Furthermore, Lee made no effort to prohibit the most shameful aspect of his invasion: the enthusiastic enslavement of Northern free blacks by Confederate soldiers.

He also had some further thoughts on deception and diversionary movements. On June 23 he proposed to Davis that P. G. T. Beauregard command a new force "pushed forward to Culpeper Court House, threatening Washington, DC, from that direction." Two days later Lee pleaded again for the scheme "even in effigy," but to no avail. Davis took no interest in this imaginative suggestion to harness the talents of his maverick commander. Despite Lee's disappointment, he privately expressed satisfaction to Major General Isaac R. Trimble that "we have again outmaneuvered the enemy." As a result of Lee's planning, Hooker had been obliged to launch a series of forced marches. "I hope with that advantage to accomplish some signal result and end the war if Providence favors us." Major Walter Taylor of Lee's staff reflected the buoyant mood of his chief when he told his sister on June 29 that "With God's help we expect to take a step or two toward an honorable peace."

The invasion of Maryland and Pennsylvania raised serious problems for Lee in terms of command and control. His preferred system had always been loose, if well considered. The logistical dimension was vital, but the more he relied on the countryside for foodstuffs the more dispersed his army became. Ewell thus received instructions that stressed the exploitation of chance. "It will depend," Lee wrote, "upon the quality of supplies obtained in that country whether the rest of the army can follow." And again: "Beef we drive with, but bread we cannot carry, and must secure it in the country." Such considerations would inevitably govern strategy and consequently, "I cannot give definite instructions ... You must therefore be guided ... by controlling circumstances around you ... keep yourself supplied with provisions, and send back any supplies, and carry out the plan you proposed so far as your judgment may seem fit."

Under the circumstances outlined by Lee, the cavalry had a vital role. Since June 12, Albert G. Jenkins's brigade from West Virginia had screened Ewell's advance. Lee believed that he had gained a two-day head start over Hooker's army, but this could easily be thrown away. To maintain the advantage, Stuart needed to monitor the Union advance carefully. On June 22, in an ambiguously phrased order, Lee enjoined Stuart to retain two brigades to guard the passes through the Blue Ridge Mountains and protect the army's rear. The remaining three brigades, Lee ordered, should advance into Maryland and be placed on Ewell's right flank. Stuart was thus entrusted to screen Lee's advance, to gain intelligence on Union movements and to assist in the gathering of supplies. A later order, issued the following day, left to Stuart's discretion whether he should "pass around" Hooker's army "doing all the damage you can, and cross the River [Potomac] east of the mountains." These second thoughts were unfortunate, for many of the errors that were committed during the Gettysburg campaign stem from it. Lee did not envisage a full-scale cavalry raid because he reiterated to Stuart that "you must move on and feel the right of Ewell's troops." Poor drafting tended to conceal the significance of this instruction.

On June 25 Stuart's force crossed the Bull Run Mountains and rode eastward. He had taken his best troops and commanders with him. He found the roads clogged with Union infantry and artillery, and concluded that he would find it difficult to carry out his tasks if he attempted to turn north. However, his solution, a drive eastward, tempted him into an over-ambitious "ride around" the Army of the Potomac that took him close to Washington, DC, and allowed the Union Army to get between him and Lee. After Stuart's departure, he received a dispatch from Lee instructing him to link up with Ewell at York, Pennsylvania. This reinforced the unfortunate impression that Stuart had acquired, namely, that his screening duties would begin there rather than immediately. As Stuart sallied east with three brigades, the Army of Northern Virginia did not lack cavalry, even if they were indifferently commanded in Stuart's absence. Longstreet was correct in thinking that Stuart should have left Wade Hampton behind to direct them. The biggest loss of all was Stuart himself. In the taxing days ahead his irrepressible enthusiasm, keen intelligence, shrewdness and experience—attributes that had made such a powerful contribution to the triumph at Chancellorsville—would be sorely missed.

For now, however, Lee thought that things had gone well over the previous two weeks and that the campaign was taking the form that he had anticipated. He delegated much to his subordinates; their sprightly maneuvers would throw up opportunities that, at a later stage, Lee would exploit with decision and tactical insight. Lee thus had an overall concept of the kind of campaign that he wished to fight; but he left the detail of *how* he would fight it until the last possible moment. Since the summer of 1862 this method, closely resembling Winfield Scott's style, had brought him a record of victories unmatched by any other Civil War commander. In this climactic campaign, Lee expected that the main body of the Army of the Potomac would arrive in Pennsylvania "broken down with hunger and hard marching, strung out in a long line, and much demoralized"; Lee would throw overwhelming strength against each corps, "crush it, follow up the success, drive one corps back and another, and by successive repulses and surprises before they can concentrate create a panic, virtually destroy[ing] the army." Although this recollection of a private conversation with Isaac Trimble dates only from the 1890s, it accords closely with the way that Lee tried to conduct the campaign as it developed.

Lee persisted in using a method, however, that would reveal serious flaws in the novel environment of Pennsylvania. The dispersal that resulted from subsistence off the country increased the likelihood of a fragment of the army becoming involved in a "meeting engagement"—an accidental coming together of armies hitherto unaware of each other's presence—at neither the place nor the time of his choosing. Dispersal also left him reliant on his subordinates. The degree of latitude that he granted his corps commanders assumed they would take the decisions he wanted them to take. It was a large assumption, for all that it reflected his enormous self-confidence. His Maryland campaign had been dislocated and his army threatened with destruction because of just such a casual attitude. In addition, in the North Lee lacked the local knowledge that he took for granted in the South, as well as the support of most of the local population and the priceless intelligence they could proffer. Unless he took energetic action, a campaign that depended on skillful maneuver could easily expose the weaknesses in his dynamic but risky generalship.

Certainly, Lee had so far failed to conceal his movements. He had no idea that Hooker was about to catch him up—or that his two-day lead was about to disappear. On June 24 Hooker's troops began to cross into Maryland. Stuart had spotted II Corps in Maryland, but Lee never received his report. Four days later, Major General George G. Meade succeeded Hooker as commander of the Army of the Potomac. (Hooker's self-confidence had never really recovered form his defeat at Chancellorsville and he had lost Lincoln's trust.) Meade immediately received an accurate briefing on Confederate movements. Lee enjoyed no such knowledge of Union troop movements. He had issued orders to Longstreet's First Corps to follow Ewell to Harrisburg; Lee intended that A. P. Hill's Third Corps should cross the Susquehanna River below Harrisburg. This northern advance would continue until the Army of Northern Virginia "encountered" Union forces.

At about 10 p.m. on June 29 these plans were thrown into disarray when a civilian scout employed by Longstreet, Henry T. Harrison, brought word of the Federal advance. Lee usually distrusted civilian scouts, but Stuart's failure to maintain contact had already perplexed Lee and lent Harrison's opinions greater importance. Lee listened "with great composure and minuteness" as Harrison told him that the Army of the Potomac had already crossed into Maryland, but was headed west toward the mountains.

Lee expressed surprise that Union forces were so close. He deduced erroneously that they were heading for the Cumberland Valley to cut his communications. As Ewell continued north-east and away from the threat, Lee had to concentrate his forces urgently to meet it. He decided to switch the axis of his advance back to the eastern slopes of the Blue Ridge Mountains, "so as to threaten Washington and Baltimore, and detain the Federal forces on that side of the mountains to protect those cities." Their previous orders were countermanded, and both Ewell and Longstreet received instructions to "move your forces to this point Chambersburg via Cashburg," 8 miles from an obscure town called Gettysburg.

Lee's shortage of cavalry worsened when Ewell failed to acquaint Jenkins with the change of plan; Jenkins's brigade would lurk uselessly in the environs of Harrisburg for a further day. In the meantime, the two other brigades, those of "Grumble" Jones and Beverley Robertson, swung to the west and rear of the Army of Northern Virginia via Berryville and Martinsburg, just as it realigned itself to the east. Lee appeared "evidently surprised and disturbed" on June 29, according to Walter Taylor, when he learned that Stuart was still in Virginia. He complained of "having no means of information about the enemy's forces."

Lee thus had no idea that Federal cavalry in the shape of John J. Buford's division had entered Gettysburg on June 30, close to his own intended point of concentration. Buford's two brigades occupied the high ground north and west of the town shielding this important road center. On the contrary, in an atmosphere described as "unusually careless and jolly," Lee moved his headquarters to Greenwood at the western access to the Cashtown Gap to "see what General Meade is after." He continued to believe wrongly that Union troops were still at Middleburg, 16 miles to the south. Just as in September 1862, Lee underestimated the capacity of Federal troops to recover from setbacks. On June 30, too, the leading brigade of Heth's division of Hill's Third Corps advanced toward Gettysburg to look for footwear. Finding Buford's cavalry instead, it withdrew. The following day, in the absence of cavalry, Hill sent forward a reconnaissance in force of two infantry brigades. Ewell was informed of these movements and acted to support Hill. Confederate infantry and Union cavalry clashed in fierce fighting. The result was a classic example of a "meeting engagement" that generated its own momentum and significance. The initial small clash drew in larger units until it ignited an unplanned general engagement.

Lee had no influence over these events. He first heard firing at about 11 a.m. while riding down the eastern side of the Cashtown Pass. He quickly indicated to his corps commanders that he had no wish to fight a battle before the army had concentrated. Lee also had no idea what enemy forces lay in front of him. "I cannot think what has become of Stuart," he muttered. "I am in ignorance as to what we have in front of us here." A great battle was nonetheless far from inevitable. By midday Heth had disengaged in the face of Major General John J. Reynolds's I Corps and later of Oliver O. Howard's XI Corps, who had arrived to reinforce Buford.

Meanwhile two of Ewell's divisions appeared to the north-east of the Union position. Fearful that the contest was going against the Confederates, Ewell sought to outflank the Union right. Lee appeared on the battlefield early in the afternoon. He became angry when informed that contact had still not been made with Stuart, and ordered that "open communication" be established forthwith. He denied Heth permission to support Ewell's fight on the right because he refused "to bring on a general engagement today—Longstreet is not up."

Over the course of the next hour Lee began to change his mind. His tactical instinct began to sense the potential for a considerable success even if that took a more limited form than a great battle. At 2:30 p.m., at long last, a courier arrived from Stuart stating that he was 30 miles away. When Hill returned for further orders, Lee replied, "Wait awhile and I will send you word when to go in." From this moment Lee committed himself to fight some kind of engagement at Gettysburg. At 3:45 p.m. a simultaneous onslaught on both Union flanks led to a splendid tactical success. This action fitted Lee's concept of throwing outnumbered Union corps back on one another until he shattered their cohesion piecemeal.

However, he was still in complete ignorance of the proximity of the rest of the Army of the Potomac. Union troops had withdrawn through Gettysburg in some confusion but had rallied on the high ground south of it. Lee preferred that Union forces be driven from this strong position: Cemetery Hill and, slightly to the east, Culp's Hill. Neither Ewell nor Hill knew anything of the ground in front of them and, lacking cavalry, had no means of finding out. Lee sent Major Taylor forward with a message that stressed the importance of gaining possession of the heights, and that, "if possible, he wished him [Ewell] to do this."

Lee himself had acted sensibly by holding back Anderson's division of the Third Corps "in case of disaster"; he had put the safety of the army first while granting Ewell discretion to take risks. He thus shared responsibility for the failure to gain Cemetery Hill and Culp's Hill on the first day of what turned out to be the Battle of Gettysburg. Such an inability to gain all the desired objectives is hardly surprising given the muddled circumstances in which the battle had begun. Lee subsequently struggled to impose a good plan on a random series of actions, a struggle made worse by a complete absence of basic intelligence about topography and the Union order of battle. Under these difficult conditions Lee and his corps commanders had done well and displayed their characteristic energy and aggression. Each small success, however, tempted Lee to seek a greater triumph and, as a result, he lost his freedom of action. Hence his investment of more and more operational capital in a small part of Pennsylvania that he knew virtually nothing about.

What should he do next? In the late afternoon Longstreet arrived on the battlefield. He, too, knew virtually nothing about the action or the ground, and immediately counselled against renewing the battle. Indeed, Longstreet then presented Lee with a proposal that he had every confidence would solve the commanding general's dilemma. The victory at Fredericksburg had persuaded Longstreet that a formula existed for Confederate success, namely, that Lee should pursue an offensive strategy by means of defensive tactics. Whether his formula was stated as clearly and as fully as Longstreet later claimed (when most ex-Confederates were agreed that Gettysburg was *the* turning point in their fortunes) might be doubted. At any rate, Longstreet argued that the army should "file around his [the enemy's] left and secure good ground between him and his capital."

Lee's relations with Longstreet are among the most controversial issues raised by his career. Lost Cause apologists tended to blame all Lee's senior subordinates for the defeat, but especially Longstreet. Longstreet's various replies to their charges were inept. What is beyond dispute is that Lee developed a much closer personal relationship with Longstreet than he did with Jackson. Longstreet himself described it as "affectionate, confidential, even tender, from first to last." A British visitor, Lieutenant Colonel A. J. L. Fremantle, Coldstream Guards, noticed this intimacy, and in his diary, *Three Months in the Southern States April–June 1863* (first published in 1864) thought "The relations between him [Lee] and Longstreet are quite touching—they are almost always together."

But they had been apart at Chancellorsville. This battle had formed the crucible into which the shared experience of great risk and attendant danger, followed by a triumph over great odds, had been poured to form the wrought-iron links of self-confidence that bound the army together. At the time Jackson received an excessive degree of credit for the battle's conception. An ambitious commander like Longstreet (whose corps had been reduced in size) assumed that after Jackson's death he should succeed to the supposed position of Lee's principal military adviser (even source of inspiration)—and receive the public credit for it. Such a position did not actually exist. Evidence of Longstreet's desire for such a special position to complement his intimate personal relationship can be found in his post-war claim that he had extracted a binding promise from Lee not to take the offensive in Pennsylvania. Lee dismissed this claim as absurd. "He had never made any such promise," Colonel Allan reported firmly. It would indeed have been quite out of character, for such a pledge would have violated the opportunistic dimension of Lee's generalship. He would never rule anything out; his dispositions depended on circumstances that could not be predicted in advance. In short, Longstreet had quite misconstrued Lee's relationship with Jackson.

As it happened, Lee had not committed himself irrevocably to continuing the battle, but to abandon this ground and the gains of July 1 demanded an alternative that offered just as much. That evening, Lee and Longstreet studied the ground intently. Lee's response to Longstreet's suggestion that he disengage was blunt. "If the enemy is there tomorrow, we must attack him." Longstreet then replied (or so he later claimed) with a quite unjustified certainty: "If he is there, it will be because he is anxious that we should attack him—a good reason, in my judgment for not doing so." Longstreet's post-war discussion tends to imply that the only alternative to his projected envelopment was a doomed frontal assault. Yet Longstreet's scheme involved risks, too. He sought tactical security by finding a strong position, but increased the danger at the operational level. Lee lacked basic intelligence, had no cavalry to screen this move and, as yet, had no idea where this theoretical "strong position" might lie. The nearer he approached the Washington defenses the less room he had for maneuver. Additionally, a movement behind the Union Army would cut Lee from his communications with the Cumberland Valley. Longstreet's scheme would not just forfeit advantages already gained, but, as Longstreet himself admitted, reduce the possibility that Lee could defeat Union corps "in detail."

The dangers of continuing to attack Cemetery Hill were nonetheless conveyed to Lee shortly afterward by Colonel Armistead Long. Lee consequently thought in terms of advancing around the Union left flank in a repeat of the Chancellorsville maneuver though this time in the opposite direction. The most urgent question was whether Ewell's Second Corps should be shifted around behind Hill's Third Corps to take up a position further south. Ewell opposed such a move because he feared that it would harm the morale of his troops. Such a redeployment would certainly sacrifice any chance of striking the Union line of communications that ran along the Baltimore Pike.

Lee's decision to hold his position exacerbated a number of his difficulties. His front ran for 5 miles. Though this was not excessively long, it took a concave shape with a semi-circular span of command. The width and shallowness of the Confederate position compared adversely to the depth and narrowness of the Union deployment, which also enjoyed the advantage of interior lines—being able to advance to threatened points more quickly than the attackers. Any attack that Lee attempted would depend on close cooperation and concentration. The Confederate position made the achievement of these two vital elements awkward. Lee could, of course, have fallen back to South Mountain and taken up a strong position there, one that would have suited Longstreet. But such an acknowledgment of the theoretical advantages of an offensive-defensive ploy should not lead automatically to the conclusion that Lee's own calculations were foolish. His army had never been more confident or strong relative to the Army of the Potomac. Lee gambled, as he had done so many times before, on the advantages garnered from the momentum already achieved, his own ingenuity and the fighting quality of his troops.

On July 2, Lee rose at dawn. Longstreet rose early, too, and took the opportunity of urging Lee to avoid a frontal attack. Lee had every intention of doing so, and wanted to find the Union flank and rear. He sent Captain Samuel R. Johnston on a reconnaissance of the ground to the south. Before Johnston reported, Lee revealed that he might be having second thoughts about the wisdom of renewing battle on this ground. Campbell Brown, a member of Ewell's staff, received instructions to tell his commander to be prepared to move in case Lee elected to "draw off by my right flank . . . so as to get between the enemy and Washington and Baltimore, and force them to attack us in position." Lee had taken Longstreet's views more seriously that morning than either Longstreet himself, or his later critics, believed.

On his return, Captain Johnston, who himself lacked knowledge of the ground, presented Lee with information that was largely inaccurate. He claimed that the Union forces were aligned along the Emmitsburg Road when in fact they were taking up position behind it on Cemetery Ridge. Nonetheless, on the basis of this faulty intelligence, Lee decided to bring Longstreet's First Corps around to the right of Hill's Third. Two of Longstreet's divisions (those of McLaws and Hood) were to attack the Union left perpendicular to the Emmitsburg Road and strike what Lee believed to be an exposed flank. At

9 a.m. Lee visited Ewell and told him to support Longstreet (in tandem with Hill) by fixing Union troops to their position on his front (i.e. depriving the enemy of freedom of maneuver by forcing him to remain in his position, usually by attacking). Both corps were to be prepared for a final crushing assault should the Union position collapse.

During the morning Lee's mood varied according to the state of his plans. Francis Lawley of *The Times* thought he looked "anxious and ruffled" during the period of uncertainty before Johnston's return. However, serenity returned once he had made the decision to attack. After about 10:30 a.m., Hill's chief of artillery observed that Lee "manifested more impatience than I ever saw him exhibit" as he endured the long delay before his orders for the attack were carried out. Longstreet's two divisions had got terribly tangled up during their approach march. The lost hours were entirely Longstreet's fault, as he had failed to grapple with the details, but Lee had no choice should he wish to persist in the attack but to acquiesce in the delay. Lee always worked through his corps commanders and became an observer once he had issued orders to them. Fremantle noticed that Lee "sat quite alone on the stump of a tree."

At long last Stuart reported later that morning. Lee instructed him to take position on the Confederate left and be prepared to attack the Union rear. This, too, was probably a mistake. Stuart's unique skills were badly needed on the right. Meanwhile, McLaws's division stumbled forward, emerging from the woods parallel to the Emmitsburg Road. To McLaws's surprise, he found a coherent front rather than an exposed flank. Daniel E. Sickles's III Corps had moved forward to the Emmitsburg Road without authorization. Longstreet, rather late in the day, decided on a personal reconnaissance. Hood's division arrived shortly afterward on McLaws's right.

He quickly grasped that Union forces occupied the ground as far south as Little Round Top. Should he advance up the Emmitsburg Road, his right flank would be enfiladed. Longstreet conferred with Lee again, the latter expressing his preference for a flanking attack but stressing the importance of "following up, as near as possible, the direction of the Emmitsburg Road." As ever, Lee allowed a considerable measure of flexibility as to how the attack should be made.

The Union line had strengthened during these lost hours, but the differences between Lee and Longstreet were only those of degree. Longstreet sought another turning movement (he had, after all, delivered an offensive stroke at Second Manassas), Lee a tactical out-flanking of the Union left. Neither sought a frontal assault on the Union position. A combination of poor knowledge of the ground and shocking intelligence failures conspired to produce an attack that bore very little resemblance to Lee's general design. Matters were worsened by Hood's decision to introduce a "digression" toward the lower slopes of Little Round Top to drive away Union skirmishers from his right.

The Confederate attack did not begin until about 4:30 p.m. Longstreet neglected numerous details in the placing of his troops. Consequently, the two divisions made a dispersed frontal assault to the north-east rather than in a northerly direction. Hood fell wounded as his division advanced and his troops plunged into the broken, rocky gullies and dales around Little Round Top. McLaws thus lacked support as he made considerable progress in shattering Sickles's over-extended front. But First Corps failed to land a power-ful coordinated punch and Meade was allowed a sufficient breathing space to send V Corps to shore up the wavering Union line. Still, McLaws had succeeded in gaining the Emmitsburg Road and

Longstreet's chief of artillery, Porter Alexander, advanced his gun line. Some units also managed briefly to get up on to Cemetery Ridge. Ewell's efforts to the north also came close to success. Meade relieved pressure on both flanks by shifting forces from the center.

"It is all very well, General. Everything is well," Lee observed cheerfully to A. P. Hill during the evening when he reported to headquarters on the Chambersburg Pike. Confederate success was perhaps more apparent than real, but Lee thought it sufficient to justify a renewal of the attack the following morning. He hoped that then "proper concert of action" might be attained. Early on the morning of July 3, Lee visited Longstreet's headquarters in a schoolhouse next to Willoughby Run, 900 yards behind Warfield Ridge. Longstreet committed the foolish error of repeating his desire to disengage and turn the Union left, a maneuver now quite impracticable. Lee pointed toward Cemetery Ridge and stated emphatically: "The enemy is there and I am going to strike him." But Lee did not envisage an unsupported frontal assault so much as an onslaught combining attacks on both Union flanks. Longstreet dissuaded him from a further attack on the Confederate right (even though he held the west base of Big Round Top). He argued that the troops were too exhausted and too vulnerable to enfilading fire. Longstreet should have been aware of this the day before.

Lee thus struggled (as he had since the battle opened) to stitch together a sensible plan of attack. That morning for the first time Lee, Longstreet and Hill went on reconnaissance together with members of Lee's staff. Lee reluctantly concluded that the only course left open to him was to fix with McLaws's and Hood's divisions while striking the weakened Union center with Pickett's division (which had arrived late the previous afternoon), supported by elements of Hill's Third Corps. Longstreet repeated his arguments concerning the exhaustion inflicted on his other two divisions. Ever loyal to Lee, Hill then offered the use of his entire corps. Longstreet's manner then became noticeably surly, probably because of the mounting evidence that his views were not being given special attention. Indeed it can be argued that too much attention has been made of Longstreet's criticisms. He had often spoken his mind before, as during the Maryland campaign, and Lee had often rejected his advice. The difference in July 1863 was that Longstreet resented the rejection more.

But Lee's trust in Longstreet's tactical skill had not been shaken by the errors of July 2. He placed him in charge of the attack rather than Hill. Despite his misgivings, Longstreet was more reliable and robust (Hill's health had already failed him the previous day). Besides Pickett's division, Longstreet would have available the two North Carolina brigades of Pender's division, Heth's division and the prospect of support by two other brigades—a total of eleven brigades in all. As at Antietam, the exigencies of battle resulted in an erosion of the lines of corps responsibility. But Lee could not use all of Third Corps because of the paramount need to guard the routes back to South Mountain. With the numbers of attacking troops smaller than the day before, Lee designed a tightly synchronized attack. The three brigades of Pickett's division should break in to the Union position and the six brigades of Heth and Pender should break through and cut the Army of the Potomac in two. Meanwhile, the remaining two brigades were to act as a reserve and flank guard. Pickett disposed of 4,500 men, the supporting force about 9,000. Once sure of success, Lee then intended to throw forward Anderson's division and a further six brigades to complete the *coup de grâce*.

At the end of the conference, Lee rode back to the Confederate center and told William Pendleton (the father of Sandie) to organize "concentrated and destructive fire" to support the infantry. In total 164 guns taken from all three corps were drawn up. Lee intended that the artillery would advance *with* the infantry and cover the advance. Consequently, he expected the Union defenders to be too demoralized to offer much resistance. Lee also intended that Ewell should put in a powerful demonstration in front of Cemetery Hill. As he rode along the Confederate line for the third time, Lee could hear firing from the left. Having put his trust in the artillery, Longstreet and providence, Lee returned to his headquarters. The bombardment began just after 1 p.m. and lasted for more than an hour.

Lee might have designed an intelligent plan, but as on the second day the execution went seriously awry. Lee had indeed homed in on the weakest part of the Union position, as Major General Winfield Scott Hancock, the commander of II Corps, recognized as soon as the Confederate advance began. At about 3 p.m. two wings of grey infantry separated by several hundred yards moved to the attack in two waves. They were an impressive sight, and numbered just under 12,000 men with 1,500 in support. Lee moved to the center of Seminary Ridge to watch the attack. Due to Pendleton's indifferent direction of the bombardment, it had continued far too long and been largely effective. Pendleton had also stationed the Reserve Artillery train too far away to sustain rapid resupply with the result that the guns ran dangerously low on ammunition. In addition, no guns accompanied the assault.

On a broilingly hot and sunny afternoon, the Confederate infantry headed for a grove of chestnut oaks, a "little clump of trees," in a converging attack. As they closed on the objective, they suffered sorely at the hands of Federal artillery whose fire, supplemented by ferocious rifled-musket volleys and unimpeded by silent Confederate guns, raked their approach. Longstreet had rather abdicated his responsibilities during the attack. The adoption later in the nineteenth century of the popular designation "Pickett's Charge" (that appropriated the tragic glory to three Virginia brigades) tends to illustrate the ambiguity of the command arrangements. To make matters worse, the thrust was not supported on the flanks. Ewell's troops did not even demonstrate in front of Cemetery Hill, but wasted their efforts against distant Culp's Hill. For the second time in two days, Lee failed to land the closely coordinated and tightly concentrated blow needed to shatter Meade's front. Longstret's men recoiled.

Defeated Confederate soldiers fled back to their lines. Lee invariably rationed his appearances at the front so as not to lessen their moral effect. He drew on all his inner resources as he rode forward to rally the broken ranks. Colonel Fremantle witnessed his efforts and thought his conduct "perfectly sublime. . . . His face . . . did not show signs of the slightest disappointment, care or annoyance; and he was addressing to every soldier he met a few words of encouragement, such as, 'All this will come right in the end: we'll talk it over afterward; but in the meantime, all good men must rally.'" Fremantle is our main contemporary source for Lee's remarkable admission that: "All this has been *my* fault—it is *I* that have lost this fight." Some have doubted that he said this, but in fact there seems no reason to question Fremantle's account. If Lee did make such a frank acknowledgment, then he was correct. As commanding general he did carry responsibility for what remained, until the last days of his military career, his only outright defeat on the battlefield.

At the earliest possible moment Lee pulled back Ewell's corps to Seminary Ridge, meaning to shorten his line and resist any Federal counterstrokes. In the event, Meade's troops did not stir. The Confederate retreat to Virginia began on the afternoon of July 4. The previous night the cavalryman, John D. Imboden, conferred with an exhausted Lee. "The moon shone full upon his massive features and revealed an expression of sadness that I had never seen upon his face." The shattered Army of Northern Virginia withdrew through the passes of the Catoctin and South Mountains. Lee hoped to cross the Potomac at Falling Waters, but Federal cavalry had burnt the pontoon bridge and heavy rainfall led to a rise in the river level leaving Lee and his troops trapped on the Maryland side. Lee prepared a strong, entrenched position near Williamsport. On July 12 the Army of the Potomac closed in. Meade, however, hesitated to attack. He procrastinated for a further day and by the time he decided to launch his attack on July 14, the pontoon bridge had been rebuilt, the waters had subsided and Lee's army had made its escape. Meade's reluctance to attack Lee's wounded army, despite the intense pressure that Lincoln brought to bear on him, illuminates one of the campaign's perennial issues. Longstreet's view thirteen days earlier that Meade could be persuaded to throw forward a reckless assault under far less advantageous conditions was a pipe dream.

Lee's return to Virginian soil brought this controversial and ambitious campaign to an abrupt end. It had proved a costly failure. Lee had sustained 22,874 casualties, although the Army of the Potomac had suffered severely, too, even on the defensive, with 22,817 casualties. Never again would Lee's army be strong or confident enough to inflict the kind of overwhelming defeat on Northern soil that would fatally damage the Union cause.

Throughout the campaign, Lee had performed below his best. Lost Cause apologists would later place the blame on his lieutenants, especially Longstreet. Certainly they had failed him, but Longstreet's sulkiness and errors were not part of a broader pattern of slowness, as Early and others suggested, but the result of a particular occasion (although Longstreet's capriciousness and casual attitude would surface again later in the year at Chattanooga and Knoxville in the Tennessee campaign). Some other writers suggest (rather like Napoleon's apologists after Waterloo) that Lee's lack of inspiration resulted from deteriorating health; but this cannot be proven and finds scant confirmation in his correspondence.

The plain fact is that Gettysburg was a battle that Lee could and should have won. However, the likelihood of defeat—the tiny margin of error allowed for—had always lurked in the background of his greatest triumphs. It was implicit in his generalship. In Pennsylvania factors that had previously favored him worked against him: intelligence, a sympathetic populace, cooperation of corps and a loose command system. Indeed, the central reason for the failure lay in Lee's devolved system of command. To work well it needed sympathetic souls. Lee needed positive responses from his subordinates, for without them he became aloof and uncommunicative. Longstreet's attitude, even if more repressed than he later claimed, introduced a tension into this delicate mix. Stuart's absence added to its unpredictable chemistry. Fremantle records that during the entire second day of the battle, Lee "sent one message, and only received one report." On the third day, Lee exerted himself greatly before the fighting began, but once Pickett moved forward he became a spectator. Such a *laissez faire* attitude worked well when the circumstances favored Lee—but at Gettysburg they did not. He should have supervised the execution of his plans more closely. On two crucial occasions, a half-understood or accepted plan unfolded in a muddled fashion. A battle that had started well ended in bloody defeat.

In his report Lee accurately summed up the reasons for his untimely failure. His plans had been crippled by "the absence of correct intelligence." In then striving "to overcome the difficulties by which we were surrounded," each further commitment increased the stakes he played for. Lee's great gamble collapsed because he proved incapable of directing, at that time and at that place, "one determined and united blow . . . by our whole line." The confidence that had served him so well in earlier campaigns came to look suspiciously like over-confidence.

Gettysburg did not carry the significance at the time that it would assume by the 1880s as the "high water mark of the Confederacy." Historians over the last half century have stressed the importance of the war in the west to the Confederacy's collapse as much as the defeat in Pennsylvania. News of the fall of Vicksburg on July 4 arrived in Washington at the same time as word of Lee's defeat. Yet the Battle of Gettysburg blunted the superb offensive edge of the Army of Northern Virginia. It was for Lee a disastrous defeat that would require a reappraisal of his entire attitude to the war's conduct.

CHAPTER EIGHT

Acme of Defensive Skill,
August 1863–June 1864

One of Lee's first acts on returning to Virginian soil was to compose, on July 13, a long and carefully drafted letter of resignation to the Confederate President. Lee claimed the Pennsylvania campaign as "a general success though the army had been denied a victory." He admitted that the "remedy for want of success in a military commander is his removal." With criticism of Lee reappearing in the newspapers, he also counseled Davis that if a commander "loses the confidence of his troops disaster must sooner or later ensue." Accordingly, Lee recommended that a "younger and abler man than myself" should be appointed to his position. Lee stressed that his declining energies had "prevented [me] from making the personal examinations and giving the general supervision to the operations in the field which I feel to be necessary." Characteristically, Lee concluded that "I have no complaints to make of anyone but myself." Davis's reply did not arrive for a month. It stated simply that to find an abler man "is to demand an impossibility." Lee, the indispensable man, would remain in command for the rest of the war.

The conduct of the Gettysburg campaign actually made little discernible mark on the confidence of Lee's soldiers in their commander. More than a month after the battle, one soldier in Wofford's brigade wrote to his mother that in comparison with the troops in Mississippi, "I wish they had such officers as we have got . . . General Lee has the confidence of our whole army." The great majority of soldiers in the Army of Northern Virginia took the view that Federal soldiers had not proved themselves superior. The authorities in Richmond believed that the army had not been severely damaged by its adventure. The head of ordnance, Josiah Gorgas, reported that 600 men per day had joined the ranks "and his [Lee's] army appears to be nearly in its original good condition."

So quickly did the army recover that many in both the ranks and in the upper echelons, like Porter Alexander, expected Lee to attempt another offensive: "We are all anxious for it, thinking that we had not a fair showing at Gettysburg." By comparison with the other disasters that befell Confederate arms in the summer and autumn of 1863—at Vicksburg, Port Hudson and Tullahoma—contemporary opinion did not regard Gettysburg as especially calamitous. It was only later that the battle came to be seen as an inauspicious turning point.

Despite the generous affirmation of presidential confidence, Lee nonetheless faced a series of grave problems that summer. He did believe that he was "too old to command this army." Some of the symptoms of his "attack" the previous spring—probably cardiovascular—lingered on. He also experienced severe back pain, wrongly diagnosed as "lumbago," that spread to his side. In April 1864 he warned his son, Custis, that his strength appeared to be ebbing and left him "less competent for duty than ever." In Lee's anxieties about the state of his health lie some of the later claims that they contributed to his Pennsylvania defeat. The evidence is not conclusive, but in reality Lee shouldered his burdens throughout 1864 with remarkable zest and stamina for a man in later middle age.

A further source of strain and distraction continued to be the lop-sided Confederate command system. At the end of July, Davis sought Lee's views on western affairs. "I need your counsel but must strive to meet the requirements of the hour," the President admitted, "without distracting your attention at a time when it should be concentrated on the field before you." Yet Lee had no responsibility or special knowledge of conditions in either Tennessee or Georgia and even less time to brief himself: for a further eighteen months his formal purview would remain restricted to his army and department. Nonetheless, on August 24 Lee again went to Richmond to advise on the deteriorating position in Tennessee. Both William S. Rosecrans's Army of the Cumberland and Burnside's Army of the Ohio had advanced toward Chattanooga and Knoxville respectively. If both these vital rail junctions were lost, the Confederacy would be unable to communicate with the Mississippi Valley and the Union would be able to strike through Georgia to the Atlantic, reducing the writ of the rebel capital to Virginia and the Carolinas. Lee initially offered to take the offensive against Meade, but after the fall of Knoxville in September Davis decided that this front had to be reinforced. Lee agreed to send Longstreet and two divisions of the First Corps (those of Hood and McLaws). In addition, two brigades were sent to succour Charleston, South Carolina.

These detachments left Lee with 46,000 men to defend the Rappahannock line. The autumn was spent fencing with Meade. During the course of these operations, Lee developed severe doubts about the ability of Hill and Ewell to conduct detached operations without close supervision. In October Hill had launched impetuous and costly attacks at Bristoe Station, losing 1,361 men and gaining nothing. "Well, well, General," remarked Lee pointedly, "bury these poor men and let us say no more about it." The following month, on Ewell's front, a pontoon bridge over the Rappahannock was burnt by Federal troops, who followed up their success by taking a sizeable number of Confederates prisoners. As a result, an attack at Kelly's Ford had to be cancelled.

Further frustration followed. At the end of November, Meade advanced toward the Mine Run, west of the Chancellorsville battle-field. Lee entrenched behind Mine Run, but Meade declined to attack his position. "They must be attacked; they must be attacked," murmured Lee, sensing a chance to regain the initiative. Early had taken command of Second Corps, as Ewell had fallen ill. Lee intended to hold Meade in position with Early and attack the Union left with two divisions. On December 2, with Lee poised to attack, Meade discovered the trap and withdrew hurriedly. These inconclusive maneuvers had cost Lee 4,255 casualties for negligible advantage.

The failure to regain the initiative highlighted the Confederates' lack of command ability in depth. Both the army and its commander had lost confidence in Ewell and Hill. Of the six divisional commanders, only Early had shown the slightest aptitude for corps level responsibilities. Lee would find himself forced to supervise the details of their operations more closely. He also faced chronic logistical problems of supplying his troops in an area already stripped of wherewithal. The plunder removed from Pennsylvania helped sustain the army up until Christmas, but thereafter the situation deteriorated. In April 1864, Lee complained to Davis, "I cannot see how we can operate with our present supplies . . . There is nothing to be had in this section for man and animals." The shortage of fodder and fresh horses especially worried Lee (fodder supplies were never more than one-third of the total requirement). A deterioration in the efficiency of the cavalry resulted, even though Stuart himself had taken the lessons of Gettysburg to heart and wrote dispatches to Lee every few hours.

Dispersal appeared to be the only solution to these logistical difficulties—and the Army of Northern Virginia accordingly spread itself over the countryside. The fertile Shenandoah Valley assumed an even greater importance in Lee's calculations. Desertion also continued to agitate him. At the turn of the year, Second Corps alone recorded 11,610 absentees.

The numerical weakness of the army persuaded Lee of the virtues of entrenchment. After Mine Run it would become part of the daily routine. As the Federal build-up began in earnest in March 1864, Lee began to worry that the new emphasis on the tactical defensive would prefigure the pattern of the forthcoming campaign. Lee still lacked the initiative: unless he could find an avenue to develop an offensive, he feared that he would have no alternative but "to conform to his [the enemy's] plans and concentrate wherever they are going to attack us." At least by April Longstreet had returned from Tennessee. His troops were stationed around Charlottesville to help guard the Shenandoah.

The Civil War entered its culminating phase in March 1864 with the appointment of Lieutenant General Ulysses S. Grant as general-in-chief of the Union armies. By far the most formidable of Lee's opponents, he exhibited a quiet determination and modesty that belied his audacity and remorseless pursuit of his objectives. He had a passion for "moving on" and never turning back. His greatest advantage over Lee lay in his appointment as general-in-chief, which allowed him to delegate most duties relating to command of his troops in the field to Meade, leaving himself free to concentrate on the direction of the campaign. He also enjoyed a significant, if not overwhelming, numerical advantage, fielding 95,583 infantry, 15,298 cavalry, 8,000 artillerymen and 274 guns. Putting aside the sick and those used up in garrisons, Grant had an "effective" force of 101,895, rather smaller than Hooker's the year before.

Lee could count on 57,811 infantry and gunners with 8,543 cavalry, plus 200 guns, giving him an "effective" strength of 61,025 men. Lee's dispositions were largely governed by logistical considerations. Yet Grant had succeeded in keeping his plans out of the newspapers, and Lee had difficulty in discerning them. Inevitably, it put him at a disadvantage in the struggle to regain the initiative. Second and Third Corps (commanded again by Ewell and Hill respectively) were in their winter camps near the Rappahannock line, with Longstreet's divisions more than a day's march away. On May 2, on Clark Mountain behind the Rapidan, Lee conferred with his divisional commanders and predicted that Grant would attempt to turn the Confederate right. But Lee had been slow to concentrate his troops to resist this move (just as in November 1862 and again in April 1863). He had underestimated the whirlwind pace of Grant's preparations.

There may have been sound logistical reasons for placing Longstreet to the south-west, but he would have to march 45 miles before he could strike the exposed Union columns as they traversed the poor roads and thickets of the Wilderness. Lee committed a serious error with this distribution, for he risked bringing on a battle before he could fully concentrate his strength.

Nonetheless, he approached the spring offensive confidently. "I have no uneasiness as to the result of the campaign in Virginia," he informed Davis. In this unruffled mood, he reflected the optimism of his troops. Lieutenant Colonel Walter Taylor of Lee's staff wrote that

"Our army was never in better spirits and in discipline and in efficiency is equal to any that ever existed." One officer in John B. Gordon's brigade wrote that "the men are now very anxious to move forward. They are also anxious that Gen[eral] Lee should carry them into Pennsylvania again." But if Lee had underestimated Grant, for his part Grant had failed to grasp the difficulties of fighting in the Wilderness or to gauge the full extent of Lee's ingenuity. He hoped to get through the Wilderness, but instructed Meade to "pitch in" if he caught fragments of Lee's army unsupported.

On May 4, as soon as he heard that Grant's advance had begun, Lee issued orders to Ewell's Second and Hill's Third Corps to march into the Wilderness along parallel roads, the Orange Turnpike and Orange Plank Road respectively. Lee rode at the head of Hill's column. He sought initially to entrap Grant in the Wilderness but not bring on a major battle before Longstreet arrived. Lee had been forced to wait until Grant revealed his hand, but the delay proved nearly fatal. The campaign would be decided by a simple formula: victory would be gained by the army that deployed first with its entire strength. Grant already had his full force at hand; Lee did not. The general who concentrated first and put in a powerful attack would win. Although Grant had expressed a wish to avoid a meeting engagement, Lee's advance to contact threatened to produce just such an encounter under the most disadvantageous circumstances for the Confederates. A gap of over 2 miles opened up between the two parallel columns, and Lee had no reserve available to fill it.

At least Lee enjoyed an advantage in intelligence gathering. While Stuart's cavalry screened the advance of the two Confederate corps efficiently, Meade had retained the bulk of his cavalry to guard his long, vulnerable trains. Stuart, dominating the area between the two armies, was accordingly able to send back a series of clear reports.

The sudden appearance of large numbers of Confederate infantry on his front took Meade by surprise. In the opening phase of the campaign, Meade held the opinion that Lee would withdraw and make a stand on the North Anna River. Lee had acted with characteristic daring in attempting to trap the Army of the Potomac in the Wilderness and force it to relinquish the initiative (as he had managed to do at Chancellorsville). For some hours Meade was caught wrong-footed. But Lee took a terrible risk in provoking Grant and Meade to mount a powerful thrust that he lacked the resources to resist.

The congested forest enabled Lee to make the most of the terrain for defense and reduce the effect of the powerful Federal artillery. But in the continued absence of First Corps, he could not overcome his numerical weakness. As the Union advance continued, the two corps of Ewell and Hill began separate engagements, but could not link up. Hill's corps was positioned 3 miles south of Ewell's, but also more dangerously, 3 miles east of Ewell's troops, thus exposing his flanks. The time and place of First Corps's arrival would be critical to the course of the Battle of the Wilderness. Lee had hoped that Longstreet would be in place by the night of May 5. This would prove too optimistic.

Grant (through Meade) concentrated his forces for an attack in the early hours of May 6. He sought to exploit the weakness in the Confederate center that the fighting the previous afternoon had revealed. Lee himself had been forced to rally a fleeing Confederate brigade near the Widow Tapp's Farm (a primitive log cabin surrounded by a clearing) under "terrific fire." "Go back boys . . . ," he shouted in his measured tones. "We want you in front now." As night fell, Hill's corps found itself in a dangerous position. His troops were exhausted and he did not have the heart to disturb them to entrench. Lee himself did not appear unduly perturbed by his predicament, believing that Longstreet would come up that night. He had not been displeased by the course of the day's fighting. The outnumbered Confederates had caught the Unionists in the Wilderness without the penalty of having to fight a general engagement. But the position would change dramatically when, that night, Grant decided to overwhelm both of Hill's flanks and then drive the Union right through the hollow Confederate center. A reinforced Union II Corps under Winfield Scott Hancock gathered for the renewed onslaught. For Lee, it was as much opportunity as threat. If Longstreet could come up in time, he could catch Hancock's troops strung out in detail in the open.

In short, Lee risked tactical destruction while he waited to concentrate a blow of operational significance that might decide the entire campaign. He is sometimes criticized for inactivity on the night of May 5, but this pattern of waiting on events resembles the Chancellorsville campaign. When the Union columns attacked early on May 6, Hill's front crumbled and his troops were driven back a mile and a half. Lee's army stared catastrophe in the face. Many of Hill's men ran back to the clearing around the Widow Tapp's Farm. Even Lee's composure seemed to buckle under the strain. He rode forward in some agitation and shouted at McGowan's brigade of South Carolinians, "My God! General McGowan, is this splendid brigade of yours running like a flock of geese?" Its commander replied that all he needed was a place to reorganize, and Lee's staff helped him do so behind the gun line.

Lee then saw troops moving through the woods to his right and trotted anxiously toward them, passing through what one observer termed "a scene of utter, and apparently irremediable confusion, such as we had never witnessed before in Lee's army." Lee shouted, "Who are you, my boys?" "Texas boys" came back the reply—an announcement of the arrival of Longstreet's advance guard. Longstreet himself arrived on the battlefield at about 6 a.m. "I was never so glad to see you," exclaimed Lee as they instantly began "close consultation." Longstreet's corps had marched over 40 miles in forty hours. It was an exceptional feat, far from the lethargic performance alleged by some of his post-war enemies. First Corps had arrived in the nick of time; more important, Longstreet's troops had not lost their tactical alignment, despite the confusion around them, and though tired they were ready for battle.

The Texas Brigade deployed parallel to the Orange Plank Road and then swung about 180 degrees, passing through the Confederate gun line at the edge of Tapp Field. It then advanced at an angle of about 60 degrees to hit the Federal troops then deploying at its furthest edge and eager to take the Confederate guns. The scenes that followed their forward movement rank among the most dramatic of the war. Lee rode on Traveller through the ranks of the brigade dressed immaculately in his "ordinary field uniform and his old army sword." He took off his hat and, in a gesture of unwonted emotional exuberance, waved it in the air and "hurrahed for the Texas Brigade." Lee seemed buoyed up by the mighty roar that he received in reply and appeared ready to lead the brigade forward himself. A Texas soldier noticed that "his form quivered with emotions." The line then passed Lee but he continued to accompany it. He was then noticed by some soldiers, one or two of whom caught Traveller's reins. Individuals shouted "Go back, General Lee, go back!" The refrain was quickly taken up, "General Lee to the rear!" Lee's horse was steered back through the ranks, and the brigade surged forward. If Lee's inspirational gesture of personal leadership reflected his fatalism and willingness to die at the head of his troops, it also indicated his nearness to defeat.

The full might of the Union offensive had been spent before Longstreet's attack drove Hancock's troops back in confusion. The crisis on the Confederate right had determined that First Corps advance along the Orange Plank Road. Longstreet would have preferred to turn Meade's left by marching along the Catharpin Road and then turning up the Brock Road behind Hancock's II Corps. As Lee lacked freedom of operational maneuver because of the gap in his center, he could not allow First Corps to undertake this much wider and deeper approach when Hill's corps tottered on the brink of defeat. Longstreet's arrival on the immediate right allowed the Army of Northern Virginia to consolidate by shuffling sideways to the left, occupying the Chewning Plateau in the Confederate center and thus closing the near fatal gap. Longstreet's infantry, however, had done more than sustain Lee's position. They had seized a line of Union breastworks and kept another under heavy pressure. One more strong push and Meade's entire left flank might disintegrate.

Lee's chief engineer, Brigadier General Martin L. Smith, had discovered a railway bed for track that had never been laid. Lee gave Longstreet permission to mount an outflanking attack while the Army of the Potomac flailed about in the Wilderness, to envelop the entire Union left and bring an abrupt end to Grant's offensive. The attacking force was drawn from four different divisions of the army, and Longstreet appointed a member of his staff, Lieutenant Colonel G. Moxley Sorrel, to coordinate it. The unsupported flank of II Corps rested on the bed and had been engaged in front by Kershaw's division. The improvised attack indeed shattered the Union left during the late morning. As panic and chaos spread, Longstreet went forward to launch a second outflanking drive in tandem with an eastward attack by Kershaw. Lee waited anxiously for word of Longstreet's progress. Instead, he received a message with the shocking news that

Longstreet had been seriously wounded in an incident eerily similar to that which led to the death of Jackson almost exactly a year before (though Longstreet would survive, albeit making a slow recovery).

Lee immediately went to the front and assumed personal command. He assessed the prospects for success, being "almost minute in his inquiries." He disapproved of Longstreet's proposed alignment, feeling that it did not grant sufficient scope for exploitation and ordered numerous changes, though as only Longstreet knew where all his brigades were the process took time. As a result, the attack did not go forward until almost 4 p.m., and, though some parts of the Union line were taken, it failed to achieve any decisive success. Later writers would claim that a tremendous opportunity had been lost and that Lee's troops might have been able to sweep triumphantly back to the Rapidan. Obviously, the wounding of Longstreet damaged the chances of a Confederate victory. But it seems unlikely that Meade, thrown back on the defensive, would have been unable to make full use of the Wilderness to parry the Confederate blows. Grant's psychological equilibrium would surely have proved a good deal more robust than Hooker's the year before. In truth, Longstreet's corps probably lacked the strength to destroy the Union left completely. Nonetheless, if Longstreet had been able to launch his attack as he had designed it, Lee would probably have emerged eventually as the outright victor in this opening round of the 1864 campaign.

Another opportunity recommended itself on the Confederate left after Meade had taken troops from the VI Corps front to reinforce his left. John B. Gordon thought the Union right flank could be attacked with profit. But having committed so much to Longstreet's front, Lee lacked reserves. Nonetheless, he gave Ewell permission to seek advantage if he could, but Meade was too astute a tactician to be caught out. He "refused"—that is, pulled back the right of VI Corps to stronger ground—and Ewell frittered away the Confederate advantage in a series of impetuous and inconclusive assaults.

The Battle of the Wilderness spluttered to a halt on the evening of May 6. The first titanic clash between Lee and Grant (in which Meade had played an important part) had resulted in a drawn battle. The Wilderness had shifted first in favor of one and then the other. Lee had certainly frustrated Grant's desire to get through the Wilderness before he could decisively defeat the Army of Northern Virginia on ground of his choosing. Lee's riposte, however, had not regained the initiative. Lee's casualties cannot be calculated exactly, but were in the region of 8,700. Grant sustained much heavier losses, of 17,666. Despite this, Grant had no intention of abandoning the campaign. On May 7 he ordered that Meade's army should continue its advance south-east toward Spotsylvania Court House.

Lee faced numerous distractions as the rest of Grant's 1864 campaign unfolded. Still, on May 7, through instinct, calculation (that Grant might try and turn his right flank again) and luck, Lee decided that Grant would attempt to seize the crossroads at Spotsylvania. At this point, Lee probably underestimated Grant's determination to continue the campaign (he thought Fredericksburg his most likely destination). Stuart picketed the road and screened the advance of First Corps, now commanded by Richard H. Anderson. Second Corps would follow if Lee's guess proved right. Anderson did not rest, started early and arrived to support Stuart's cavalry at about 7 a.m., before the Union infantry.

However, Lee's concentration was complicated by two other developments. First, on May 9 Grant sent Major General Philip H. Sheridan and his cavalry corps of 10,000 troopers on a raid that struck Lee's line of communications and threatened Richmond. Lee had little choice but to order Stuart to intercept him. He did so two days later at Yellow Tavern, where Stuart was killed while attempting to shore up his crumbling left flank. Second, Major General Benjamin F. Butler's Army of the James had attempted to march on Richmond itself. Since April 23 General P. G. T. Beauregard had taken command of a new department, including Virginia south of the James and North Carolina. Beauregard attacked Butler at Drewry's Bluff on May 16, forcing him to withdraw to City Point and entrench along the Bermuda Hundred, a tongue of land between the confluence of the James and Appomattox rivers. Beauregard commanded about 20,000 troops—a significant detraction from Lee's strength as the crisis at Spotsylvania moved rapidly toward its bloody climax. The only advantage for Lee in this fluid situation was that Sheridan absented himself from the Army of the Potomac until May 24 while on his cavalry raid; the Union Army, lacking cavalry, stumbled forward blindly. For the remainder of the campaign, the Confederate cavalry was commanded effectively by Lee's choice as Stuart's successor, Wade Hampton.

Lee persisted in his desire to keep Grant away from Richmond. His skill as an engineer allowed him to compensate for his numerical inferiority by exploiting the terrain to his advantage as well as systematically entrenching his troops. By such delaying tactics, he still hoped to erode Northern support for the war. In other words, with Grant every bit as resolute as Lee, Lee found himself increasingly forced to attain his strategic aim by defensive means. When two ingenious and resourceful commanders are determined to fight it out, the result is often a battle of attrition.

By May 9 Lee had succeeded in getting his three corps into a position at Spotsylvania blocking Grant's advance. His line ran for about 3 miles along a shallow ridge the flanks of which were guarded by the Po and Ny rivers, running left and right respectively. The tree line ran about 200 yards from the Confederate works, offering a clear line of fire. Anderson occupied the left, Ewell the center and Third Corps, commanded temporarily by Jubal Early (because Hill had fallen ill), the right. The only potential cavity in the line lay in the center, where Ewell had decided to occupy two pieces of high ground to the north that resulted in an exposed salient—the "Mule Shoe"—which stretched almost a mile from the base line by 1,200 yards in width. This extension of the front required more men and guns to hold it. Yet though Lee ordered the construction of a shorter line at the base of the salient, due to the intense strain of preparing the defenses of the position in time, his instructions were not carried out.

The seemingly interminable Battle of Spotsylvania lasted more than ten days. Yet the fighting, although it seemed of unremitting intensity to the participants, was actually concentrated in two crucial days. On May 10 Grant ordered Meade to launch an attack on the Confederate left toward Laurel Hill, combining V and VI Corps reinforced by two divisions from II Corps. Meanwhile, Burnside's IX Corps would distract Lee with probing attacks on the Confederate right. The V Corps attacks gained some temporary successes but were eventually driven back. Consequently, Lee was shocked to learn that units of VI Corps had penetrated his front, thanks to the efforts of a specially trained force commanded by Brigadier General Emory Upton. Lee at once assumed the duties of a corps commander and rode to the point of heaviest fighting. When persuaded to leave, he said coldly, "Then you must see to it that the ground is recovered." Fortunately, Upton received no support and was pushed out of the line by nightfall.

On the late afternoon of May 11 Lee suspected that Grant might be on the move. He decided to shift batteries from the salient so that they could be put on the road hurriedly. "Allegheny" Johnson, the divisional commander at the apex of the salient, objected to these orders, but it is doubtful if Lee knew this. The weather continued murky and dull, with heavy rain and thick fog. Shortly after 3 a.m. on May 12, soon after Lee had risen and dressed (this was his habitual rising hour on campaign), he heard heavy firing from the direction of the Mule Shoe. He mounted Traveller hurriedly and rode toward the commotion. He passed streams of Confederate soldiers running to the rear. "Hold on!" he shouted. "We are going to form a new line. Your commanders need your services. Stop men!" Some rallied, but those that ignored him received an additional reproof: "Shame on you men, shame on you; go back to your regiments!" Then Lee heard the startling news that under a cloak of fog the Union II Corps had shattered his line. He had no idea what units remained from which to cobble together some semblance of a defensive line.

In scenes of confusion and mounting panic, Lee (unlike on the morning of May 6) kept calm. Johnson's division had been destroyed, and Rodes's seemed to be facing destruction. Twenty guns had also been lost. Ewell was frantic in his efforts to extricate Rodes's men, and seemed close to a complete breakdown, shrieking and chasing retreating soldiers. "General Ewell," Lee rebuked him sternly, "you must restrain yourself; how can you expect to control these men if you have lost control of yourself? If you cannot repress your excitement, you had better retire." One commander exhibited some steel— John B. Gordon. He had managed to organize two brigades and sundry regiments for an assault on the Union lodgement. Lee put spurs to his horse and took position before his troops, as if to lead them into battle. Gordon remonstrated with Lee, and then, with members of his staff, blocked his path. The cry of "General Lee to the rear; Lee to the rear!" resounded through the woods once more. For a second time, Lee stared defeat in the face. Gordon's troops were at any rate organized, while II Corps had become disorganized by the extent of its unexpected success. With support from other Confederate brigades acting on their own initiative, Gordon drove the Union troops back in frenzied fighting.

Lee then rode off to find Mahone's division and bring it over to the center. En route he narrowly escaped death when Traveller suddenly reared and a shell passed underneath him, missing Lee's foot by inches. He then encountered Harris's brigade and sought to lead it into action, too, only to be met with a barrage of shouts, "Go back General, go back! For God's sake go back!" Lee revealed himself as pertinacious in the extreme when his lines were breached. He replied to the entreaties of his men: "If you will promise me to drive those people from our works, I will go back." Lee's generalship had always sought to control events; now that they were escaping his clutches, he exhibited qualities of personal leadership that offered the ultimate sacrifice and the acceptance of what fate might have in store for him.

Yet he still had not given up hope completely. While the Confederate counterattack had driven the Union intruders back to the parapet of the Mule Shoe, now rechristened the "Bloody Angle," they had not been driven from his works completely and ferocious fighting continued around the parapet. Lee insisted that the Union forces must be driven away from the line: if they could shelter behind it, they would be provided with a base for the renewal of their assault. An orderly retreat could not be organized until the front had been restored. Lee had given fresh orders for the construction of a new line across the base of the salient; the front had to be held until it could be completed. Lee simply had no choice but to hold his line irrespective of the cost.

Some relief naturally had to be found for the Second Corps. Lee trotted off to examine the position on the left and then crossed to the right. He deduced immediately that no troops could be taken from Anderson, but on the Confederate right, where things were quieter, Lee believed that he could use Wilcox and Heth's divisions in a counterstroke aimed at the Union left, reminiscent of the flank attack in the Wilderness. He proposed to take advantage of a small salient on Heth's front to concentrate and then screen the advance behind Oak Wood, circling around it to strike the Union flank.

The one advantage for the Union of Grant's opportunistic but frequently piecemeal assaults was that they kept Lee on the defensive. Thus, Lee's preparations for his counterstroke were foiled by an attack ordered by Grant on Burnside's IX Corps front. Grant had become anxious about a gap that had opened up between II Corps and IX Corps. Fierce Confederate counterattacks had begun to break between these two corps and endangered the integrity of the Union line. Had Lee been able to throw forward his attack, he might at the very least have been able to knock the Army of the Potomac off-balance. As it happened, Third Corps's artillery took a terrible toll of Burnside's infantry, with Lee supervising the tactical details so closely that he issued orders for the guns to change their range. Even with the repulse of the IX Corps assaults, Lee found that he could not unleash a counterstroke because the Union entrenchments had been extended and strengthened. Alas, Second Corps had to continue to slug it out in position, under hellish conditions. At about midnight, Lee (who had been working himself virtually without a break for twenty-one hours) gave orders for a retirement to the new line along the base of "Bloody Angle."

Lee's burden of responsibility would have crushed a lesser man. Yet he had to endure one more blow. He received confirmation of the news of Stuart's death at about 8 p.m. on May 12. Lee was so overcome with grief that he retired to his tent for a while. Stuart killed, Longstreet wounded, Hill ill, Ewell on the brink of collapse (he finally stepped down on May 27, replaced by Early): Lee appeared to be commanding his army single-handed, with only his moral authority to keep it functioning. His new subordinates needed close supervision: reliable though they may have been, they were uninspired. Lee's command style adapted accordingly.

Over the next few days Grant concentrated on consolidating his position. Likewise Lee supervised the strengthening of the Confederate line, placing an abattis, or rampart, of thorns and fallen trees just in time to aid the repulse of a renewed assault on May 18 at the Bloody Angle. Success here was cancelled out by a badly planned foray by Second Corps at Harris's Farm that resulted in 900 unnecessary casualties. Though this Confederate sortie delayed Grant's attempt to turn the Confederate right again until May 21, it left little doubt in Lee's mind that Ewell had lost his grip on corps operations.

The ordeal at Spotsylvania thus came to its anti-climactic end. The line had held, but only just. Lee had endured some bad luck and been near to defeat. Nonetheless, he had drawn prodigiously on his own resources, not least his qualities of personal leadership and tactical improvisation, and had succeeded in repulsing Grant. Still, he had not regained the initiative, and the cost of these efforts—actually to retake ground of little intrinsic tactical value—had been high among his regimental officers. His losses were higher than at the Wilderness: 8,000 men (including 4,000 prisoners) were lost in the fighting of May 10–12, giving an estimated total of about 10,000, whereas after twelve days' fighting (including the Wilderness) he had inflicted 36,872 casualties on Grant.

Grant made the most of his possession of the initiative by

advancing around the Confederate flank. On the evening of May 20, Lee asked Ewell whether the Union "rear is weak enough for you to strike at it?" He lacked the time to wait for an answer because he had little alternative but to anticipate another Union attempt at envelopment. Ewell received new orders to push south-east at first light. Grant made for the North Anna River via Guiney's Station. During the advance he pushed II Corps out ahead in an effort to entice Lee into the open in order to attack an isolated corps. Lee could not be tempted. The defense of the Virginia Central Railroad, over which he drew supplies from the Shenandoah Valley to Richmond, was simply too high a priority. Lee still exuded confidence. "Whatever route he [Grant] pursues," he assured Davis, "I am in position to move against him and shall endeavor to engage him while in motion." He remained sensitive to the accusation that after Spotsylvania he had given up territory without a fight, and stressed to the President the advantages of pulling back to the North Anna River. "We have the advantage of being nearer our supplies and less liable to have our communications . . . cut by his cavalry and he is getting further from his base."

Lee found the movement to the North Anna a strain, not least as he was able to snatch only a few hours sleep each night. The Union advance to the river had been on a broad front, and Lee exploited it brilliantly. He concentrated his artillery on the high ground above Ox Ford and then refused his entrenched flanks at angles of 45 degrees to form an equilateral triangle. With Hill (now restored to command of Third Corps) on the left, his flank resting on the Little River, Anderson in the center and Ewell on the right, his three corps were mutually self-supporting in a virtually impregnable line. Grant's forces were widely scattered, by contrast, broken by the terrain into three segments by the North Anna River; his flanks, linked only by two crude bridges and poor roads, were between 15 and 20 miles apart. Lee had turned the tables against Grant with a dazzling display of defensive skill. Yet suddenly struck down by illness—his surgeon diagnosed "intestinal inflammation"—Lee was unable to deliver an intended crushing counterstroke. There are no orders, it is true, to substantiate claims that Lee planned to deliver this *coup de grâce*, but this is not surprising given Lee's opportunistic methods and his heavy reliance on oral orders. To use a strong defensive fastness as a spring-board for an offensive was characteristic of him throughout this campaign, and there seems no reason to doubt that was his intention when the odds, for once, favored him. In frustration at the wasted opportunity, Lee retired to his headquarters at Hanover Junction, bemoaning: "We must not let them pass us again. . . . We must strike them a blow."

Lee's position on the North Anna was so strong that it deterred attack. Once more Grant side-stepped around the Confederate right. On May 28 he crossed the Pamunkey River and then maneuvered around another formidable position that Lee had taken up behind Totopotomoy Creek. Lee gained one major advantage. As Grant shifted toward the coast, Lee could secure the Virginia Central Railroad more strongly, in turn, guaranteeing the defensibility of Richmond. He paid heavily, however, in sacrificing room for maneuver. He had gained space in which to out-maneuver Federal forces ever since the Seven Days' Battles. Two years later he had been pulled, struggling all the way, back to the coast where Grant enjoyed the enormous advantage of command of the sea. Grant appeared boxed in but in reality his control of the river estuaries strengthened his grip on the initiative.

Lee's plight was at least partially eased by the arrival of reinforcements. Major General John C. Breckinridge's victory at New

Market on May 15 allowed Davis to transfer his division from the Shenandoah Valley to Lee's front; similarly, Beauregard (reluctantly) sent Hoke's division after his success at the Bermuda Hundred. After receipt of these reinforcements, Lee sought to strike the Army of the Potomac as it approached Cold Harbor in columns. This important crossroads lay on the direct route to the James River via the Chickahominy River. A botched approach march signaled further erosion of structures of the Army of Northern Virginia under the remorseless pressure of the preceding month's fighting. After Sheridan's cavalry seized Cold Harbor, Lee withdrew into a series of interlocking trenches, with the artillery frequently placed ahead of the infantry so that the guns could enfilade massed Union columns. He made his headquarters at Gaines' Mill. Grant assaulted his works on June 1 but was repulsed, although some progress had been made on the Union left. This minor success encouraged a second assault on June 3, having allowed Lee a further day to strengthen an already formidable position. This attack, actually planned by Meade, was disjointed and effortlessly thrown back. In all, Grant suffered 10,000 casualties for no gain (3,000 on June 1 and 7,000 on June 3). But Cold Harbor proved a victory that Lee could not exploit. The initiative still lay in Grant's hands, and the improved Union entrenchments put a Confederate counterattack out of the question.

Checked north of the James River, Grant decided to transfer operations to its south bank. This complex and audacious river crossing took place over June 13–14. The James River formed the boundary between the departments of Lee and Beauregard. Grant successfully exploited the division of responsibility. Lee, worn out by an arduous campaign, had realized for some days that Grant might well succeed in "crossing the river and taking possession of Petersburg." But discerning Grant's intention did not by itself solve his problem. He could not switch his entire army to the south bank of the James until he was absolutely sure that Grant had moved all his forces in that direction. Lee had also been forced to send two of his three cavalry divisions to protect the Virginia Central Railroad from another of Sheridan's raids (a clever diversion ordered by Grant). Due to the resulting lack of cavalry, he lost contact with the Union columns on June 13–14 and did not move to Beauregard's relief until June 17.

Confederate decision-making during this period of crisis fell between four different men with varying levels of responsibility. Davis had done well logistically, but consistently failed to provide a coherent strategy. General Braxton Bragg, the President's military adviser, and the two field commanders thus worked in a vacuum. Davis relied heavily on Lee's informal advice, but requests for this could be a nuisance when Lee faced innumerable problems of his own. As Grant crossed the James, Davis sent Lee an importunate request that he advise him on who should succeed Lieutenant General Leonidas Polk (killed at Pine Mountain, Georgia) as a corps commander in the Army of Tennessee. Lee could not afford to take the time to comply effectively with this request. Lee's hesitation over Grant's movements across the James thus reflected systemic weaknesses in the command system rather than any personal failing. Despite the problems of coordination Grant encountered, the Union command system enjoyed an advantage in empowering one man to control the movement of scattered forces. Throughout the advance on Petersburg, Grant maintained the twenty-four-hour lead he had snatched at the outset over his two Confederate opponents.

Fortunately, thanks to Beauregard's aptitude for bluff (he marched his troops backward and forward, creating dust clouds to make his army seem larger than it was) and his skilfully sited breastworks, 5,400 men succeeded in holding a line 10 miles long, and he deterred cautious Union generals from taking their objectives. Major General William F. Smith, commander of XVIII Corps of the Army of the James, ranked among the most cautious. His troops had been badly mauled at Cold Harbor, and even though he received support from Hancock's II Corps he failed to occupy Petersburg when he could just have marched in. The defenses at Petersburg held on by a thread, but it was just enough. The troops of the Army of Northern Virginia filed into the trenches in the early hours of June 18. Lee reaped the benefit of the moral ascendancy he had acquired over so many of his Union opponents.

During the great campaign that ran as an unbroken sequence of engagements and maneuvers over six weeks, Lee had enjoyed both good luck and ill. But he had enjoyed his best luck at its end. On the North Anna, Lee had summarized his dilemma well to Jubal Early. He preferred to "settle this business" north of Richmond. "We must destroy this army of Grant's before he gets to the James River. If he gets there, it will become a siege, and then it will be a mere question of time." Lee had prevented Grant from defeating him either north or south of the James River, and he had fought general engagements on ground of his choosing—no mean achievement. Indeed the campaign illuminates Lee's dazzling skills as a defensive commander. The Army of Northern Virginia during these hectic, relentless weeks inflicted losses on the Army of the Potomac comparable to its own fighting strength—55,000—while sustaining losses of about 30,000.

Lee's outstanding eye for defensible ground and his skill at making the most of it frustrated Grant at every turn. Yet Lee had hoped to use his defensive successes as the base for a counterstroke that would throw Grant back. Mainly due to the dynamic and aggressive style of the Union general-in-chief's direction of operations, this opportunity never arose. Or, when it glimmered before Lee's eyes, as at the Wilderness or North Anna, it was dashed by cruel fate or infirmity.

All Lee's biographers dwell on the colossal responsibility that rested on his shoulders. The future of the Confederacy rested there. If a stray shell had felled him at Spotsylvania, it is difficult to see how the Army of Northern Virginia could have survived his loss. His stamina and calm deliberation were hard evidence that he was not too old to command an army, as he himself feared. However, one significant criticism of his conduct is that he failed to make better use of his staff, though in this regard Grant and Sherman were equally at fault. Lee's failure to make more use of his staff as a planning tool is perhaps typical of Civil War generals as a whole. His tolerance of his wholly inadequate chief of staff, Colonel Chilton (until he was promoted and transferred, in March 1864), is one of the great mysteries of his career. Lee, perforce, tended to work around him. Walter Taylor of Lee's staff wrote in March 1864 that when he put a question to Chilton, his answer "was so very muddy and exhibited such ignorance of the situation that I was convinced I was to receive no help from this quarter." Lee did not replace Chilton during the spring campaign, though Taylor became a kind of *de facto* chief of staff. Lee used his staff to help him administer the army rather than help him plan. Porter Alexander thought this tendency "an inherent weakness" of the Confederate Army, the lack of "an abundance of trained and professional soldiers in the staff to make constant studies of all matters of detail." Lee, in other words, relied too much on his own resources and ingenuity, and thus on rapid improvisation.

Yet through sheer strength of character and leadership, Lee had conserved his army as a powerful fighting force despite great perils. His tendency to err on the side of caution is more noticeable after his withdrawal to Cold Harbor. It must have occurred to Lee by this date—as his men took up position in the defenses around Petersburg—that a siege had been imposed on him again. Defeat was thus "a mere question of time." Only two hopes beckoned: that his army could be preserved and that William T. Sherman be prevented from taking Atlanta, Georgia. Then, possibly, the patience and enthusiasm of Northern public opinion for the war would be exhausted before the presidential election in November 1864. Hence Lee's caution during the crossing of the James. But, in accepting the siege he had feared since taking up field command two years before, Lee was taking the biggest risk of his career.

CHAPTER NINE

Slow Disintegration,
June 1864–April 1865

The siege of Petersburg imposed an unbreakable defensive caste on Lee's strategy. The town of Petersburg, on the south bank of the Appomattox River, although small (with a population of 18,266), held the key to Richmond's defense. It served as the junction for five railroads: to the east ran the City Point Railroad and the Norfolk and Petersburg Railroad; to the west, the Southside Railroad from the Shenandoah Valley; to the south, the Petersburg and Weldon Railroad linked the Confederate capital to the coast; a single line ran north linking Petersburg to Richmond. In addition, Petersburg also lay close to two roads vital to the maintenance of any defensive system, the Jerusalem Plank Road (which ran parallel to the Weldon Railroad) and the Boydton Plank Road heading south-west. Richmond quite simply could not be held should this communications hub be lost.

The siege of Petersburg resembled other great sieges of the mid nineteenth century in retaining an open flank. Confederate defenses were extended but never formed a concentric ring. A chance to turn them always existed, though conversely the Confederates (like the Russians during the siege of Sevastopol in 1854–55) could continually resupply and reinforce the beleaguered city. Lee's prime aim was to shield his strategically vital railroad network. Railroads had always played an important part in Lee's success. Once the campaign in Virginia became more static, Lee gave a higher priority to preventing the Union Army from cutting them. Otherwise fixed points could not be sustained logistically for any length of time. Operationally, however, the longer the siege continued and the further the Confederate lines were stretched, the more important the roads became in shifting troops about to meet threats at various points.

Grant enjoyed the advantages of a larger army and control of the James estuary. His control of the sea conferred flexibility on Union operations and rendered his supply lines almost invulnerable. Grant thus sought to stretch Lee's lines to breaking point. He also denied Lee the initiative by shifting troops to the north bank of the James with the aim of seizing the high ground south of Richmond around Deep Bottom. Once Lee's attention had been engaged to the north by this diversion, Grant would launch his main thrust—an envelopment south and west of Petersburg. A chance always existed, of course, that the stabs toward Deep Bottom could result in a breakthrough and entry into Richmond itself. Lee could not tell with certainty whether an attack north of the James would remain just a diversion.

The Union effort to turn Lee's right began on June 22 with a rapid advance down the Jerusalem Plank Road intended to cut the Weldon Railroad, followed by an effort to swing around and seize the Southside Railroad. A. P. Hill counterattacked energetically and caught the Union flank exposed. Another effort the following day, however, prefigured the dreary pattern that so many of these operations would acquire. Lee had to issue orders via Beauregard (who remained technically in charge of Petersburg's defenses until October). The riposte was botched. As Lee admitted, "some misunderstanding [occurred] as to the part each division was expected to have performed." Nonetheless a Union cavalry raid, launched in tandem with the advance down the Jerusalem Plank Road, was brought to a halt at Ream's Station. Its commander, James Harrison Wilson, escaped with most of his force, but suffered 1,600 casualties and lost sixteen guns and several hundred wagons. Wilson had still succeeded though in destroying some 60 miles of track, plus a number of stations, bridges and water tanks. Lee had no choice but to transfer traffic to the roads, especially the Boydton Plank Road.

The front lay quiet for a month. The lull, after two months' incessant fighting, allowed Lee to mark his thirty-third wedding anniversary in peace. He wrote to his wife recalling many "hopes and pleasures it [their wedding day] gave birth to! God has been kind to us, and how thankless and sinful I have been." Although he took the opportunity of visiting friends in Richmond, he did not allow himself the luxury of a short break. On the contrary, his attention shifted to the Shenandoah Valley. Grant's campaign in Virginia involved a renewal of the offensive toward Lynchburg under the command of Major General David Hunter. Hunter's efforts were initially successful, but Lee expressed reluctance to weaken his force at Petersburg. But he did acknowledge that "unless a sufficient force can be had in that country to restrain the movements of the enemy, he will do us great evil." Lee sent Breckinridge's division back to the Shenandoah Valley but came under pressure to do more.

Lee's hand had already been forced when two weeks earlier, on June 8, he had ordered Wade Hampton's cavalry to intercept a raid on the Virginia Central Railroad by Sheridan's troopers. Davis urged him to send more help to the Shenandoah Valley, and Lee responded reluctantly, "I think this is what the enemy would desire." Over the next two weeks, Lee changed his mind when he grasped that Grant's method of launching a series of concentric attacks could be turned against him. Lee deduced that he could hold a heavily fortified Richmond with fewer men (he had about 55,000 in total) and thus could create a field detachment to advance down the Shenandoah Valley toward Washington, DC. It could strike at the Union railroads, especially the Washington and Baltimore Railroad. "Grant would be compelled," Lee concluded, "either to weaken himself so much for their protection as to offer us an opportunity to attack him, or that he might be induced to attack us."

On June 12 Lee decided to give command of the field detachment to the newly promoted Lieutenant General Jubal Early. Second Corps would be often styled "the Army of the Valley" over ensuing weeks. Lee had tactfully prevented Ewell from returning to field command by the suggestion that he take charge of the Richmond defenses instead. Lee argued that Early's force should be permitted to cross into Maryland. Confederate strategy, he told Davis, should be "to draw the attention of the enemy to his own territory." Early received instructions, like all Lee's senior lieutenants, to "be governed by your good judgment." He set off on June 13 and his initial successes—the defeat of Hunter at Lynchburg, his rapid advance up the Valley and victory at the Monocacy in Maryland, which allowed him to approach the ramparts of Washington, DC, itself on July 11–12— encouraged Lee to seek the complete dislocation of Grant's campaign in Virginia. Early, in effect, mounted a strategic indirect approach toward the Federal capital in a presidential election year. The political and propaganda dividends that beckoned were enormous.

In the strategic game of poker that Lee played with Grant, he played an indifferent hand brilliantly. Grant came under enormous pressure to withdraw large parts of the Army of the Potomac at Richmond and send them to the environs of Washington. Lincoln even urged him to return himself. Grant consistently defended the wisdom of his concentration before Richmond and his ability to maintain the offensive. Nonetheless, he could not ignore the President's blandishments, and sent VI Corps back to Washington, arriving just in time to shore up the city's defenses as Early approached. The Confederates fell back on the evening of July 12. If Early had broken into the city even for a short period, Lee would have forced Grant to acknowledge that his Virginia campaign had failed, and, moreover, that his movement south of the James had exposed Washington to disaster. This would have been a propaganda victory of no small magnitude. As Lee pointed out to Davis, the campaign would have succeeded in "teaching them they must keep some of their troops at home and that they cannot denude their frontiers with impunity." By a very narrow margin, Lee failed to break Grant's grip on Petersburg. Thus Grant eluded the pressures to make the protection of Washington, DC, not the taking of Petersburg, his objective.

On the Petersburg front, however, Grant almost recouped his fortunes—and Lee came very close to defeat—on July 30 at the Battle of the Crater. In a "spectacle . . . of appalling grandeur," to use the words of one Union soldier, a hole—a crater 170 feet long, 60 feet wide and 40 feet deep—was blown in the Confederate defenses. Lee had received warning on July 1 that Federal troops were digging tunnels underneath the center of the Confederate lines at Elliott's salient, about a mile and a half south of the Appomattox River. The universal opinion at Lee's headquarters held that it was impossible to dig tunnels of more than 500 feet. Countershafts and listening galleries ordered by Lee failed to find them. To distract Lee's attention,

Grant ordered II Corps north of the James to probe toward Richmond from Deep Bottom. Lee sent Kershaw and Field's divisions, plus two divisions of cavalry, to cover the capital. This left only three divisions (Hoke, Johnson and Mahone) with a small reserve (part of Wilcox's division) to cover the Petersburg sector—a total of 18,000 men.

At 2 a.m. on July 30 Lee sent out a warning that a Union attack might be imminent. Within an hour and three-quarters of the mine's detonation Lee knew that his line had been ruptured. As at Spotsylvania, his orders were simple: the Federal troops had to be driven back. Lee sent Colonel Venable of his staff to Mahone, who told him to secretly withdraw his two brigades from the line and rush to cover the gap. Lee rode out to meet them. Once satisfied with their progress, he left their direction to Mahone and went to discuss the crisis with Beauregard at the Gee House, 500 yards behind the crater and from where they could observe the battle.

Fortunately for Lee, although Union troops had taken 200 yards of the Confederate line to the left of the crater, and 30 yards to its right, they had failed to exploit this tremendous success. Instead, they had crowded into the crater to gaze at it in wonder, and had then crowded up behind it, making movement impossible. The Confederate command system was given several hours to recover: troops were rallied and decisions, once taken, acted upon energetically. The gap was sealed, the Confederate gun line re-established and the crater area bombarded. A rapid advance of 1,600 yards would have gained Petersburg from the south-east, but lethargy and incompetence prevailed on the Union side. The Confederates averted catastrophe by initiative, aggression and determination. Lee's divisional commanders were superior to their Federal counterparts, and Lee himself was present at the decisive point. At 10 a.m. Mahone's division put in a successful counterattack and Union resistance collapsed into a hysterical stampede. Lee reported to the War Department, "We have retaken the salient and driven the enemy back to his lines with loss." He had won a very lucky victory. The Army of the Potomac suffered 3,798 casualties (including 1,101 prisoners); the Confederates just under 1,500, most being sustained during the initial detonation of the mine. Although Lee had been caught out, his powers of recovery were remarkable. But this defensive success could not alter the state of siege imposed on his army.

After this failure, Grant returned to his practice of probing the enemy's flanks to find a weakness. He aimed to stretch the Confederate lines until they snapped, especially to the south and west. Grant knew that Lee had made a sizeable detachment to stab at Washington and could not be strong everywhere; eventually he would find a weak point. The Petersburg and Shenandoah campaigns remained intimately connected. Lee still hoped that Early would force the withdrawal of more Union troops northward, an acknowledgment of failure before Petersburg. But Lee could not achieve this by relying on defensive methods. After August 6, he sent Kershaw's division and two cavalry divisions to reinforce Early.

Grant determined to exploit this reduction in Lee's strength by attacking at either end of his long, tenuous defensive line. II Corps and three cavalry divisions were sent to Deep Bottom on the north bank. At the same time, efforts were made to dig a canal at Farrar's Island, so that Federal gunboats could raid Richmond without running the gauntlet of the batteries at Drewry's Bluff. Lee sent a further 5,500 Confederate troops north; by the first week of August, one-third of Lee's army had been sent to counterbalance Grant's deployment. Grant sought to disguise his plan with a series of complicated movements in which II Corps returned to the south bank and then retraced its steps to the north bank again, this time accompanied by X Corps, in a desperate effort to break into Richmond.

Lee himself went to Chaffin's Bluff to monitor events. He had become anxious about the vulnerable position held by Field's division. It held two sides of an equilateral triangle in front of the main defenses, covering the three roads into Richmond from the south and east of the city. On August 16 Field's position was indeed overrun before Lee could take remedial action, but the division rallied, and the following day Lee planned a counterattack with cavalry support. It successfully restored the Confederate left flank on the Charles City Road. Grant then recalled II Corps to the south bank and X Corps withdrew into the Deep Bottom lodgement. Lee was prevented from extinguishing this irritating outpost by a warning from Beauregard that Federal troops were advancing on the Weldon Railroad to the south. He immediately sent Rooney Lee's cavalry to the right flank; by August 19 all the infantry sent to reinforce the Confederate left had been hurried back to the right flank.

Grant had intended to launch a simultaneous attack on the Weldon Railroad in the vicinity of Ream's Station to cut Lee's direct links with North Carolina. V Corps destroyed several hundred yards of track on August 17 before running into Hill's Third Corps in the congested woods around Globe Tavern. Lee again decided to go to the point of maximum danger himself. He arrived on the hot afternoon of August 21. The initial fighting had favored the Confederates, and Hill succeeded in exploiting the gaps that had opened in the front of two Union divisions and turning their flanks; his troops took 2,700 prisoners. Lee hoped to exploit this success with a rapid counterattack that would drive the Unionists from the Weldon Railroad and get it back into working order at the earliest possible date. Alas, V Corps withdrew into a specially prepared position that allowed it to retain its hold on the railroad and simultaneously cover the angle of the junction of the Jerusalem Plank Road. At this unpropitious moment, Hill launched a disjointed attack which the entrenched Union infantry repulsed easily. Lee instantly understood that further effort would be futile.

He thus acquiesced in the loss of the Weldon Railroad from Rowarty Creek to Petersburg. The defense of the Petersburg–Richmond line depended henceforth on the Southside and Richmond–Danville Railroads. The loss of the Weldon could not have come at a worse time: having already consumed all its corn, Richmond relied on the harvest for replenishment. Lee was accordingly forced to use the roads parallel to the Weldon Railroad to haul corn, via Wilmington, North Carolina, over the last part of its journey into the city. This setback highlighted for Lee the continuing danger that Grant might "endeavor to compel the evacuation of . . . [Richmond] by cutting off our supplies." It was a danger that could not be eased by tactical successes. On August 25, Confederate cavalry had succeeded in getting behind II Corps at Ream's Station, while Heth's division smashed into its left flanks, inflicting 2,602 casualties for the loss of 720. Yet however much a victory of this kind raised morale, it made no difference to the strategic situation.

By the end of the summer Lee had no choice but to confront the harsh fact that despite his creditable defense of the Petersburg–Richmond line, he had not broken Grant's grip on the two cities. On the contrary, he had only just succeeded in keeping their lines of communications open, not least to the Confederacy's sole surviving port, Wilmington, North Carolina. His right flank might yet be turned. As Lee's lines eventually stretched for 35 miles, his span of command became increasingly attenuated and his numerical weakness more significant. Lee juggled with his available resources with great skill, but he could only hold the lines; his capacity to do anything else diminished as they continued to lengthen—even should Early and the Second Corps return to Richmond.

The Virginia Central Railroad remained intact, but Lee could do little more than shore up his line by bringing the cavalry back to Richmond. In short measure, the new Federal commander in the Shenandoah Valley, Philip Sheridan, inflicted two defeats on Early at the Opequon and Fisher's Hill (September 19, 22). "Without some increase of strength," Lee had warned on August 23, "I cannot see how we can escape the natural military consequences of the enemy's numerical superiority."

Following Sheridan's success in the Shenandoah, Grant increased the pressure on Lee at Petersburg with a fifth offensive, this time toward Peeble's Farm, 5 miles to the south-west. Union troops were to advance and secure the Boydton Plank Road as a springboard for an assault on the Southside Railroad. This operation showed that the numerous roads radiating from Richmond did as much to expose Lee's lines of communications as to facilitate them. Characterized by charge and countercharge, the action at Peeble's Farm, from September 28 to October 2, proved a partial Union success. A ferocious attack thrown forward by Hill was halted by an out-flanking Federal counterstroke that drove his troops back in confusion. Grant's troops thus inched their way toward the Southside Railroad (despite the loss of 2,898 casualties compared with the Confederate loss of 1,300).

North of the James River, Benjamin F. Butler's Army of the James succeeded in taking Fort Harrison and then besieged Fort Gilmer. Lee rushed to the scene and ordered an immediate counterattack by Anderson's First Corps. Eight brigades were assembled, but the affair did not prosper. Even spirited appeals by Lee did not work, riding to the front rank and waving his hat in the air. "I had always thought General Lee was a very cold and unemotional man," one soldier reflected, "but he showed lots of feeling and excitement on that occasion . . . imploring his men to make one more effort to take the position for him." But such efforts had failed, and Lee refused to renew the attack, contenting himself with redrawing the Confederate lines to cut off Fort Harrison and secure the front.

Lee had to react to one further effort by Grant on October 24 to attack both ends of his defenses, with a thrust along the Williamsburg Road toward Richmond coupled with a stab toward Burgess' Mill, where the Boydton Plank Road crossed Hatcher's Run. Lee could clearly perceive the grim logic of Grant's plan. "If the enemy cannot be prevented from extending his left," he had predicted two weeks previously, "he will eventually reach the Appomattox [River] and cut us off from the [S]outh side altogether."

Lee also had to adjust to two further developments, one good, one bad. On October 19, Longstreet returned to duty. Lee delighted in passing responsibility for the northern sector to his dependable lieutenant. Longstreet thought Lee "seemed worn by past labor, besides suffering . . . from sciatica, while his work was accumulating and his troubles multiplying to proportions that should have employed half a dozen able men." The same day, Early attacked Sheridan's army at Cedar Creek and was eventually repulsed. The news arrived the following day. "I have weakened myself very much to strengthen you," Lee had complained to Early on October 12, but a week later the investment reaped a very disappointing dividend. Early's defeat meant that the game was up in the Shenandoah Valley. Lee could no longer exploit this window of Union vulnerability during the last days of the presidential election. Lincoln's return to office seemed guaranteed. Sheridan followed up his victory with a sustained program of devastation in the Shenandoah; the effects of this have probably been exaggerated, but even so they gravely complicated Lee's logistical difficulties.

On October 27 the Union advance at Burgess' Mill began. Frustrated by poor maps and thick woods, the stumbling Union movement came to a halt before a blocking position taken up by Wade Hampton's cavalry along the Boydton Plank Road, supported by infantry. On November 1 Lee arrived himself to examine the position. He had recalled the defeated Second Corps to Richmond, with John B. Gordon taking over the command. Lee feared an immense Union concentration on the Richmond front as he lacked the means to create powerful diversions. He expected Grant to attack, but warned James Seddon that "I do not see where I am to get troops to meet him, as ours seem rather to diminish than to increase."

In November 1864 the extension of Lee's span of command demanded a shift of headquarters. He needed to find suitable accommodation west of Petersburg because here lay his true vulnerability. Walter Taylor and Mrs. Lee had persuaded him to accept an invitation to use Edge Hill, a comfortable house 2 miles west of Petersburg. Headquarters were duly moved, but to Taylor's consternation Lee did not enjoy its comforts, "for he is never so uncomfortable as when comfortable." Lee preferred to move back into tents; the staff had no choice but to follow his wishes. Then, "Lo! The next morning he informed me he thought we had better move back and so back I came . . . and as I could find no better place . . . I took possession of the same house we had vacated . . ."

Lee's small and overworked staff had been placed under unprecedented strain since the opening of the campaign in May, and illness had taken its toll. This small group came under even greater pressure after February 6, 1865, when a reluctant President Davis appointed

Lee to the position of general-in-chief of the Confederacy. The promotion threatened Lee's harmonious relationship with Davis. The President had been alarmed by wild talk that Lee should supplant Davis and be granted dictatorial powers. The conferment of the appointment, long resisted by Davis, resulted from the maneuvers of his enemies in Congress. Though Lee had distanced himself from their cabals, Davis treated him with suspicion for several weeks in February. "As I have received no instructions as to my duties," he told the adjutant general tactfully, "I do not know what he [Davis] desires me to undertake." Yet during these difficult weeks, Lee repaid Davis's loyalty to him, and gradually something of the old warmth returned to their exchanges.

Working under such strain and faced with multiplying problems at every turn, it is not surprising that Lee's frustration worked itself out in irritability and bitter sarcasm: he became very difficult to please. He received no enlargement of his staff and had no choice but to instruct that "all special reports and communications" for the general-in-chief "be addressed . . . for the present to the headquarters of the Army of Northern Virginia." Lee quickly made two requests of Davis. First, that Davis issue a presidential proclamation pardoning all deserters if they returned to the ranks. (The following month he would support those who favored the arming of black slaves as a means of finding fresh troops.) Secondly, that General Joseph E. Johnston be restored to command and reorganize the remnants of Confederate forces in North Carolina. Davis disliked Johnston because of the latter's closeness to his congressional critics, but he agreed reluctantly if Lee took responsibility for it (and Johnston reported directly to him).

February 1865 had witnessed a series of raids in the area around Hatcher's Run (a small stream running parallel to the Southside

Railroad about 10 miles west of Petersburg). It was obvious to Lee that Grant would resume his remorseless effort to turn his right flank in the spring. He became increasingly despondent over his prospects. His instincts told him that Petersburg should be abandoned, but he could not risk his army in the open in winter on poor roads. For political reasons (not least the preservation of what remained of his own prestige), Davis still insisted that Richmond continued to be held. Lee went so far as to warn the last Confederate Secretary of War, John C. Breckinridge, that "I fear it may be necessary to abandon all our cities, and preparation should be made for this contingency." Davis responded with an adamant refusal to admit that defeat was even a possibility. "The President is very pertinacious in opinion and purpose," Lee wrote in terms of measured under-statement. He revealed "remarkable faith in the possibility of still winning our independence." Lee could not avoid admitting to himself that this looked increasingly unlikely; but even a private admission of defeat only sharpened the dilemma he faced.

Lee found it difficult to work with Davis during these last few months. The interminable meetings Davis called were especially onerous. They served mainly as a means of reassuring the President without ever confronting—let alone taking—decisions to cure the Confederacy's terminal problems. On February 22, Lee confided to Longstreet that should Sherman continue to march through North Carolina, unite with John M. Schofield (who had taken Wilmington) and then drive on Richmond from the south, "we shall have to abandon our position on the James River, as lamentable as it is on every account." Davis would not accept the logic of this argument.

Lee had no alternative but to seek a military success at Petersburg that might frustrate Grant's build-up and prevent him from extending his line westward. Not least Lee had to find a vulnerable point east of Petersburg that Grant valued so much that he would pull in his flanks to reinforce it. The idea was a desperate gamble— all too typical of the hopeless plight of the last days of the Confederacy and Lee's loyal commitment to it, despite his private doubts. Lee entrusted the operation to Gordon of Second Corps. According to the latter's self-serving *Reminiscences* (1904), Lee called him to his headquarters in early March and outlined the Confederacy's dire predicament. Lee expressed a view already common among other senior Confederate generals that they should "make terms with the enemy, the best we can get." Lee then rehearsed an alternative, the abandonment of Richmond and withdrawal toward North Carolina to unite with Johnston. If the two Confederate forces could link up, Lee might be able to defeat Sherman before Grant could come to his aid.

Lee delegated to Gordon the details of the plan. Gordon selected Fort Stedman as his objective, located on the front of IX Corps. He created an ingenious plan. In the early hours of March 25, three specially trained squads opened up the avenues of advance; then fifty axe men removed all obstacles; these were followed up by three storming parties of 100 men each led by officers who knew the names of their Union counterparts and thus could bluff their way into Stedman. After the fort had fallen, the attackers were required to continue their advance and seize the three batteries that lay beyond.

Lee was at the front during the initial approach, and after things went well, returned to headquarters. However, as the attackers fanned out behind Stedman, they failed to locate the batteries (they were not positioned where Gordon had calculated). Union defenders reacted more rapidly and powerfully than anticipated and Gordon's troops became pinned down in a small pocket around Stedman. Gordon's plan had been more appropriate to a divisional than a corps level attack, and he had made no provision for artillery support. At 8 a.m., on hearing of Gordon's predicament, Lee ordered an immediate cessation of the attack. Confederate losses numbered 4,000, with Union casualties only a quarter of that number. The defeat at Fort Stedman appears as an alarming portent of the greater collapse soon to come.

Grant's concentration had been almost completed a few days before with the arrival of Sheridan's three powerful cavalry divisions from the Shenandoah Valley. Grant decided to open his spring offensive early, and on March 29 Sheridan's troopers arrived at Dinwiddie Court House. Lee could not ignore this threat, as an orderly evacuation of Richmond (notably of the heavy equipment) required that Sheridan be kept away from the Southside Railroad. Lee believed that with luck he might have between ten and twelve days to evacuate the Richmond–Petersburg line. He sent Pickett's division plus Fitz Lee's cavalry to Five Forks, a crossroads north of Dinwiddie Court House, with orders of great simplicity: "Hold Five Forks at all hazards."

It might have been preferable if Lee had instead ordered the seizure of Dinwiddie Court House, because its possession allowed Sheridan to complete his concentration and bring up V Corps to support him. In any case, Pickett let him down. Although his troops entrenched, Pickett and Fitz Lee could not resist the temptation to take some rest. On March 31, Sheridan attacked their position while they were absent at a picnic on the infamous shad bake. With its front shattered and simultaneously outflanked, Pickett's division ceased to exist as an organized entity—5,250 Confederate casualties were lost. At first, Lee did not appreciate the full significance of this defeat.

In fact, the Confederate right flank had been shattered. Sheridan wasted no time in exploiting his victory by pushing on to the

Southside Railroad. Lee had no reserves that could come to the aid of the right, and, in any case, he now faced a general assault all along the line as Grant sensed that victory was his for the taking. VI Corps steamrollered its way into the Confederate line west of Petersburg, shattering Hill's cohesion. Lee recalled Longstreet's First Corps from the north bank of the James, but it could not arrive in time to save the position. Lee conferred with Hill at Edge Hill but a staff officer disturbed their deliberations to warn, "General, the lines are broken out front. You will have to go." Hill galloped off frantically, and shortly afterward was killed in a skirmish trying to reach his troops. Lee hurriedly ordered the abandonment of headquarters: "It is absolutely necessary that we should abandon our position [at Petersburg] tonight, as we run the risk of being cut off in the morning." Taylor had this telegraphed to Richmond as shot and shell landed on Edge Hill while Lee made his escape. "This is a bad business, Colonel," Lee observed to Armistead Long as they rode off. "Well, it has happened as I told them it would. The line has stretched and it has broken."

When Lee heard of Hill's death, he muttered, "He is at rest now, and we who are left are the ones to suffer." The fatalism conveyed by this remark underlines Lee's sense not just of the inevitability of defeat but the uncertainty of its outcome. It also voices his desire, evident for more than ten months, to die at the head of his troops rather than suffer humiliation, arrest and persecution. Everywhere he turned, Lee faced catastrophe. If he tarried too long at Richmond and allowed Sherman to occupy Burke's Junction, an intersection of the Danville Railroad with the Lynchburg Railroad, he would be trapped. News soon pressed him for further decisions, because after the success of a concentrated thrust of II and VI Corps, supported by XXIV Corps of the Army of the James, Sutherland Station had been lost and with it all use of the Southside Railroad. Lee remained calm in face of these calamities, and took the decision to abandon the capital. At 10 a.m. on April 2 he dictated a telegram to Breckinridge that ended, "I advise that all preparation be made for leaving Richmond tonight."

Writers sympathetic to the Confederacy tend to assume that Lee's surrender at Appomattox a week later was a foregone conclusion. They look at the recent record, Fort Stedman and Five Forks, minimize Lee's field strength and assume that Grant's numerical superiority resembled that of Xerxes. Finally, the scheme to link up with Johnston is judged impracticable. In short, Lee's defeat resulted from his chronic numerical inferiority and other material factors quite beyond his control. This is quite untrue. The Army of Northern Virginia remained a cohesive entity, numbering just under 50,000 men; but Lee's troops could be tempted to desert once they had left the shelter of their fortifications, and this cohesion would crumble if the army failed to resupply itself en route. Lee got his army away safely, and he might well have escaped Grant's clutches if the logistical system had not broken down. The plan to attack Sherman was not fantastic. His army lacked cavalry and advanced on a very broad front. Johnston had almost knocked him off balance by attacking an isolated portion of his force at Bentonville in March. Reinforced by Lee's army, the chances of doing this again multiplied.

Lee's main difficulty, other than resupply, resulted from the baleful legacy of Five Forks. Grant's army was closer to Burkeville than Lee's. Consequently, the Army of Northern Virginia had to get ahead of Grant's pincers before it could maintain any lead that had been gained from the precipitate abandonment of Richmond. In other words, Union troops lay between Lee and Johnston, and the former had to march west before he could turn south.

Lee issued orders to head for Farmville and the Southside Railroad. He thought, too, that orders had been dispatched for rations to be sent to Amelia Court House, so that food would be waiting for the army during its arduous march (instead he would find ammunition). In fact, the food had gone to Danville and Lynchburg. When the troops arrived at Amelia Court House and found nothing to eat, morale plummeted. Lee lost his temper when he saw ammunition boxes, but quickly regained his composure; he looked nonetheless "anxious and haggard" but put on a brave face in an effort to minimize the disaster. He ordered that the rations be sent forward from Danville and attempted to collect provisions from the surrounding country, but little was brought in. He passed the day reorganizing the army for the next stage of the march. Longstreet's First Corps would form the vanguard, Third Corps and Anderson the center, while Gordon's Second Corps and Ewell's garrison troops would bring up the rear.

At dawn on April 6 the march resumed, and the famished troops staggered along clogging, muddy roads, men dropping from the ranks in increasing numbers. Far from swinging south-west to Burkeville, Lee had to head north-west to Paineville before crossing the Appomattox River at High Bridge. With II Corps in close pursuit, Lee tried to allay the sense of growing anxiety. He said firmly to his son, Rooney, "Keep your command together and in good spirits, general: don't let it think of surrender. I will get you out of this." But as the weary, bedraggled Confederate column crossed Sayler's Creek, it became spread out. In the later afternoon Union cavalry got in between the infantry and the trains and caused mayhem, while VI Corps attacked its rear. Ewell had no choice once surrounded but to capitulate. At the very least 15 percent of Lee's army had become prisoners. Once Lee grasped the full extent of the defeat, he exclaimed: "My God! Has the army been dissolved?" Not yet, but the second reorganization that Sayler's Creek required cost Lee time he could ill afford.

After April 6 Lee lost his chance to escape his encircling Union pursuers. Sayler's Creek, an outright defeat, also cost him the cohesion of his army. It had broken into two fragments, and once the troops arrived at Farmville, with II Corps scurrying at its heels, the troops could be offered little respite. Lee turned the army north in a desperate effort to keep the route to Lynchburg open. One officer blamed the high command for the growing disorder in the ranks. They "seemed to shut their eyes" to straggling "and rode in advance of their brigades in dogged indifference." But in reality, without sustenance, there was little that Lee could do under the circumstances. To threaten the army with draconian disciplinary measures would also threaten it with disintegration. Only the balm of good news would revive morale, but the news continued to get worse. Confederate rations had arrived at Appomattox Station, but Sheridan's cavalry had got there first. On the evening of April 7, Grant wrote Lee a letter suggesting that he should surrender. Lee showed it to Longstreet, who replied tersely, "Not yet." But Lee took the precaution of inquiring what terms Grant might offer. The following day Lee could not fail to discern the opinion among his senior officers. William Pendleton conveyed the feelings of one group that they should surrender. "Oh, no," Lee retorted unhesitatingly, "I trust that it has not yet come to that." But the series of desperate measures forced on Lee to keep the army moving at all—cutting the trains right back, so that the wagons only carried ammunition, the reduction of the artillery to two battalions—accentuated by the logistical collapse, only underlined the desperate straits that the army found itself in. Even if it escaped, what could it *do*? During this ill-planned retreat the fighting power of the Confederacy's premier field army had been so whittled away, that undoubtedly the scheme to link up with Johnston from April 6 onward began to resemble fantasy. In the meantime, Sheridan's troopers trotted into Appomattox Court House to block Lee's path and Grant's reply to Lee's enquiry about terms arrived.

Grant made it clear that he would require one condition, namely, that all surrendered men "shall be disqualified from taking up arms again, against the Government of the United States until properly exchanged." Lee replied mildly, hoping to negotiate a general settlement and thus enable him to judge how Grant's terms "may affect the CS Forces under my command and to tend to the restoration of peace."

This was a subtle move using his authority as Confederate general-in-chief to gain more time. Since April 2 Lee had not heard from the Confederate government. So he decided to make one last effort to escape his pursuers. He asked Gordon to make it. Fitz Lee's cavalry and what remained of Gordon's Second Corps would attack Sheridan's cavalry blocking the escape route west. If his men broke through, Longstreet's First Corps would exploit and the army would follow hurriedly. At 5 a.m. on April 9, Gordon made his attack. The Union cavalry slowly fell back to reveal the infantry of no less than two Union corps, V and XXIV. There could be no escape. As soon as Lee heard this grave news, he called for Longstreet. On his arrival, Lee was already attired in full dress uniform, sash, sword and gold spurs. Lee asked for Longstreet's opinion on their plight. After reviewing the position, Longstreet concluded gloomily, "Your situation speaks for itself." Lee announced that he had decided to meet Grant and seek his terms for surrender, although he would rather "die a thousand deaths." Before he set out for this first historic (but hurriedly arranged) meeting with Grant at the McLean House in Appomattox Court House, it had been made clear to Lee that Grant would only treat for the surrender of those forces under his immediate command.

Lee waited in McLean's parlor for thirty minutes, Grant eventually arriving at about 1 p.m. Grant attempted some reminiscences of the "Old" army, until Lee (anxious in case fresh terms might be imposed upon him rather than those previously discussed) brought his attention back to the business in hand. Grant then wrote out his terms without interruption, paused, looked at Lee's sword and added an addendum. Lee cleaned his spectacles and read the document carefully, evidently relieved that there had been no substantive change. Officers on receipt of their paroles were allowed to keep their side arms, swords, horses and baggage (extended to private soldiers where appropriate) after swearing an oath not to take up arms again. Regimental officers were to do so on behalf of their men. They would then be allowed to go home and would not be "disturbed" so long as they kept to the terms of their parole. There would be no mass arrests or arbitrary justice. Lee said the document would have "a very happy effect upon my army."

Some 28,231 soldiers and 63 guns were surrendered. Lee then returned to his lines to encounter the most loyal Confederates in his ranks curious to know their fate. They greeted their commander with simultaneous expressions of affection and dismay on learning that he had agreed to capitulate. "Men," Lee shouted, "we have fought the war together and I have done the best I could for you." He then gave way to the emotions that he had briefly displayed at the Wilderness and Fort Harrison and withdrew to an apple orchard to gather his thoughts and feelings. During the succeeding days he succumbed to a deep depression that he could not throw off for some time.

Lee remained a loyal Confederate to the end. Whatever his private doubts, he showed an iron determination to serve his chosen cause and continue the war by joining forces with Joseph E. Johnston. As general-in-chief he bore responsibilities that were his duty to carry out and they could not be evaded. Nonetheless, he refused to let the war degenerate into a guerrilla struggle that would wreck the existing social structure of the South.

At the beginning of the Appomattox campaign Lee enjoyed a reasonable chance of escape, even though the siege of Petersburg had eroded his troops' attacking edge. The Union material and numerical superiority cannot be ascribed as the sole reason for his defeat. Lee did commit errors on the retreat. There is nothing shameful about this. Even the greatest commanders make mistakes, as Napoleon did in 1814, going on to commit even greater blunders in the Waterloo campaign the following year. Under adverse circumstances, Lee's underdeveloped staff system collapsed after the loss of Richmond—just when its skills were needed most. Even Lee's self-confidence could not compensate for staff errors. As Lee himself wrote in his final report to Jefferson Davis, the failure to place rations at Amelia Court House "was fatal, and could not be retrieved." Whatever the source of the error though, Lee must bear responsibility for it.

CHAPTER TEN

The Reckoning

At Appomattox Lee's military career came to an abrupt end. Lee had lost his home at Arlington (confiscated in 1861) and had no choice but to repair (with his son Custis and Walter Taylor) to Richmond and the house on 707 East Franklin Street where Mrs. Lee had set up a temporary home for more than a year. His first thoughts on a future occupation turned to farming. For some months, though, his future appeared blighted by the prospect of being indicted for treason. On June 20, 1865, he received General Grant's personal assurance that the new President, Andrew Johnson, who had succeeded the assassinated Lincoln two months earlier, would abide by the terms agreed at Appomattox. Lee remained a paroled prisoner of war, but the threat of indictment did not lift until Christmas Day 1868 when Johnson issued his proclamation of general amnesty.

During these troubled months Lee's Confederate loyalties sustained him. He felt that "true patriotism" lay in "the desire to do right" rather than in consistent loyalty to one cause. He cited George Washington's withdrawal of loyalty to Great Britain as an exemplar "not branded by the world with reproach." But Washington had led the victorious side and thus gained the victor's laurels; Lee had not, and benefited immeasurably from the liberality with which after 1865 the Federal government treated the former rebels. He quickly learned to behave with due prudence.

The summer of 1865 passed quietly before Lee received a visit from Judge John W. Brockenbrough with the news that he had been elected president of Washington College in Lexington. Brockenbrough offered him a salary of $1,500 plus a residence, and a 20 percent share of tuition fees. Washington College had been damaged by Union troops in 1864 and would rely on Lee's fame to revive its fortunes. After initially hesitating (because Lee surmised that a treason indictment might have damaged the college), he accepted the offer. His decision to enter the world of higher education, justified by a passionate belief that the South's future depended on its youth, began the process of restoring his finances. Lee's remaining stocks slowly recovered and earned interest of about $3,500 per year. By 1868 his annual income amounted to some $8,000.

Lee's attitude to Federal Reconstruction reveals a marked ambivalence. In February 1866 Lee received a summons to appear before the Congressional Joint Committee on Reconstruction. He dodged its questions with the disclaimer that he was "living very retired" and enjoyed "but little communication with politicians." He tried to avoid involvement with the public controversies surrounding Reconstruction. In 1867 he resisted all efforts to persuade him to run as a candidate for the Governorship of Virginia. He counseled all former Confederates to "omit all epiphets or remarks calculated to excite bitterness or animosity between different sections of the country."

His core beliefs were rather more strident, however wise his plea for discretion appears in retrospect. In the summer of 1868 he took a vacation at White Sulphur Springs, Virginia. In collaboration with

General Beauregard, the former vice-president of the Confederacy, Alexander H. Stephens, and others, he issued the "White Sulphur Paper." This document attempted to advance the cause of one of the Democratic candidates for the party's nomination in the 1868 presidential election, Union Major General William S. Rosecrans. Rosecrans appeared sympathetic to the views of white Southerners. Lee hoped to see a restoration of the *status quo ante bellum* that had prevailed in 1860. Alas, the "Union as it was" could never be restored; key issues had moved on irrevocably. The Union itself had changed forever. In the event, Rosecrans did not win the Democratic nomination. When General Grant, the Republican candidate, easily won the 1868 presidential election, Lee wrote bitterly, "I grieve for posterity, for American principles and American liberty."

He tended to keep such views to himself. His public service, refusal to parade his bitterness in public, his sense of justice, thoughtfulness, forbearance, combined with numerous acts of personal kindness to Northerners and Southerners alike, did much in the South to nurture the Christ-like image that gained such a hold after his death. Humane and progressive attitudes to higher education marked his work at Washington College. During the Civil War if a subordinate let him down because of lack of military knowledge, Lee would instruct a senior member of his staff, "'Suage him, Colonel, 'suage him"; meaning thereby that a kind but instructive word should be written in reply. Lee transferred this approach to higher education. He abolished onerous rules, such as compulsory attendance at chapel, because he felt that students should *want* to attend. He created "schools," the equivalent of modern university departments. And he gave a lot of attention to the repair of buildings and grounds with an eye to improving facilities for students just as much as enhancing the college's appearance and reputation.

His name continued to provoke hostility from many Northern politicians. In 1867 he had testified before the grand jury inquiring into the degree to which Jefferson Davis was responsible for the outbreak of the Civil War. Davis seemed a useful scapegoat on whose shoulders all the blame could be unloaded easily without the inconvenience of trying the entire Confederate leadership. Lee rallied to help his old chief and undercut the prosecution case by taking responsibility for all his own actions. In 1868 two incidents involving the students of Washington College brought Lee unwelcome publicity. The first involved the harassment of a former Union soldier devoted to the education of freedmen; the second, the near lynching of a young black man (saved by Lee's personal intervention) who had severely wounded Judge Brockenbrough's son when he had pulled a gun during a fight. Leading Northern political figures denounced what they assumed to be Lee's malign influence over the young.

In March 1870, Lee took a trip south to Savannah, Georgia, in the hope that warmer climes might improve his health. The journey became a triumphal tour that took a further toll on his ebbing strength. Huge crowds turned out everywhere to greet him. "Why should they come to see me?" he asked in some perplexity. "I am only a poor old Confederate." When he returned, exhausted, to Virginia, a young girl introduced to him muttered, "We had heard of God, but this was General Lee." In October 1870 Lee died after a brief illness brought on by a stroke resulting from angina pectoris, followed by pneumonia.

This book has sought to re-evaluate Robert E. Lee as a great commander by, first, detaching him from the exaggerated praise that arose from his identification with the failed Confederate cause; and second, by confronting directly the critical, indeed hypercritical, assessments of more recent historians who have reacted against the pieties of the Lost Cause.

A review of his record reveals that Lee's qualities as a commander simply do not need embellishment. Indeed it is perhaps symptomatic of the Southern uncertainty over its future in 1865 and its passionate desire to control the type of writing about its past that Lost Cause advocates presented Lee as a flawless commander, infinitely superior to any of his Northern counterparts. This attitude seems dubious, not least because in style Grant and Lee were very similar—especially in their fundamentally opportunistic approaches. But the effort to present Lee as perfect inevitably provoked a critical reaction that has been as misleading as the sugary effusions of Lee's most dedicated champions.

Lee demonstrated a number of fine qualities as a commander: vision, imagination and decisiveness. Lee always *commanded*; his gentlemanly manner could not disguise that he never deferred to "councils of war," and although he often sought the advice of his lieutenants, he never allowed himself to be dominated by it, indeed, frequently disregarded it. Lee was lucky in his subordinates, and their success is testimony to the skill with which he selected them. His greater command difficulties after 1863 owe more to the South's lack of command talent in depth than to any other factor. Stonewall Jackson's initial greater fame tended to conceal the degree to which Lee himself was the prime stimulus for his army's campaigns. He did not (contrary to Longstreet's expectation) rely on a senior counsellor or guide.

Another aspect of his generalship concealed by his personality was his reliance on deception. Although Lee was the embodiment of gentlemanly openness and courtesy, when in command of an army

Lee could show the most underhand cunning. Likewise, the penchant for gambling he inherited from his father, kept sublimated by the strictest control in his private life, worked its way out while on campaign in a readiness to take risks—not to hazard rash gambles, but calculated (and sometimes breathtaking) audacity.

He also showed stamina to *win* and not just to avoid defeat. The Prussian observer, Major Justus Scheibert, thought Lee's features "registered a nature ruled by will and intellect—mostly will." He also exhibited a marked and effortless charisma. Probably his greatest achievement was the building of an army, sustained over time and adapted to changing priorities, to carry out his designs. Lee created an enduring organization for the Army of Northern Virginia, a sense of purpose and a great confidence in itself and its leaders. The resulting dash, flair and élan allowed the Army of Northern Virginia to implement Lee's plans with a high level of initiative and aggressive confidence. At all levels, it out-fought the Army of the Potomac until the last days, invariably moving more quickly and with ferocious power. Lee achieved this in a military system more noted for petty squabbling than organizational efficiency. Other Confederate commanders (with the exception perhaps of Joseph E. Johnston) were either feckless adventurers, or men like Braxton Bragg, who were temperamentally incapable of winning the loyalty of their troops.

Lee's successes would not have been possible without his superb qualities as a leader. General Fuller was the first to acknowledge their excellence. "His bravery magnetized them [his troops], for Lee had no fear of danger." He did not habitually go to the front and get in the way of his subordinates. But if things went wrong, as Fuller acknowledged, "he immediately rode forward." He showed himself and deployed his formidable moral authority to inspirit wavering troops. He was a sterner disciplinarian than he is often given credit for, despite his mild way; but he adopted a paternal tone that disguised his harsher, regular soldier's instincts. His appeals struck a chord with young, volunteer soldiers that bound them to him.

Lee demonstrated great military versatility. He was equally accomplished on the offensive, the defensive and in siege warfare. Unlike Grant, however, he did not conduct any sieges, as he lacked any kind of siege train; but he was besieged at Petersburg for ten months, conducting its defense skillfully. If Lee had a special talent, it was for maneuver, either the envelopment of the enemy's entire army—the turning movement—or the outflanking attack. He developed these skills to such a degree that he acquired an enormous psychological sway over Union generals in the east. His greatest victory was thus over the *minds* of opposing generals. This only waned after Grant's arrival from the west, but the hold persisted over Meade and most of his subordinates until the eve of Appomattox. Such ascendancy allowed Lee to reduce the odds against him by demoralizing the command system of the Army of the Potomac and fragmenting its fighting power. His record does display one significant shortcoming: that he failed to relate his moral advantages to the needs of the pursuit.

Nevertheless, Lee gained two advantages in the war for public opinion. First, he made serious inroads into the Northern determination to continue the war. He did this in 1862 and 1863 by offensive means, and in 1864 by clever use of defensive methods. His successes stimulated the activities of the peace party among the Democrats in the North. In Lee's pursuit of his strategic aims, the choice of Virginia as the decisive theater was the right one. The eyes of the North, the South and the European powers were on the eastern theater, not the west. Here lay the "cockpit" of the conflict and the theater that afforded most political and strategic advantage to the Confederacy. Conversely, a defeat here would have had disastrous effects. Lee was absolutely right to argue that the Confederacy could only gain its independence by its own efforts, and be seen to be doing so. Virginia was the only theater where this could be achieved quickly and with dramatic effect.

Second, Lee bolstered faltering Confederate enthusiasm for the war. In June 1862 the South tottered on the brink of defeat. While the Army of Northern Virginia remained in the field for almost three further years, success seemed possible. An Irish observer quickly realized the importance Southerners attached to "the prestige which surrounds his [Lee's] person and the almost fanatical belief in his judgment and capacity wh[ich] is the one idea of an entire people." Once Lee surrendered, all hope that the Confederacy might continue disappeared. "The life of the 'CS' is gon" when General Lee and his army surrendered, sighed a North Carolinian soldier on April 9, 1865. Lee, in short, enabled the Confederacy to believe in itself and fight on for three more years than seemed likely in the spring of 1862. To avoid defeat for so long was a remarkable achievement.

But Lee *did* fail. He *was* defeated, for all his fine qualities and skill. He did not succeed in gaining his strategic aims. Thus the nature of his achievement will always remain controversial. Criticism of his methods and chosen strategy will invariably stem from his defeat. The encomiums lavished on Lee's genius have rendered any evaluation of his generalship difficult. The only alternative seems to be criticism, and much of this has proved shallow, unfair and indiscriminating. Criticism can always focus on actions that Lee might have taken—on what he failed to do—that might have brought a Southern victory. Lee offered a strong strategic prognosis, and implemented a defensive-offensive strategy until the autumn of 1863. It more clearly reflected what Southerners expected and wanted at the time. It did prove more costly than he expected; but despite the cost, if Lee had gained a great victory on Northern soil, it would have reduced the casualties sustained during the remainder of the Civil War.

Certainly, Lee's forays north of the Potomac seemed to expose his weaknesses as a commander. His confidence in himself after two runs of consecutive victories, in 1862 at Seven Days and Second Manassas, and in 1863 at Fredericksburg and Chancellorsville, spilled into over-confidence. His faith in himself and his troops persuaded him to underestimate the Union capacity to recover and to believe that he had more time at his disposal than he had actually been granted. His dispositions became casual, his direction of the staff poor; the clarity of orders issued by his headquarters left much to be desired and confused commanders on the spot. All of these factors conspired to produce disappointing results at the crucial moment. In Lee's style of warfare, the dividing line between great victory and shattering defeat was very fine indeed. Often his tactical skill came to his rescue and saved him, as at Antietam, and during the retreat from Gettysburg, from the full effects of strategic miscalculation and downright error. Under these trying circumstances, Lee showed himself an improviser of the highest caliber.

Finally, consideration needs to be given to the prevalent view that Lee, as the embodiment of the cavalier spirit, was an "old-fashioned" general. This seems a spurious label. In his understanding of the relationship between war, public opinion and propaganda, combined with his careful nursing of his relations with the civil power, especially Jefferson Davis, Lee appears sophisticated and modern-minded. His understanding of the psychology of volunteer soldiers is also impressive, as is his willingness to train their untutored commanders with sympathy and perceptive advice. All of these attributes aided his success. In the end, the discussion must return to those sterling and impressive qualities that brought outstanding operational triumphs. These can be taken for granted rather too easily. Robert E. Lee made command of an army appear easy when it is taxing and complex.

Lee's victories were won against the odds. The Lost Cause arguments, modified by a later generation of Southern scholars like Freeman and Dowdey, contain a solid vein of truth. Virginia was the most important theater for the Confederacy; Lee prevailed while outnumbered and operating at a severe material disadvantage. The image of the great Confederate laboring against the odds is not wholly false. This is an unusual experience for American commanders, who usually enjoy the benefits of plenty. Lee remained a loyal Confederate until 1865. His victories remain among the greatest humiliations ever inflicted on the armies of the United States. Nonetheless, the link with the other American commander, George Washington, who battled against the odds, is a just one. For this reason, Lee still ranks among the very finest of American generals, for like his hero, Washington, he managed to achieve much with the most meagre resources.

Guide to Further Reading

The literature on Lee is enormous, but a lot of it has been influenced by the canon of the Lost Cause and has a clear polemical message. One of the best ways to understand the historical Lee is to come to terms with its overall shape. By far the best survey of the continuing influence of the Confederate experience and the trauma of defeat is Gaines M. Foster, *Ghosts of the Confederacy: Defeat, the Lost Cause and the Emergence of a New South, 1865 to 1913* (New York: Oxford University Press, 1987). A racy journalistic account of the prevalent neo-Confederate revival that discusses continuing Lost Cause sympathies, is Tony Horwitz, *Confederates in the Attic: Dispatches from the Unfinished Civil War* (New York: Pantheon, 1998).

As for Lee himself, the chapter in Dixon Wecter, *The Hero in America* (New York: Charles Scribners' Sons, 1941), remains a good starting point. The most detailed survey of Lee's reputation and its changing phases is Thomas L. Connelly, *The Marble Man: Robert E. Lee and His Image in American Society* (New York:

Alfred A. Knopf, 1977). This book exemplifies Connelly's strengths and weaknesses as a historian. It combines valuable intellectual history with carelessness over detail and over-indulgence of his prejudices. In the lengthy fifty-page epilogue, that essays "a reappraisal" of Lee, it is instructive to compare the material that Connelly quotes with his comments on it. Connelly's work should be viewed as a counterblast to the pieties of the Lost Cause. It also includes material on the parallels drawn between Lee and George Washington.

For the literary device of reducing mythological material to forms or "guises," see Marcus Cunliffe, *George Washington: Man and Monument* (London: Collins, 1958). Then consult Mason L. Weems, *Life of Washington*, edited by Marcus Cunliffe (Cambridge MA: Harvard University Press, 1962).

There are three essential works that underpin any interpretation of Lee the historical rather than mythical figure. The first and most important is *The Wartime Papers of R. E. Lee*, edited by Clifford Dowdey and Louis H. Manarin (New York: Bramhall House, 1961). In the absence of a comprehensive, multivolume edition of Lee's papers, this volume, though by no means complete, includes Lee's most important personal and military correspondence and reports from 1861 to 1865. It can be supplemented by *Lee's Dispatches*, edited by Douglas Southall Freeman and Grady McWhiney (New York: Putnam, 1957). The third key volume is *Lee: The Soldier*, edited by Gary W. Gallagher (Lincoln: University of Nebraska Press, 1996), that includes three memoranda on Lee's postwar conversations about his campaigns, Jubal A. Early's important 1872 address at Washington and Lee University, numerous nineteenth-century assessments of Lee and those made by modern historians, and ends with an annotated bibliography of the two hundred essential works on Lee. The present work rests on the foundations provided by these books; they are indispensable to the serious student of Lee.

Other contemporary sources remain of value. A. L. Long, *Memoirs of Robert E. Lee* (New York: J. M. Stoddart, 1887) is reverential. Lee's nephew, Fitzhugh Lee's biography, *General Lee,* first published in "The Great Commanders Series," edited by James Grant Wilson in 1904 by Appleton, is now available in a paperback edition (New York: Da Capo, 1994). It is well written and garnished with shrewd assessment. *Lee's Adjutant: The Wartime Letters of Colonel Walter Herron Taylor, 1862–1865*, edited by R. Lockwood Tower (Columbia: University of South Carolina Press, 1995) is much more candid and less respectful than Taylor's later memoir, *Four Years with General Lee* (New York: D. Appleton, 1877). Robert E. Lee Jr., *Recollections and Letters of Robert E. Lee* (Westminster: Archibald and Constable, 1904), contains more about his family life and character than his campaigns. James Longstreet's side is put forcefully though not always wisely in *From Manassas to Appomattox* (Philadelphia: Lippincott Co., 1896).

Lee biographies are of a high quality despite a certain partiality among the older books. By far the most important is Douglas Southall Freeman, *R. E. Lee*, in four volumes (New York: Scribner's, 1934–35). This book undoubtedly ranks among the greatest American biographies. Also notable is Clifford Dowdey, *Lee: A Biography* (London: Gollancz, 1970), a vivid and full one-volume treatment in the Freeman tradition, although occasionally more strident in its sympathies. The best modern biography, and certainly the most subtle psychological study of Lee's character, is Emory M. Thomas, *Robert E. Lee: A Biography* (New York: Norton, 1995). All these books are by Southerners. Among shorter books, Earl Schenck Miers, *Robert E. Lee* (New York: Alfred A. Knopf, 1956) can be recommended as an example of the pro-Lee Northern view.

Insight can also be gleaned by consulting works written by professional soldiers, especially those by Europeans. Eyewitness accounts offer key sources. Lieutenant Colonel A. J. L. Fremantle, Coldstream Guards, *Three Months in the Southern States, April–June 1863* (Lincoln NE: University of Nebraska Press, 1991) gives an exciting account of Gettysburg. Less descriptive and more analytical, though no less pro-Confederate, is the German view, *A Prussian Observes the American Civil War: The Military Studies of Justus Scheibert*, edited by Frederic Trautmann (Columbia: University of Missouri Press, 2001). The most outstanding book by a sympathetic British writer is Major General Sir Frederick Maurice, *Robert E. Lee: The Soldier* (Boston, New York: Houghton Mifflin Co., 1925). Colonel G. F. R. Henderson's views can be found in *The Civil War: In the Writings of Col. G. F. R. Henderson*, edited by Jay Luvaas (Chicago: University of Chicago Press, 1958). Much more critical is Major General J. F. C. Fuller, *Grant and Lee: A Study in Personality and Generalship* (London: Eyre & Spottiswoode, 1933), and remains the standard source for criticisms of Lee's strategy. For the changing context of British evaluations, see Brian Holden Reid, *Studies in British Military Thought* (Lincoln: University of Nebraska Press, 1998).

Turning to Lee's critics among modern historians, the most important work is Thomas L. Connelly and Archer Jones, *The Politics of
Command: Factions and Ideas in Confederate Strategy* (Baton
Rouge: Louisiana State University Press, 1973). Alan T. Nolan's
Lee Considered (Chapel Hill: University of North Carolina Press,
1991) imitates Connelly's essential line without adding substantive
detail. Shorter essays by both authors are included in *Lee: The Soldier* (1996). The essential context to these views, not least the pervasive influence on American military writing of the Vietnam Syndrome, is explored in Brian Holden Reid, "The Influence of the
Vietnam Syndrome on the Writing of Civil War History," *RUSI
(Royal United Services Institute) Journal*, vol. 147 (February
2002).

The most powerful reply to the Connelly–Nolan critique is provided by Gary W. Gallagher in two volumes of his essays based on
wide research and a firm understanding of political pressures and
contemporary Confederate opinion, *Lee and his Generals in War
and Memory* (Baton Rouge: Louisiana State University Press,
1998) and *Lee and his Army in Confederate History* (Chapel Hill:
University of North Carolina Press, 2001). Gallagher is not uncrit-
ical of Lee, but his approach is balanced while remaining sympathetic. He makes a convincing case that Lee's illustrious reputation
was not a retrospective invention but rooted in favorable opinion
expressed during the Civil War itself.

Other sympathetic studies of specialist aspects of Lee's career
include Richard M. McMurry, *Two Great Rebel Armies* (Chapel
Hill: University of North Carolina Press, 1989), which explains
why Virginia made such an important contribution to the Confed-

erate war effort. Steven E. Woodworth, *Davis and Lee at War* (Lawrence: University Press of Kansas, 1995) explores his relations with the Confederate President, and perhaps makes too much of their differences in emphasis. J. Boone Bartholomees, *Buff Facings and Gilt Buttons: Staff and Headquarters in the Army of Northern Virginia, 1861–65* (Columbia: University of South Carolina Press, 1998) is a detailed assessment that needs some kind of comparative dimension. Jennings Cropper Wise, *The Long Arm of Lee,* two volumes (Lynchburg, VA: J. P. Bell Co., 1915) remains the most detailed study of Lee's artillery. The best work on his soldiers' experience is J. Tracey Power, *Lee's Miserables: Life in the Army of Northern Virginia from the Wilderness to Appomattox* (Chapel Hill: University of North Carolina Press, 1998).

On the moral sway that Lee exploited, the central work is Michael C. C. Adams, *Our Masters the Rebels* (1978; reprinted in paperback with the new title, *Fighting for Defeat: Union Military Failure in the East, 1861–1865* (Lincoln: University of Nebraska Press, 1992). Marcus Cunliffe challenged the idea of an antebellum Southern military tradition in *Soldiers and Civilians: The Martial Spirit in America, 1775–1865* (Boston: Little, Brown & Co., 1968). Bruce Collins, "The Southern Military Tradition, 1812–1865," in John White and Brian Holden Reid, eds., *Americana: Essays in Memory of Marcus Cunliffe* (Hull: University of Hull Press, 1998) supports his view. On the idea that there existed a superior Confederate moral spirit, Wiley Sword, *Southern Invincibility: A History of the Confederate Heart* (New York: St. Martin's Griffin, 1999) offers a disappointingly episodic treatment.

On Lee's campaigns, only a sample of works can be offered here. The fullest account is Douglas Southall Freeman, *Lee's Lieutenants: A Study in Command,* three volumes (New York: Scribner's, 1942–44). There has been surprisingly little discussion of command techniques in the Civil War. A starting point is Brian Holden Reid, "Command and Leadership in the Civil War, 1861–1865," in Susan-Mary Grant and Brian Holden Reid, eds., *The American Civil War: Explorations and Reconsiderations* (London: Longman, 2000). The finest discussion of Lee's first offensive before Richmond in the context of efforts to finish off the war in the summer of 1862 is Stephen Sears, *To the Gates of Richmond: The Peninsular Campaign* (New York: Ticknor and Fields, 1992). Brian K. Burton, *Extraordinary Circumstances: The Seven Days Battles* (Bloomington: Indiana University Press, 2001) is a clear and detailed tactical study of its subject but offers little new insight on the higher conduct of the campaign. The most detailed account of Second Manassas that still keeps the larger issues in clear focus is John J. Hennessy, *Return to Bull Run* (New York: Simon and Schuster, 1993), a model campaign study. Stephen Sears has also produced a wonderfully graphic and controlled account of the Maryland campaign, *Landscape Turned Red: The Battle of Antietam* (New York: Ticknor and Fields, 1989). The most stimulating works on Lee's strategy are two books by Joseph L. Harsh, *Confederate Tide Rising: Robert E. Lee and the Making of Confederate Strategy, 1861–1862* (Kent, OH: Kent State University Press, 1998) and *Taken at the Flood: Robert E. Lee and Confederate Strategy in the Maryland Campaign of 1862* (Kent, OH: Kent State University Press, 1999). They rebut the misguided notion that Lee failed to evolve a grand strategic view.

A brief, authoritative account of the two battles on the Rappahannock line is Daniel Sutherland, *Fredericksburg and Chancellorsville: The Dare Mark Campaign* (Lincoln: University of Nebraska Press, 1998). Stephen W. Sears, *Chancellorsville* (Boston: Houghton Mifflin, 1996) is the most authoritative modern study. Specialist aspects can be explored in *Chancellorsville: The Battle and the Aftermath*, edited by Gary W. Gallagher (Chapel Hill: University of North Carolina Press, 1996). Two contrasting books on Gettysburg can be recommended: Steven E. Woodworth, *Beneath a Northern Sky: A Short History of the Gettysburg Campaign* (Wilmington, DE: SR Books, 2003) and Noah Andre Trudeau, *Gettysburg: A Testing of Courage* (New York: HarperCollins, 2002). The former is concise and to the point, the latter more expansive. The symbolic importance of the battle's third day is assessed in Carol Reardon, *Pickett's Charge in History and Memory* (Chapel Hill: University of North Carolina Press, 1997).

On the climactic 1864–65 campaign, the first port of call is Mark Grimsley, *And Keep Moving On: The Virginia Campaign, May–June 1864* (Lincoln: University of Nebraska Press, 2002) that brings some new points of view to old questions. Gary W. Gallagher explores particular aspects in another edited volume, *The Wilderness Campaign* (Chapel Hill: University of North Carolina Press, 1997) and also in a companion volume on *The Spotsylvania Campaign* (Chapel Hill: University of North Carolina Press, 1998). Noah Andre Trudeau, *The Last Citadel: Petersburg, Virginia, June 1864–April 1865* (Baton Rouge: Louisiana State University Press, 1991) is a reliable and complete account, but its presentation, in the form of a present day, breaking news story, sometimes rather jars. On the final campaign, Burke Davis, *To Appomattox: Nine*

April Days (New York: Rinehart, 1959) and Jay Winik, *April 1865* (New York: HarperCollins, 2001) present graphic accounts of the road to Lee's surrender, though Winik is much more sophisticated in his treatment of the episode. On the dilemmas facing Lee and other Confederates, see Mark Grimsley, "Learning to Say 'Enough': Southern Generals and the Final Weeks of the Confederacy," in *The Collapse of the Confederacy,* edited by Mark Grimsley and Brooks D. Simpson (Lincoln: University of Nebraska Press, 2001). These last two works have much that is sensible to say on the complex process of bringing a great war to an end and resolving the tricky dilemmas that Lee's Confederate loyalties threw up.

Index

Guadaloupe Hidalgo, Treaty of (1848), 61

Hagerstown, 122, 124, 126, 127, 128

Hampton, Wade, 121, 174, 206, 221, 230

Hancock, Major General Winfield Scott, 188, 201, 203, 216

Hannibal, 37, 39

Harper's Ferry, 62, 66, 124–25, 126, 127, 128, 129

Harrisburg, 122, 163, 171, 176, 177

Harrison, Henry T., 176

Harrison's Landing, 102, 104, 109

Hatcher's Run, 229, 231–32

Henderson, Colonel G. F. R., 43, 146

Heth, Major General Henry, 177, 178, 187, 210, 227

Hill, A.P., 108, 198, 207, 211, 212; Lee reforms army, 91, 168; Seven Days' Battles, 93, 94, 95, 98, 99, 100; Second Manassas, 116; Battle of Antietam, 132–33, 134; Battle of Fredericksburg, 145; quarrel with Jackson, 150; invasion of the North, 169, 176; Battle of Gettysburg, 177, 178, 179, 182, 183, 184, 186–87; Lee doubts abilities of, 195–96; Battle of the Wilderness, 199–201; siege of Petersburg, 220; defense of Richmond, 226, 227; action at Peeble's Farm, 228; collapse of Confederacy, 235; death, 235

Hill, Senator Benjamin, 30

Hill, D. H., 91, 117; on Lee, 100; Seven Days' Battles, 93, 101; campaign against Pope, 113; Maryland campaign, 121, 122, 125, 126, 127, 129; Battle of Antietam, 132; Battle of Fredericksburg, 139–41; joins Army of Tennessee, 150

Hitchcock, Lieutenant Colonel E.A., 53

Hoke, Major General Robert, 214, 224

Holmes, Major General Theophilus, 92, 96, 97, 99

Hood, John B., 195; Seven Days' Battles, 95; Second Manassas, 114, 115; raggedness of army, 138; Battle of Fredericksburg, 143, 144, 145; Battle of Gettysburg, 183, 184–85, 186

Hooker, Major General Joseph: Burnside loathes, 136; Battle of Antietam, 130; Battle of Fredericksburg, 142, 144, 145; reforms army, 147, 149; tactics, 150–52; Battle of Chancellorsville, 152, 154–62;

176; and Lee's invasion of the North, 167, 168–69, 172, 173, 176

Horwitz, Tony, 27–28

Hotchkiss, Major Jedediah, 156, 158, 163

House of Representatives, 46

Howard, Oliver O., 178

Huger, Benjamin, 92, 94, 96–101, 103

Humphreys, Major General Andrew A., 145

Hunter, Major General David, 221, 222

Imboden, John D., 189–90

Jackson, Stonewall, 42, 75; crosses Potomac, 76; relief of Virginia, 90, 91, 92; Seven Days' Battles, 93, 95, 98–101, 103, 104, 108–109; defense of Richmond, 107, 108–109; Battle of Cedar Mountain, 109; Second Manassas, 112–14, 116, 117; Maryland campaign, 122, 124–28; Battle of Antietam, 129–31, 134, 167; promotion, 138; Battle of Fredericksburg, 139, 141, 142–43, 145; quarrel with A.P. Hill, 149–50; wants to attack Sedgwick, 153; Battle of Chancellorsville, 154–58, 181; death, 27, 164, 167–68, 171, 181, 204; posthumous reputation, 29, 246

Jackson, Colonel Thomas J., 66

James, Henry, *The Ambassadors*, 79

James River, 73, 74, 76, 96, 97, 99, 148, 206, 214–15, 216, 218, 220, 232

Jenkins, Albert G., 173, 177

Jerusalem Plank Road, 219, 220, 221, 227

Johnson, "Allegheny," 208

Johnson, President Andrew, 242

Johnson, Colonel Bradley T., 123

Johnston, Albert Sidney, 48, 66, 67

Johnston, General Joseph E., 65, 164, 239, 241, 247; friendship with Lee, 48; in Winfield Scott's field staff, 53; leadership style, 66; First Manassas, 67; McClellan threatens Richmond, 73–76; Battle of Seven Pines, 77–78; Lee replaces, 79, 80; character, 81; strategy, 89, 91; Lee persuades Davis to restore to command, 231; and Sherman's advance, 236

Johnston, Peter, 48

Johnston, Captain Samuel R., 183, 184